CAVE IN THE SNOW

CAVE IN THE SNOW
A WESTERN WOMAN'S QUEST
FOR ENLIGHTENMENT

VICKI MACKENZIE

Tenzin Palmo

BLOOMSBURY

Published by Bloomsbury Publishing, New York and London
Distributed to the trade by St Martin's Press

PICTURE CREDIT

All photographs supplied by Tenzin Palmo; the author wishes
to thank the copyright holders for permission to reproduce
their photographs in this book.

Map on page ix by Neil Hyslop

A CIP catalogue record for this book
is available from the Library of Congress

ISBN 1-58234-045-5

First published in Great Britain in 1998 by Bloomsbury Publishing Plc
First U.S. edition published in 1998 by Bloomsbury Publishing

This U.S. paperback edition published 1999
10 9

Typeset by Hewer Text Ltd, Edinburgh
Printed in the United States of America
by R.R. Donnelley & Sons Company,
Harrisonburg, Virginia

For my mother, Rene Mackenzie (1919–1998), the first spiritual woman in my life; with deep gratitude for her unfailing love, wisdom and support.

Contents

Map of Lahoul   ix
Chapter One: The Meeting   1
Chapter Two: The Wrong Place   8
Chapter Three: The Dawning – Finding the Path   19
Chapter Four: The First Step   32
Chapter Five: The Guru   41
Chapter Six: Fear of the Feminine   51
Chapter Seven: Lahoul   65
Chapter Eight: The Cave   77
Chapter Nine: Facing Death   96
Chapter Ten: Yogini   111
Chapter Eleven: Woman's Way   125
Chapter Twelve: Coming Out   139
Chapter Thirteen: The Vision   153
Chapter Fourteen: The Teacher   163
Chapter Fifteen: Challenges   176
Chapter Sixteen: Is a Cave Necessary?   190
Chapter Seventeen: Now   202
Bibliography   209
Acknowledgements   211
Author's Note   213

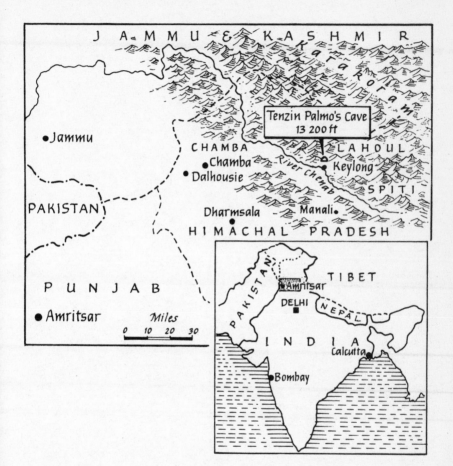

ONE

The Meeting

In retrospect, it was a curious place to meet her. The time was midsummer, the place Pomaia, a little town perched among the magnificent hills of Tuscany about an hour's drive from Pisa. It was late afternoon and the air was filled with the aroma of dry heat and the scent of pine needles. The once-grand mansion with its ochre-coloured walls, high arched doorways, and castellated roof shimmered in the August sun and only the sound of the cicadas broke the silence of the siesta. In a few hours' time the town down the road would come alive for the evening. The small shops selling that odd assortment of salami, biscotti and sandals would open and the old men would gather in the square to discuss municipal business and the affairs of the regional Communist party. The sheer lusciousness of Italy, where all things seem to conspire to bring pleasure to the senses, could not have contrasted more radically with the world that she had come from.

The first time I saw her she was standing in the grounds of the mansion under the shade of a copse of trees – a somewhat frail-looking woman in early middle age, with fair skin and a rather rounded back. She was dressed in the maroon and gold robes of an ordained Buddhist nun and her hair was cropped short in the traditional manner. Standing all around her was a group of women. You could see at a glance that the conversation was animated, the atmosphere intimate. It was an arresting scene, but on a month-long Buddhist meditation course not particularly unusual.

I and about fifty others had gathered there, drawn from all over the world, to attend the course. These events had become a regular and welcome part of my life ever since I had stumbled upon the lamas in Nepal back in 1976 and discovered the richness of their message. Lively discussions, such as those I was witnessing, were a welcome break from the long hours of sitting cross-legged listening to the words of the Buddha or attempting the arduous business of meditation.

Later that night, eating dinner under the stars, mopping up the olive oil with large chunks of bread, the man sitting next to me drew my attention to the woman again. She was sitting at a table, once more surrounded by people, talking enthusiastically to them.

'That's Tenzin Palmo, the Englishwoman who has spent twelve years meditating in a cave over 13,000 feet up in the Himalayas. For most of that time she was totally alone. She has only just come out,' he said.

The glance now was more than cursory.

Over the years, I had certainly read about such characters – the great yogis from Tibet, India and China who forsook all worldly comfort to wander off to some remote cave to engage in profound meditation for years on end. These were the spiritual virtuosi, their path the hardest and loneliest of all. All alone, I read, dressed in a simple robe or flimsy loincloth, they faced the fiercest of elements – howling gales, raging blizzards, freezing cold. Their bodies became horribly emaciated, their hair grew matted and long to their waists. They faced wild animals and gangs of robbers who, having no regard for their sanctity, beat them into bloody pulp and left them for dead. But all this was nothing compared to facing the vagaries of their own minds. Here, cut off from the distractions of ordinary life, all the demons lying just beneath the surface began to rise up and taunt. The anger, the paranoia, the longings, the lust (especially the lust). They too had to be overcome if the victory was to be won. Still they persevered. What they were after was the most glittering prize of all – Enlightenment, a mind blown wide open to encompass universal reality. A state in which the unknowable was made known. Omniscience, no less. And accompanying it a sublime happiness and an inconceivable peace. It was the highest state of evolution humankind could ever achieve.

So I had read. I never thought I would actually meet such a person but here in Pomaia, Italy, was a character who had seemingly stepped out of the pages of myth and legend and who was now sitting casually among us as though she had done nothing more momentous than just got off a bus from a shopping trip. Furthermore this was not an Eastern yogi, as the tales had told, but a contemporary Westerner. More astonishing still, a woman.

The mind buzzed with myriad questions. What had driven a modern Englishwoman to live in a dank, dark hole in a mountainside like a latter-day cavewoman? How did she survive in that extreme cold? What did she do for food, a bath, a bed, a telephone? How did she exist without the warmth of human companionship for all those years? What had she gained? And, more curiously, how had she emerged from that excessive silence and solitude as chatty as a woman at a cocktail party?

The immediate rush of curiosity, however, was quickly followed by unabashed admiration and a little awe. This woman had ventured where I knew I would never tread. Her thirst for knowing, unlike mine, had pushed her beyond the safe confines of a four-week meditation course with its exit clause guaranteeing a speedy return to ordinary life. Retreat, I knew from pitifully small experience, was infinitely hard work involving endless repetition of the same prayers, the same mantras, the same visualizations, the same meditations – day in, day out. You sat on the same cushion, in the same place, seeing the same people, in the same location. For someone steeped in the modern ethos of constant stimulation and rapid change, the tedium was excruciating. Only the tiniest shimmer of awareness, and the unaccustomed feeling of deep calm, made it worthwhile. Ultimately retreat was a test of endurance, courage and faith in the final goal.

The next day I saw her again in the garden, this time sitting alone, and seeing my chance I approached. Did she mind if I joined her for a little while? The smile stretched from ear to ear in greeting and a pair of the most penetrating blue eyes gazed steadily into mine. There was calmness there, and kindness, laughter too, but the most outstanding quality was an unmistakable luminosity. The woman virtually glowed. In fact she was a most interesting-looking person – she had sharp

features, a long pointed nose and small neat ears. Maybe it
was her cropped hair and lack of make-up but there was
also something decidedly androgynous about her, as though
a sensitive male were lodging within.

We began to chat. She told me that she was now living in
Assisi in a small house in the garden of a friend's place, and
was enjoying it immensely. She had been called there, she said,
when her time in the cave had come to an end. It seemed a
natural place to go. I learnt that she had been ordained back in
1964, when she was just twenty-one, long before most of us even
knew Tibetan Buddhism existed. That made her, I reckoned, the
most senior Tibetan Buddhist nun in the Western world. Thirty
years of celibacy, however, was a long time. Hadn't she ever
wished for a partner, marriage or children in all those years?

'That would have been a disaster. It wasn't my path at all,'
she replied, throwing back her head and laughing. I hadn't
expected such animation after twelve years in a cave.

What had led her there, to that cave, I asked.

'My life has been like a river, it has flowed steadily in one
direction,' she replied, and then added after a pause, 'The
purpose of life is to realize our spiritual nature. And to do
that one has to go away and practise, to reap the fruits of the
path, otherwise you have nothing to give anyone else.'

Wasn't there anything she missed?

'I missed my lama, apart from that nothing. I was very happy
there and had everything I wanted,' she said quietly.

But wasn't going to a cave an escape, an evasion of the trials
of 'ordinary' life, I went on, quoting the argument most levelled
at hermits by those of us engrossed in the mundane.

'Not at all. To my mind worldly life is an escape,' she retorted,
quick as a flash. 'When you have a problem you can turn on the
television, phone a friend, go out for a coffee. In a cave, however,
you have no one to turn to but yourself. When problems arise
and things get tough you have no choice but to go through with
them, and come out the other side. In a cave you face your own
nature in the raw, you have to find a way of working with it
and dealing with it,' she said. Her logic was irrefutable .

It was a memorable meeting. Tenzin Palmo was, as I had
witnessed from a distance, remarkably open and affable.

She was talkative and highly articulate too, and displayed a sharp, penetrating mind. She had also revealed a distinctive down-to-earth quality which immediately dispelled any clichéd notion of a 'spaced-out meditator'. And behind the vivacity was a profound stillness, an immense inner calm as though nothing could, or would, disrupt her, no matter how galvanic. All in all, I concluded, she was a woman of stature. When the course was over I thought it unlikely our paths would ever cross again. Then one day, some months later, I picked up a Buddhist magazine and found inside an interview with Tenzin Palmo. About half-way through, buried in the middle of the text, was one small sentence:

'I have made a vow to attain Enlightenment in the female form – no matter how many lifetimes it takes,' Tenzin Palmo had said.

I stopped. The effect of her words was electrifying, for what Tenzin Palmo had stated in that casual, almost throwaway manner was nothing short of revolutionary. What she had promised was to become a female Buddha, and female Buddhas (like female Christs and female Mohammeds) were decidedly thin on the ground. Certainly there had been plenty of acclaimed women mystics and saints in all parts of the world, but the full flowering of human divinity had, for the past few thousand years at least, been deemed the exclusive domain of the male. The female body, for some reason, had been seen as an unfit or unworthy vessel to contain the most sacred. Now Tenzin Palmo was publicly announcing that she was intending to overthrow all that. It was a bold, courageous statement. A reckless one, even. One that could easily be dismissed as a piece of bravado or wishful thinking, had it not been Tenzin Palmo with her track record of exceptional meditational ability and tenacity who had made it. It could just be possible that she might do it! If not in this lifetime, then maybe the next or the next.

My hopes rose. This was something I had been waiting for for years. From the very beginning of my search into Buddhism I had been told that we all possessed the seed of full awakening, men and women alike. It was our birthright, our natural inheritance, the lamas had said from their high brocaded thrones. Buddhahood was there shining within, like a pearl of great price, and all we had to do was to uncover it. The responsibility was ours, and ours alone. How the philosophy had appealed to an independent woman making her own way in the world! It took lifetimes of diligence and effort, the lamas continued, but if we set out on this journey eventually the magnificent prize would be ours.

That, at least was the theory. In actuality, however, examples of female spiritual excellence were decidedly thin on the ground. Yes, there were female Buddhas aplenty in paint and plaster – paying homage to the ideal of feminine divinity in all its diverse and wonderful forms. You could find them dotted all around temple walls and throughout the monastery gardens, worthy objects of veneration and prayer. Some were beautiful, some peaceful, others powerful or overtly erotic. But where were the living examples? The more I looked the more I could see no sign that women were getting anywhere in the spiritual selection stakes. The lamas who taught us were male; the Dalai Lamas (all fourteen of them) were male; the powerful lineage holders who carried the weight of the entire tradition were male; the revered Tulkus, the recognized reincarnated lamas, were male; the vast assembly of monastics who filled the temple halls and schools of learning were male; the succession of gurus who had come to the West to inspire eager new seekers were male. Where were the women in all of this? To be fair, it was not just Tibetan Buddhism which was so testosterone-heavy, but Buddhism from Japan, Thailand, Sri Lanka, Burma – in fact from all Eastern countries with the possible exception of Taiwan. (Even my own home-grown religion, Christianity, with its insistence on a male God and its fear of female priests, was no better.) Where were the female gurus for us women to emulate? What in fact did female spirituality look like? We had no idea. The fact was that in spite of the Buddha's word that we could all advance up the spiritual evolutionary ladder to Enlightenment there was no proof that women could actually do it. To the women practitioners sitting at the lamas' feet earnestly trying to follow The Way, it was discouraging to say the least.

How urgently we needed hope that the impossible could become possible. How badly we women needed champions to lead the way. It was time. The twentieth century had seen the steady and inexorable emancipation of women in all areas of life, except that of religion. Now, at two minutes before the millennium, it seemed that the last wave of female emancipation was poised to begin. If it happened it would also be the greatest. The ultimate women's liberation was surely a female Buddha, an omniscient being. In the light of her great intention, Tenzin Palmo's already remarkable achievement of enduring twelve years of meditation in a Himalayan cave was suddenly thrust into the realm of universal endeavour.

I decided to seek her out again. There was now so much more to know. Who exactly was she, where had she come from, what had she learnt in that cave, what had prompted her to make that vow – and would she mind being the subject of a book? Reluctantly, very reluctantly, she agreed, and then only on the grounds that it would inspire other women, and help her own project currently under way to facilitate women's enlightenment. And so over the next year I tracked her down, in Singapore, London, Seattle, California and India where she was leading a very different way of life, and gradually pieced together the elements of her extraordinary and, some would say, most unnatural life. I spoke to people who had known her and visited the places which had been central to her life. With great difficulty I even found her cave and, having climbed to that thin-aired altitude and witnessed for myself her dwelling place, marvelled with new appreciation at what she had accomplished.

This then, is Tenzin Palmo's story – a tale of one woman's quest for Enlightenment.

TWO

The Wrong Place

The world that Tenzin Palmo came from could not have been further removed from the one that she was to find herself in.

She was born in a stately home, Woolmers Park, in Hertfordshire, in the library to be exact. This was not because she was of blue blood, far from it, but because on 30 June 1943, the day of her birth, Hitler's Luftwaffe were blitzing London and the capital's maternity hospitals had been evacuated to the relative peace of the home counties. Something must have gone terribly wrong with the mathematics, because although she was technically overdue and was induced she arrived into this world with no eyelashes, no fingernails, no hair and was, even her mother said, quite ugly; however, in spite of the wizened child's unprepossessing appearance, her mother was filled with romantic aspirations for her and promptly named her Diane after a popular French song that had caught her fancy – but, she insisted, it had to be pronounced in the French way which, with the English pronunciation, came out as 'Dionne'. This was how she was known until her ordination as a Buddhist nun some twenty-one years later, when she took the second name of Tenzin Palmo.

Home for the first twenty years of her life was above a fish shop at 72 Old Bethnal Green Road, Bethnal Green, just round the corner from the historical Old Roman Road in the heart of London's East End. It was about as far away as you could get from the soaring snow-capped mountains and vast open vistas of the Himalayas where her soul was to run free. Today, 72 Old Bethnal Green Road does not exist and Bethnal Green itself, with its elegant squares, tiny lanes and proximity to the City, is in danger of becoming chic; but when Tenzin Palmo got there it was a mass of rubble after the Blitz, and this was how she thought it had always looked before she was old enough to know better. It was crowded, blackened, smog-filled, with hardly a tree in sight. For as long as she could remember she never felt she belonged: 'I had this intense feeling that I was in the wrong place. Even now I never feel "right" in England,' she said.

Her father, George Perry, was a fishmonger, owning the shop downstairs. George was a small man, twenty years older than his wife, and liked to enjoy himself. He frequented the 'horses', the 'dogs', the music-halls, and as a Pearly King would dress up in his suit of pearly buttons whenever occasion demanded. He'd been gassed in World War 1, and suffered badly from bronchitis as a result. Working in a cold, wet fish shop didn't help. He died at the age of fifty-seven, when Tenzin Palmo was just two.

'Sadly, I never knew him, but I heard he was a very kind man. I remember being told how my mother, being so much younger, used to like to go out dancing with her dancing partners and he encouraged her, having a meal ready on the table when she came home. I know he very much wanted me after having two sons from a previous marriage. But for me he was out of the picture,' she said.

It was left to her mother, Lee Perry, a former housemaid, to bring up Tenzin Palmo and her brother Mervyn, six years older. Lee was by all accounts a remarkable woman. She was feisty, open-minded, optimistic in the face of adversity and, most significantly for this story, a spiritual seeker and a staunch supporter of Tenzin Palmo in all her endeavours throughout all her life. They were very close.

'My mother was wonderful. I admired her enormously,' she said 'She worked extremely hard and was always interested in new ideas. She was also a free spirit. When she met my father he was separated but not divorced from his first wife but she moved in with him and had two children by him anyway, which was quite unusual in those days. By the time his divorce came through she still didn't marry him because she had got used to her independence.'

The environment that Tenzin Palmo was brought up in could

not have been more quintessentially English. All around her were the Cockneys, the 'real Londoners', renowned for their sharp wit, quick tongues, and latterly for winning Brain of Britain competitions. The East End then was a friendly place to live in. Tenzin Palmo knew everyone in the neighbourhood, her Uncle Harry owned the pub over the road, the street life was lively and the bomb sites provided the children with excellent adventure playgrounds.

In spite of all this, however, the seeds of the unusual life she was to follow were there from the start, proving in her case that nature won over nurture.

She was an introspective and reclusive child, having friends but never wanting to bring them home. 'I wasn't interested. I knew there was something else I had to do with my life,' she said. 'I just really liked being by myself. I was very happy just to sit and read. I remember again and again my teachers lending me books, which they didn't do with other children.' She was also curiously drawn to the East, although there was no thriving Asian community in the East End as there is today and nobody in her family was remotely interested in the Orient. 'I would spend hours alone drawing Japanese ladies in flowing kimonos. I can still see all the intricate patterns I painted on them. When the first Chinese restaurants opened in the West End I would beg my mother to take me there so that I could see some oriental faces.' There was also her inexplicable fascination with nuns, especially the contemplative orders. 'I liked the idea of the enclosed nuns, the sort that go in and never come out and spend all their life in prayer. The idea of that kind of lifestyle was enormously appealing. Once I went into a neighbourhood shop and the shopkeeper asked me what I was going to be when I grew up. I replied quite spontaneously, "A nun". She laughed and said I'd change my mind when I grew older and I thought, "You're wrong!" The problem was I didn't know what kind of a nun I was going to be.'

There were other anomalies. Just as she felt perpetually displaced in England, she also felt strangely 'wrong' as a girl. 'I was very confused by being a female,' she explained. 'It just didn't feel right. I kept hearing adults say that when you reached adolescence your body changed and I would think, "Oh good, then I can go back to being a boy.'" This enigma, like many others, would be explained later.

If her temperament was ideally equipped for a future life of solitary meditation in a cave, her body could not have been less well suited. Her entire childhood was dominated by a series of illnesses which left her so enfeebled that her doctors and teachers advised, when she left school, that she should never take up any career that was remotely taxing. She was born with the base of her spine twisted inwards and tilted to the left, making the whole of her spinal column off-balance. To compensate she developed round shoulders, the hunched look which she carries to this day. It was an excruciatingly painful condition which left her with weak vertebrae and prone to lumbago. As a child she went three times a week to hospital for physiotherapy but it didn't help (although later yoga did). When she was a few months old she got meningitis, recovered and then got it again. She was rushed to hospital, where her parents could only view her from behind glass. Staring at the undersized baby lying there with her stick-like limbs and huge blue eyes, a distraught Lee declared, 'She's going to die.' 'Oh, no, she's not. Look at those eyes! She's longing to live,' replied George.

Then there was the mystery illness which baffled doctors and left her hospitalized for months at a time. She lost much schooling, at one time spending eight months at the famous Great Ormond Street Children's Hospital, and was so generally weak that her school arranged for her to have regular compulsory convalescent periods at the seaside, at the council's expense.

'No one knew what it was, but two or three times a year I would be completely debilitated with high fevers, and terrible headaches. I was very sick. Personally, I think it was a karmic thing because when I got older it just disappeared, and I was never seriously ill in the cave,' she said. 'Because of these very high fevers I used to have a lot of out-of-body experiences,' she continued. 'I used to travel around the neighbourhood but because I was a little girl I wouldn't go far from home. I didn't want to get lost. So I would just wander around the streets, floating above everything, looking down on people for a change, instead of always looking up at them. I tried it again when I was a teenager but I got scared so I never developed the ability.'

There were accidents too, which also brought fascinating consequences, such as the time when she playing with a ball inside the house and her nylon dress brushed against the electric fire. Within seconds she was a mass of flames. Fortunately Lee happened to be at home and not in the fish shop, as she herself was sick. The young Tenzin Palmo rushed into her mother's room with her dress ablaze, screaming. Lee leapt out of bed, wrapped her in blankets and dashed her to hospital.

'The amazing thing was I had no pain, even though my back was one big red, raw mess. I remember being wheeled down the hospital corridor with the doctor holding my hand and telling me what a brave girl I was for not crying. But it wasn't hurting at all. I stayed in hospital for ages with this frame holding the sheets off my body but I was left with no scars. Later, when I was older, my mother told me that when she had seen me engulfed in flames she had prayed fervently that my pain be taken from me and given to her instead. I was interested because by then I had heard about the Buddhist practice called Tong Lin where you breathe in the suffering of others to relieve them of their misery, and give out in its place all your health and well-being in the form of white light. My mother had done this profound practice absolutely spontaneously! Furthermore, it worked. She said that although her prayer was absolutely sincere she never received the extra pain of my burns. She was amazing. She did that, even though she was in agony herself,' she said. 'Actually I think I came into this family because of her,' she added quietly, referring to her inherent belief in reincarnation, and by implication that she had chosen this Western life in a female body for some specific purpose.

When she was not ill, life in the East End went on as normal. It was a decidedly no-frills existence. Tenzin Palmo shared a bedroom with her brother Mervyn, the bath was brought out once a week, and money was in desperately short supply. She explained: 'After my father died my mother took over the fish shop, only unbeknown to her an uncle who was managing the shop was gambling on the horses. The family ended up being enormously in debt and my mother had to work doubly hard to make ends meet.'

Financially strained and fatherless they might have been, but it was, nevertheless, a happy, normal childhood, something that would hold her in good stead later when she faced her years of solitude. There were penny bus rides to the parks and museum, and the occasional treat of a Walt Disney film. Added to this was the forbidden delight of the fish shop's smoke holes (the last remaining ones in London), two large brick chimneys in the back yard blackened with tar, and lined with shelves for smoking the haddocks and bloaters. They were dangerous but fun.

'To be honest we never thought much about being poor, it was simply how we lived. We always had enough to eat and one's goals in those times were so much more modest,' she remarked. 'We didn't miss having a father at all! In fact, we got on very well without one. I noticed that we didn't have any conflict or tension in our house, whereas there often was in my friends' houses.'

Tenzin Palmo grew up to be a pretty child, still thin, but with those same huge blue eyes. Her bald head had given way to a mop of light brown curls. She was so engaging to look at, in fact, that later her monastery in India insisted on pinning up a picture of her at this age. 'I reached my peak at three – after that it was downhill,' she laughs. She fought with her brother, whom she idolized, following him in umpteen pranks which he thought up. 'I used to be dressed up as the guy for Guy Fawkes night, sitting motionless on the pavement for hours! And once he got me to approach strangers on Hampstead Heath asking them for money for the bus ride home, telling them our mother had abandoned us. He's always said ever since that it was him who put me on the path of the begging bowl!'

She liked her two schools, Teesdale Street Primary School and the John Howard Grammar School, whose motto from Virgil was singularly apt: 'They Can Because They Think They Can'. She was a good pupil, though not outstanding, doing well in English, history and IQ tests, which she always topped. 'This doesn't mean I was necessarily intelligent, merely that I have the sort of mind that can do intelligence tests,' she said modestly. She also invariably took the annual progress prize, an accolade which she also dismisses. 'Basically it meant you had done your best, which in my case wasn't true. I didn't try hard at school at all because fundamentally I didn't find the subjects very interesting.'

As might be expected in this tale, however, it was in the spiritual arena where the most interesting developments were taking place. Lee was a spiritualist and every Wednesday at 8 p.m. the neighbours would arrive at 72 Old Bethnal Green Road for their weekly seance.

'We used to sit round this huge mahogany table with legs the size of tree trunks which had come from some grand house and one of the neighbours who was a medium would go into trance and get messages from the spirit guides. I remember one night my mother made some joke about the spirits not being very strong and they took up the challenge. They asked the greengrocer, a woman of about 18 stone, to sit on top of the table then they lifted the whole thing up, this huge heavy piece of furniture, and it sailed around the room with the greengrocer perched on top. We all had to run into the corners to get out of the way,' Tenzin Palmo recalled.

She never doubted the authenticity of what was going on. It was her house, she knew there were no trapdoors and no one was being paid. 'I gained a lot from those experiences,' she continued. 'There is no way now anyone could tell me that consciousness does not exist after death because I have so much proof again and again that it does. It's not a belief, it's a knowledge, a certainty. I also learnt that there are many dimensions of being that are absolutely real, which we are not normally conscious of. And because of the seances we talked about death a lot in our family, in a very positive way. We discussed what it was all about and what happened next. It was one of our major topics of interest. And I'm enormously grateful for that. Many people avoid thinking about death and are mainly afraid of it, and if you're not it removes an enormously heavy burden from your life.

'For me, death is the next stage on, another opening up. We've done so many things in the past and now we are to go on to an infinite future. This gives much less anxiety about this life because it is seen as a little waterdrop in a big pool. And so for this lifetime you do what you need to do for this lifetime and it doesn't matter about all the rest because you've probably already done it before or else you'll do it in the future. It gives one a sense of spaciousness, and hope.'

From an early age, however, Tenzin Palmo was showing signs of a penetrating mind and a highly questioning nature – qualities that she was to carry with her all her life. She was never going to be an easy believer. 'I didn't like the way spiritualism hooked people in so they didn't let go and get on with their lives. Those seances became the very centre of our neighbours' existence, increasing their attachment. I also thought that on the whole people asked such stupid questions,' she said. 'They didn't get down to the profound issues that I thought really mattered. They were mostly interested in chit-chat with their dead relatives. Personally I thought it was a waste of the spirit guide's time and knowledge.'

The 'issues' that were preoccupying the young Tenzin Palmo were both precocious and profound. They were also curiously Buddhist: 'I couldn't have put it in these words but what concerned me was how we get beyond the dilemma of constantly coming back and having to experience again and again the inherent suffering in our existence.'

There was one particular incident from her childhood which illustrated perfectly the way her mind was working: 'I was about thirteen and was coming home with my mother after visiting an aunt and uncle,' she recalled. 'We'd had a very pleasant evening and were waiting for the bus. Sitting at the bus stop I had this sudden flash – that we were all going to die, and before that we were all going to get old and probably sick too. We hadn't been talking about these things, it just came to me. I remember watching the buses going past all lit up with the people inside laughing and talking and thinking, "Don't they know, don't they see what is going to happen?" I said to my mother that life was really very sad because of what we had to go through. And my mother who had had a terrible life really, struggling to bring up two children, with incredibly awful health and so many financial problems replied: "Yes, of course there's a lot of suffering in life but there are good things too." I thought, she's missed the point! There are good things BUT underlying it all is the fact of ageing, sickness and death, and that negates all the other things.

'But people couldn't see it, they were so indifferent. I could never understand why. Didn't they understand this is a terrible situation we're all trapped in? I felt it really, really in the depths of my being,' she said with great feeling. 'However, since nobody understood what I was talking about, and just thought I was being incredibly gloomy, I stopped discussing it.'

Interestingly, what the young girl was worrying about in the East End of London was exactly the same issue that had troubled the young Prince Siddhartha in India back in 560 BC when he had left his sheltered palace and been confronted with a diseased man, an ageing man and a corpse. These ungainly sights had had such a shocking impact on his sensibilities that he had abandoned his easy, privileged existence and gone searching for the reasons that lay behind the human condition with all its attendant suffering. After many years of wandering, testing and trying the various spiritual methods on offer, he finally found his answer under the boddhi tree in Bodhgaya where, in profound meditation, he broke through the barriers of ignorance and attained Enlightenment. In doing so he became the Buddha, the Fully Awakened One, and triggered off a religion which was to inspire millions down the ages who tried to emulate him. But they were mostly in the East.

There was, however, another larger question which was preoccupying Tenzin Palmo, one which was to form the *raison d'être* of the entire course of this present life. It was the very touchstone of Buddhism. 'I wanted to know, how do we become perfect? Ever since I was small I had this conviction that we were in fact innately perfect and that we had to keep coming back again and again to rediscover our true nature. I felt that somehow our perfection had become obscured and that we had to uncover it, to find out who we really were. And that was what we were here for. I asked my mother if she believed in reincarnation and she replied that it seemed very logical to her and she didn't see why not, so that part of the question seemed OK.'

Getting the answer to the rest of it was more of a problem. She asked the spirit guides.

'First of all, I asked, "Is there a God?" And they said, "We definitely don't think there is a God in the sense of a person, but ultimately we feel there is light, and love and intelligence." That sounded good to me. So then I asked them the number one question in my life, "How do we become perfect?" And they replied, "You have to be very good and very kind." And I thought, "They don't know." At that point I completely lost interest in spiritualism as a path,' she said.

She next turned to the local priest, Father Hetherington, whom she liked on account of the fact that he was tall, ascetic and monk-like. She would go to her local Anglican church occasionally with Lee, appreciating its pseudo-Gothic architecture.

'He replied, "Well, you have to become good." And, "You have to become good and you have to be kind." And I thought, "That's not it!" Of course you've got to be good and kind, that's the foundation. But Perfection! That's something else. I knew a lot of people who were good and kind, but they certainly weren't perfect. It was something more. What was the *more*, that was what I wanted to know,' she said, her voice taking on the urgency she had felt when she was a child.

Christianity, her home-grown religion, had never had any resonance for Tenzin Palmo. In fact it posed more dilemmas than solutions. Her fundamental problem was that she could not believe in the idea of God as a personal being. 'To me, he seemed like Father Christmas,' she said. 'I can also remember being particularly puzzled by the hymns. I used to sing at school "All things bright and beautiful, all things great and small, all things wise and wonderful, the Lord God made them all", and at the same time I would be wondering, "Well, who made all things dull and ugly then?" It was the same with the harvest hymns, praising God for the sunshine and rain. In that case, I thought God must also have brought the drought and the famine.' Tenzin Palmo, it seemed, was confronting the problem of 'duality', good and evil, dark and light, big and small, looking for an answer that transcended the opposites.

She kept looking, looking for something. She wasn't sure what. When she was thirteen she tried reading the Koran, she attempted yet again to understand Christianity. It remained an enigma. At fifteen she took up yoga and through that was introduced to Hinduism. That satisfied her somewhat, but only to a point. Once again her stumbling block was God.

'The problem was that all these religions were based on the idea of this external being who it was our duty somehow to propitiate and come into contact with. That simply didn't have any inner reference for me. If it is meaningful for you it absolutely works, but if it isn't you're left with nothing. You need to believe in this transcendent being in the first place and have a relationship with it in order to make any progress. If you don't, like me, there is nothing to get going on,' she explained. 'I remember entering into a discussion with my future sister-in-law who was a good friend of the family. She was Jewish and was arguing that Jesus was not the son of God. Carrying on her argument I got to the point that there was no God. To me it was like this tremendous revelation. 'Yeah! That's exactly how I feel.'

When she was a teenager she turned to the Existentialists, reading Sartre, Kierkegaard and Camus 'in a very superficial way'. The trouble here, she found, was that although they were asking all the right questions, and stating the problem about the human condition, they were not coming up with the answers.

She kept searching.

At school a teacher read them Heinrich Harrer's book *Seven Years in Tibet*, about his journey to the Land of Snows and his friendship with the Dalai Lama. And Tenzin Palmo marvelled that such a being existed in this world. And when she was around nine or ten years old she saw a programme on the temples in Thailand. On one temple there was a frieze depicting the life of the Buddha. She turned to Lee and asked her who he was. 'He's some kind of oriental god,' her mother replied. 'No, he lived and has a story, like Jesus,' Tenzin Palmo replied, with conviction. It was only a matter of time before she found out exactly what that story was.

THREE

The Dawning – Finding the Path

The breakthrough happened one day when Tenzin Palmo and
her mother were about to go to Germany to spend Christmas
with Mervyn, Tenzin Palmo's brother who had joined the RAF
and was stationed there. It was 1961, and Tenzin Palmo was
eighteen. She had left her grammar school a year earlier and
had started work at the Hackney Library, a nice, quiet job just
as her teachers had recommended. It suited her methodical,
meticulous mind and great love of books admirably. She had
hoped to go to university to study English and philosophy
but Lee could not afford it and Tenzin Palmo had consoled
herself with the thought that earning money would get her
out of England quicker. 'The homesickness for the East was
agonizing at times,' she said. Needing something to read for
her German holiday, she took three books from the library: a
Sartre, a Camus and one other which she grabbed at the last
moment because someone had just brought it in. It had a nice
image of the Buddha on the cover but it was the title, *The Mind
Unshaken*, that caught her eye. In Germany she read the Sartre
and the Camus but for some reason had ignored the Buddhist
book. In the airport on the way home, however, there was an
eight-hour delay and as it was a military establishment with no
shops or amusements on offer she had no alternative to relieve
her boredom but to open its pages. She had got half-way through
it when she turned to her mother and said in a small, surprised
voice: 'I'm a Buddhist.' Lee Perry replied in her down-to-earth
way: 'That's nice, dear, finish reading the book and then you can
tell me all about it.' Tenzin Palmo was not so phlegmatic.

'To me, it was astonishing. Everything I had ever believed
in, there it was! Much better stated than anything I could have

formulated for myself, of course, but nonetheless! That view! It was exactly as I thought and felt. And together with that was this absolutely clear and logical path to get us back to our innate perfection.'

To be precise, what she had actually found in those pages was the Buddha's confrontation with the very same conundrum that had so struck her when she saw the people on the bus – the universal problem of ageing, sickness and death. 'The other thing I liked very much was the teaching on rebirth and the fact that there was no external deity pulling the strings. Also, when I encountered Hinduism there was a lot of emphasis on atman (soul) and its relationship with the Divine. When I first heard the word "atman" I felt this nausea, this revulsion against even the word. Buddhism, on the other hand was talking about non-atman! There was no such thing as this independent entity which is "Self" with capital letters and blazing lights. To me this was so liberating. It was so wonderful finally to find a religion, a spiritual path which proceeded from that.' As with so many other strange predilections in her life, her inexplicable nausea over the word 'atman' would be made clear later on.

But finally she had found it. 'That book transformed my life completely,' she continued. 'I remember three days later walking to work and thinking, "How long have I been a Buddhist? Three days? No, lifetimes."' She did not know then how right she was.

Having discovered her path, Tenzin Palmo wasted no time stepping on to it. 'If you're going to do something, you might as well do it properly,' was her motto throughout all her life. This was no easy task in the Britain of 1961. Today Buddhism is booming, with hundreds of books being published on the subject and meditation centres mushrooming everywhere (even Bethnal Green's old fire station has metamorphosed into an exquisite Buddhist temple, an oasis of calm amidst the noise), but when Tenzin Palmo first stumbled upon the Buddha's message she was very much on her own. Nevertheless, what she managed to discover she took on board with the zest and naïvety of a new convert.

'I kept reading that the main thing in Buddhism was to be without desire, so I thought "Right". I proceeded to give all my clothes to my mother for her to dispose of and I started going around in this kind of yellow Greek tunic type thing. It went straight down and I wore it with a belt and black stockings,' she said, laughing at the memory. 'I stopped wearing make-up, I pulled my hair back, wore sensible shoes and stopped going out with boys. I was desperately trying to be desireless.'

That phase didn't last long. Shortly afterwards she discovered the Buddhist Society in Eccleston Square, just behind Victoria Station, founded in 1924 by the judge Christmas Humphreys. Humphreys arguably did more than any other person to introduce the British public to the ways of Eastern spiritual thought. He was a fascinating character who managed to combine a distinguished career at the bench with an unconventional interest in alternative medicine, astrology, ESP and Buddhism. He mingled with such luminaries as C.G. Jung, the Zen Master Dr D.T. Suzuki and the royal family of Thailand, and was one of the first to meet and welcome the Dalai Lama when he was newly exiled. When Tenzin Palmo found her way to the Buddhist Society it was the oldest and largest Buddhist organization in the West. Still, it was a small building with a very limited membership.

'I walked through the door and discovered that all the other people there were not wandering around in yellow tunics! "I've gone wrong somewhere," I thought. "Maybe it was a mistake to give away all my clothes." I told my mother and she gave me the key to a wardrobe where she had locked them all up. She hadn't got rid of them at all. She never said a word, she just waited. Really, she was so skilful.'

At Eccleston Square Tenzin Palmo immersed herself in the treasures of Theravadan Buddhism, the 'Southern School' which existed in Sri Lanka, Burma, Thailand, Vietnam and Cambodia. She learnt about the Buddha's Four Noble Truths, his brilliant and logical diagnosis of the human condition and its cure: the truth of suffering; the truth of the cause of suffering; the truth of the cessation of suffering and the truth of the path of liberation. It was the distillation of his great revelation under the Boddhi tree when he became Enlightened. She discovered his Eightfold Path: right view, right thinking, right speech, right action, right living, right effort, right concentration, right meditation, the Buddha's blueprint for conducting either the secular or meditative life. They were the very foundations of the path. Tenzin Palmo lapped it up. 'It was like being at a banquet after you've been starving,' she said. Zen, with its riddles and clever intellectual gymnastics, the other form of Buddhism on offer at the time, filled her with despair. 'I can remember lying in bed sobbing because it was completely beyond me! It was so full of paradoxes. Now I enjoy Zen but if that had been the first book I'd picked up I would never have gone on,' she said.

Feeling her way along, she made herself an altar covered in a buttercup-yellow bath-towel and put on it a statue of the Buddha, given to her by a woman from whom she had bought two Siamese cats. It was typical of the way things were coming to her at that time. The statue had been on the woman's mantelpiece, brought back from Burma by her merchant seaman husband, and when the woman discovered that Tenzin Palmo was a real Buddhist she spontaneously handed it over. In front of her altar she did prostrations, naturally, energetically and with great joy. 'When I first went into the Buddhist Society and saw a shrine my first impulse was to prostrate. Then I thought, "Oh no, no, no! One can't do that! Buddhists wouldn't do such a thing." So I didn't but it was very painful not to. Later I saw pictures of people in the East prostrating in front of the Buddha image and I was so happy. I prostrated and prostrated and prostrated. It just felt so right,' she said.

Somehow she also came across the Tibetan mantra 'Om Mani Padme Hung', which calls on Chenrezig the Buddha of compassion, and began to recite it in her own way, with surprising results.

'I didn't know anything about it,' she said. 'I thought you had to say the mantra all the time, so I started saying it continuously, first verbally and then in my heart. Actually it was very like that Russian in *The Way of a Pilgrim* saying the Jesus Prayer, although I didn't know about him either at that stage. I just kept saying it in my heart. The effect was very interesting very quickly. Although I was working at the time I found I could function very well while still reciting the mantra in my heart. What it did was to split off a part of my mind so that I had this kind of observing consciousness which was resounding with the "Om Mani Padme Hung". It gave me space in which I could develop awareness of what was going on rather than being right in the middle of it.'

But something was not quite right. While she knew without any shadow of a doubt that Buddhism was for her, there were aspects of the Southern School which worried her. Particularly disconcerting, to Tenzin Palmo's mind, were the Arhats, those great heroes who had attained Nirvana having eradicated for all time all traces of ignorance, greed and hatred. As such they never had to be born again into this world of suffering. They were free! It should have been just what Tenzin Palmo was after, but they never appealed.

'There was no talk about love in all that. I loved the Buddha and would cry tears of devotion whenever I thought of him. I wanted to be like the Buddha but I didn't want to be like the Arhats. They seemed so cold. Actually I think that was rather an unfair representation and I'm now much kinder to Arhats but then it really worried me. If you have a ginger cake and you don't like the ginger you're in trouble. So although I loved Buddhism I didn't like where the Theravadan path was leading. It was not where I wanted to go. There was something missing but I didn't know what it was. All I knew at the time was that the Theravadan way wasn't right.'

She kept refining her search, seeking the exact path to suite her needs. A few months later she came across a book by Nagarjuna, the famous second-century Buddhist saint and philosopher, and in it found a definition of a Bodhisattva, the 'spiritual hero' who elects to forsake Nirvana in order to return over and over again to this world to help free all sentient beings. 'Immediately I knew. That's what I want! That's the goal! To do it not for oneself but out of compassion for all beings. The idea of being a Bodhisattva really resonated.'

The revelation of the exact avenue she wanted to take brought with it, however, one enormous problem. Nagarjuna, the founder of Mahayana Buddhism, the 'Big Vehicle', was revered and followed primarily in Tibet. And Tibetan Buddhism in the sixties was almost unknown and what was known was not liked. Stories had filtered out of Tibet, brought by those intrepid travellers who had managed to steal into the Forbidden

Country, barred to outsiders – stories of magic and psychic phenomena which had become more fantastic in the telling. Lamas could 'fly', could materialize and dematerialize things at will, they could turn themselves into animals or whatever form they wished, they could travel improbable distances in next to no time by a strange trance-like jumping method. In Tibet there were spirits and genies and alien-looking idols with many arms and legs, fangs and bulging eyes. As a result Tibetan Buddhism was dismissed by the largely intellectual members of the London Buddhist Society as shamanistic, esoteric and basically degenerate. Unlike the chaste lines of Zen and the straight dogma of the Theravada, Tibetan Buddhism was simply too exotic, too odd. No one thought it would ever catch on.

At this point Tenzin Palmo, as a new and keen member of the Buddhist Society, promptly turned her back on Tibetan Buddhism and all it stood for. But it was not to let go. While she was browsing through yet another book she came across a brief description of the four schools of Tibetan Buddhism Nyingmapa, Sakya, Gelugpa and Kargyupa. 'When I read the word "Kargyupa" a voice inside said, "You're Kargyu." And I said, "What's Kargyupa?" and the voice said, "It doesn't matter, you're Kargyupa." And my heart dropped. Being a Tibetan Buddhist was the last thing I wanted to be.'

Throughout Tenzin Palmo's story this same voice was to make itself heard again and again at strategic points, guiding her, warning her, steering her in the right direction. She always heeded it, regardless of what her head might be telling her. 'Actually it's been pretty hard to ignore – it's made itself fairly strong at times,' she said.

Following the dictates of the Voice, Tenzin Palmo contacted the only person she knew in London who had any knowledge of Tibetan Buddhism, who, over afternoon tea, handed her the Evan-Wentz biography of Milarepa, Tibet's most beloved poet-saint, cave-meditator *par excellence* and founder of the Kargyupas. It was a riveting tale. Milarepa was a swashbuckling spiritual hero of the eleventh century who had led a spectacularly disreputable youth during which he had practised black magic to avenge his family's wrongs, killing several people in the process. Finally seeing the error of his ways he had sought out a guru, the renowned Marpa the Translator, who had brought the Buddhist texts from India, beseeching him to give him the Saving Truths. Marpa took one look at the young reprobate standing before him and promptly set him about the Herculean task of building a high stone tower. When the task was completed Marpa surveyed the work and brusquely told Milarepa to dismantle it replacing each stone to the place it had come from. This process was repeated four times until Milarepa, bleeding and almost broken, had expiated his foul deeds and proven his determination. Marpa now bestowed on him the secret initiations and teachings he yearned for.

Armed with these, a staff, a cloak, a bowl and nothing else, he disappeared into the Mountain of Solitude where, freezing cold and with nothing to eat but nettles, his body became skeletal and his flesh turned entirely green. His meditations worked, however, because he learnt to raise the ecstatic mystic heat, keeping him warm in those sub-zero temperatures, and farmers reported seeing him flying over the valleys. When, after years of dedicated effort, he finally emerged to teach, flowers rained down and rainbows appeared in the sky.

> All worldly pursuits have but one unavoidable and inevitable end, which is sorrow:
> Acquisitions end in dispersion; buildings in destruction; meetings in separation; births in death.
> Knowing this one should, from the very first, renounce acquisition and heaping up, and building and meeting,
> And, faithful to the commands of an eminent guru, set about realizing the Truth, which hath no birth or death.
> That alone is the best science.

His words were recorded by the faithful disciple Rechungpa, who was to have an important part to play much later in Tenzin Palmo's life.

When Tenzin Palmo put the book down she was converted. While such esoteric stuff may have been anathema to the respectable and conventional members of the Buddhist Society, Tenzin Palmo was in her element. 'The talk of the Pure Lands, of spirit realms, of heavens and hells that I found in that book blew my mind. These were levels of existence that I knew about from the seances at home. After all, I was brought up with tables floating around the room! And to me concepts such as Milarepa flying were completely feasible because I'd done the same thing myself as a child when I was sick and went out of body. But these elements were completely lacking in Theravada and Zen. Those paths were so rationalistic it bothered me. No one was mentioning spirit. I have a pretty logical mind and I'm not gullible, but when I come across genuine expressions of higher human potential I take notice,' she said.

The obvious next step was to find a teacher, 'an eminent guru' as Milarepa had put it, to guide her, as he had found Marpa. 'I knew I had to look for a teacher, not just any teacher, but *the* one,' she said. 'I don't think I ever questioned the fact that I would find him, that he would be Kargyu and that he would be in India because that was where all the Tibetan refugees had gone. I made up my mind then that I would go there to look for him,' she added. But this was not to happen yet.

In the meantime life was not all serious spiritual inquiry. Tenzin Palmo had another side. She was a teenager, she was pretty, she had long curly hair and was described as 'bubbly' by those who knew her. As she had grown older she had not only got used to being in a female body but had actively begun to enjoy it. She had discovered boys and they had certainly discovered her. Life in the heart of London was fun. It was the early sixties, the time of Elvis Presley, Ricky Nelson, Beatniks, Radio Luxembourg and rock'n' roll. The cult of youth was just beginning, and Tenzin Palmo threw herself into it with all the enthusiasm she could muster.

'I wore stiletto heels, and pretty clothes, went to jazz clubs and loved dancing. I was a great Elvis Presley fan (he was my big renunciation when I became a Buddhist!). In fact I had a very hectic social life and had lots of boyfriends, especially Asians. Funnily enough, I was never attracted to Western men. One thing I was always completely sure about, though, I never wanted to get married. I was very clear about that. I can remember when I was sixteen and about to be a bridesmaid for the third time – a friend said, "Don't do it! Three times a bridesmaid never a bride!" And I replied, "That's a silly superstition but let's hope it works, it will add that little bit extra." I wanted to be independent. I didn't want to have my head filled with thoughts of one person.'

The two sides of Tenzin Palmo inevitably clashed, throwing her into an inner struggle which was not to be resolved for some years. 'On the one side I was this frivolous, fun-loving young woman and on the other I was serious and "spiritual". I would vacillate between putting on my flared skirt and petticoats and the black stockings and flat shoes. Those two sides were at war. At the time I was frightened the frivolous side would win,' she said. The split caused other difficulties. 'I had friends who belonged to each side and who never mixed. One day I went to a gathering where I'd invited both sets. I arrived late, and by the time I walked through the door they were totally confused because the only thing they had in common was me and it seemed as though they were talking about entirely different people. That gave me a real sense of crisis. How am I going to resolve this, I wondered. And at that moment I heard this voice inside me again saying: "Don't worry about it. When the time comes to renounce, you will renounce. You're young, enjoy yourself! Then when the time comes you'll really have something to give up." Hearing that, I relaxed.'

She continued to date boys, go dancing and on one occasion got properly drunk on Chianti during an Italian holiday. Underneath the levity, however, she had not forgotten her quest to find a guru. On the Buddhist grapevine, she had heard of an Englishwoman called Freda Bedi who had married an Indian, become a Buddhist and started a small nunnery for Kargyupa nuns as well as a school for young reincarnated lamas in Dalhousie, in northern India. It was as good a place as any to begin her search. Tenzin Palmo duly wrote to Freda Bedi explaining that she was also Kargyu and would like to offer her services in whatever way she could, although she was only a trainee librarian and didn't know really what she could do. Freda Bedi wrote back: 'Please come, come. Don't worry, just come!'

The door was open but stepping through it was difficult. Getting to India required money, more than Tenzin Palmo could ever amass from the Hackney Library. She decided to look for a higher-paying job. She was never ambitious in the worldly sense – careers, success, personal accolades meaning nothing to her. 'I have never been driven to prove myself in that sense,' she said. Having made up her mind, fate or karma once again played into her hands.

'Almost immediately I saw a job advertised at the School of Oriental and African Studies in Bloomsbury and went along for an interview with the Chief Librarian, a Mr Pearson. He had just come back from Burma and India, so I was absolutely fascinated and plied him with all these questions. He asked me if I would be willing to take library exams and I said, "No, because I'm going to go to India to help the Tibetan refugees." With that I thought I'd lost the job. Mr Pearson then asked me when I planned to leave. "As soon as I can save up the money, in a year or two," I replied. When I walked out of his office I saw all these other people lining up for the job. A few days later I got a phone call. It was Mr Pearson. "Well, we had such a fantastic interview I forgot to talk about things like how much money you want and the hours," he said. "We'd be very happy to welcome you to our library."'

Mr Pearson had clearly taken Tenzin Palmo's personal mission to heart. Once she was installed in the library, he arranged for her to take Tibetan lessons at SOAS's expense and during the library's time with the renowned Tibetologist David Snellgrove, one of the rare people who had actually travelled to Tibet in the 1950s. These elementary lessons were to prove invaluable later when she was faced with being in an all-Tibetan community with only Tibetan texts to read. At the time, however, this unexpected boon had some dire moments. 'Snellgrove was terrifying. He used to stand in front of us and utter these crushing remarks. I used literally to shake before going into the classroom. The nice thing was he had these three Bonpo lamas (the religion from pre-Buddhist Tibet), staying with him. They were the first Tibetan lamas I ever met.'

Over the next year a few other Tibetan lamas were to trickle into England, lamas who spearheaded the first wave of the implantation of Tibetan Buddhism to the West. Tenzin Palmo, as one of the first Westerners ever to embrace the unfashionable faith, was in a perfect position to meet them. Her mother, Lee, always interested in new things and open to fresh ideas, especially in the matter of spirituality, would invite them home for lunch and dinner, and they, knowing no one in this strange land, were only too happy to mix with people who were showing some interest in Tibetan Buddhism.

Among them was Rato Rinpoche (who now runs Tibet House in New York and who starred in Bertolucci's film *The Little Buddha*) and the brilliant, charismatic and latterly notorious Choygam Trungpa. Trungpa went on to make his mark in a number of ways: he not only wrote a number of best-selling early Buddhist books including *Cutting through Spiritual Materialism* and *Journey Without Goal*, but he established the first British Tibetan retreat and meditation centre, 'Samye Ling' in Scotland. Later he moved on to the USA where he founded the equally successful and still thriving Naropa Institute in Boulder, Colorado, which has produced some of America's most prominent Buddhist teachers. As well as being a high lama, an accomplished meditation master, a brilliant scholar and gifted communicator, Choygam Trungpa in his later years also became known for his unconventional and scandalous behaviour, which threw his organization into chaos.

None of this had yet happened when the nineteen-year-old Tenzin Palmo met the young and obscure Choygam Trungpa. Like the other lamas of that time he was wandering around lost and ignored, no one having any idea of the calibre of the teachers who had come among them. Tenzin Palmo happened to be at this cross-over point, ready.

'Shortly after I met him he turned to me and said: "You may find this difficult to believe, but actually back in Tibet I was quite a high lama and I never thought it would come to this but please, can I teach you meditation? I must have one disciple!"'

Tenzin Palmo was only too willing. She became a private pupil of the talented Trungpa. Now instead of having only a few books to turn to for guidance, she had a living resource. She was delighted. 'I felt, this is the genuine thing at last, even though Trungpa was nothing like how I imagined a monk or lama should be. He wasn't at all beautiful. He was very plain and didn't know much English but there was something there,' she said.

In the coming months Trungpa demonstrated some remarkable capacities. 'On one occasion he began talking about the
Tibetan lamas' powers to "make weather", claiming that it
was easy to bring about hailstorms but not so easy to prevent
them once they were on their way. We were fascinated,' recalled
Tenzin Palmo. 'The next week my mother and I went to visit
him in Oxford where he was staying. It was a warm sunny day
in mid-July, with a gorgeous deep-blue sky, and as we got off
the coach this little black cloud came tripping along and the
next minute we were in the middle of a small hailstorm right
over our heads.'

On a more serious level, he was there to meet her barrage
of questions and to engage in heated arguments which both
of them enjoyed. He told her many things which she didn't
understand at all at the time but which made sense later on.
And he gave her her first meditation lessons, teaching her how
to observe the mind, how to make it relaxed but alert at the
same time. Tenzin Palmo was in her element. 'I thought it was
wonderful. I always felt meditation was the essence of the path
and I had great faith in Trungpa,' she said. At the time she could
not have articulated precisely why meditation was so important,
nor what it did. Now after thirty years of solid practice she
can explain exactly what the business of 'looking inwards' is
all about: 'Our mind is so untamed, out of control, constantly
creating memories, prejudices, mental commentaries. It's like a
riot act for most people! Anarchy within. We have no way of
choosing how to think and the emotions engulf us. Meditation
is where you begin to calm the storm, to cease the never-ending
chattering of the mind. Once that is achieved you can access the
deeper levels of consciousness which exist beyond the surface
noise. Along with that comes the gradual disidentification with
our thoughts and emotions. You see their transparent nature and
no longer totally believe in them. This creates inner harmony
which you can then bring into your everyday life.'

But Tenzin Palmo also experienced at first hand the more
controversial side of Trungpa. She was neither upset, nor
outraged (unlike his recent detractors), nor did she take the
high moral ground. Quite the contrary. 'I can remember the
first time I met him. As I walked in the room he patted the seat

next to him on the sofa, indicating I should sit beside him. We were in the middle of afternoon tea, eating cucumber sandwiches and talking about deep Buddhist subjects when suddenly I felt his hand going up my skirt. I didn't scream but I did have on stiletto heels and Trungpa was wearing sandals! He didn't scream either, but he did remove his hand very quickly,' she said laughing as she recalled the event.

Trungpa was not to be deterred. 'He was always suggesting I sleep with him. And I kept saying "No way",' she continued. 'The fact was, he was not being truthful. He was presenting himself as a pure monk and saying that meeting me had swept him off his feet etc. which I thought was a load of baloney, although I did think he was "pure" because I couldn't see how a high Tibetan lama would have had the opportunity to be otherwise. And I certainly was not going to be the cause of any monk losing his vows. I didn't want anything to damage Mahayana Buddhism. If he had said to me, "Look, my dear, I've had women since I was thirteen and I have a son, don't worry about it," which was true, I would have said, "Let's go," because what would have been more fascinating than to practise with Trungpa? None of the men I knew were anything like him,' she said with surprising candour, referring to the fact that in the higher stages of Tibetan Buddhism in tantra, one takes a sexual partner to enhance one's spiritual insights. 'So, he lost out by presenting that pathetic image!' she added.

In spite of the sexual skirmishes Tenzin Palmo and Choygam Trungpa remained good friends. 'He definitely had something. Even though he was very casual and certainly never acted in a way I expected a lama to act, he was special,' she acknowledged. He was also instrumental in encouraging Tenzin Palmo to go to India to find her guru. By February 1964 Tenzin Palmo, now aged twenty, had saved the £90 needed for the sea passage to India. It was the cheapest way she could find, but earning just £8 a week, it had been a slow process. Her ship, *Le Vietnam*, was to sail from Marseille, in the south of France. A train, a Channel crossing and another train were necessary before the journey proper could begin. Trungpa was amongst the group who came to Victoria station to wave her off.

FOUR

The First Step

As the train pulled away from the platform leaving her mother, her country, for she didn't know how long, Tenzin Palmo was dry-eyed. Her travelling companions, Ruth Tarling and Christine Morris, who were also headed for Freda Bedi's school, were in floods of tears, however. 'I couldn't understand it. I was extremely happy. Finally I was off. This was the moment I'd been waiting for years,' Tenzin Palmo said.

She was carrying two big bags containing an odd assortment of gear – six nightdresses, lots of soap and a big sweater which one of the London lamas wanted her to deliver to his brother in India. 'I was carrying all the wrong things. Why I needed six nightgowns I'll never know, and India makes perfectly good soap,' she laughed.

Le Vietnam was a banana boat crewed by Ethiopians, Vietnamese, Sudanese and Algerians, recruited from the former French colonies. This was India on the cheap. There were no deck quoits, no cocktail parties, no luxury swimming pool, and just a handful of passengers, all making their way slowly eastwards to India and beyond. The voyage took two weeks, stopping off at Barcelona, Port Said, Aden, and Bombay before sailing further eastwards. Tenzin Palmo knew a girl who lived in Bombay and had written to her asking if she could stay for a few days while she orientated herself.

The leisurely pace of the voyage suited Tenzin Palmo's mood perfectly. 'It was like being in a bardo state, that world in between death and rebirth. You're not part of the past and not yet in the future. I had this limited time where I could just be on the boat, before the next chapter. It was a lovely way to travel.'

The journey was to prove memorable, however. True to all

good sea voyage stories, there was a ship-board romance. Also accompanying Tenzin Palmo was a young Japanese man whom she had only recently met. Like many of her suitors, he had fallen deeply in love with the vivacious and intelligent woman. Tenzin Palmo from her side had been extremely attracted to the tall Asian man, who came from a good family and was Buddhist as well. They had decided to travel together, the Japanese man intending to take the boat on to Tokyo. Inevitably, once on board romance flourished and one night under the stars he proposed, albeit in a most unusual way.

'He told me he was going to say something and that I had to say "Hei" at the end. I said OK, thinking it was a game. He went on for about five minutes, stopped, looked at me and I said, "Hei". I asked what I had agreed to, and he said, "You've just agreed to marry me." I burst out laughing. I thought he was joking. We hardly knew each other. I didn't think he was serious, but he was.'

Tenzin Palmo vacillated, caught once more between the two sides of herself. 'The thing was he was so beautiful and such a lovely person. He had such a good heart. My friends said I'd better marry him quick because I wasn't going to find someone like him again in a hurry. And it was the first time I'd ever met anyone who I felt "This one I want to be with." Still, deep inside me, I didn't really want to get married. My idea was that we'd live together for a while, he would get fed up with me because he was so incredible and I was really nothing and then I'd really understand that this life was suffering, as the Buddha had said. I could then come back and be a nun. That's what I was thinking,' she said.

'The problem was I never actually said "No." When I suggested we live together he was horrified and said it was out of the question. The family, the tradition would never allow it. It was unthinkable. We had to get married. At that moment all the warning bells went off and I felt this terror of becoming entrapped.'

Caught in the two-way pull between the need for physical and emotional intimacy and the ever-present call of the spirit she decided to keep her options open. They made an agreement. Tenzin Palmo would stay in India for a year and then go to

Japan. As it turned out, the Japanese boyfriend almost got his way sooner than he expected. Disembarking at Bombay Tenzin Palmo discovered, much to her dismay, that there was no one waiting on the docks to meet them as arranged. Taking control of the situation, the Japanese boyfriend left the girls with the luggage and went to look around.

'He came back absolutely appalled. "This is a terrible place. It's hell. I can't leave you here," he said. I didn't know what to do. "If someone doesn't come for us in half an hour I will come on with you to Japan," I finally agreed. We had waited for another twenty minutes when a man suddenly came rushing towards us waving a letter. "You wrote to my daughter – but she is not at home, so I opened it. It only came by this morning's mail. I rushed here immediately," he said. Such is the fine-timing of fate. I remember crying myself to sleep that night, thinking of leaving my boyfriend. The next morning, however, I woke up and felt quite cheerful! Ah, never mind, I thought.'

So Tenzin Palmo and her girlfriends made their way to Dalhousie, in northern India, and Freda Bedi's school for young lamas. It was March when they arrived, Tenzin Palmo having trudged the last two hours through the snow in sandals. Her feet might have been wet but her spirits were ebullient: 'I was going up into the mountains and more and more Tibetans were appearing. When I finally reached Dalhousie there were thousands of them. There were snow mountains all around, the sky was bright blue – it was so lovely.'

She continued: We found Mrs Bedi in the kitchen standing over a stove which was gushing out smoke with no heat coming from it at all. She was cooking porridge made with some Tibetan cheese. It was disgusting. She was a tall, plump woman in her mid fifties with blue eyes, an aquiline nose and grey hair pulled back in a bun. I remember she was wearing a maroon sari made of heavy woollen cloth, which made her look enormous.'

Freda Bedi was indeed a fascinating character, now a legend within Tibetan Buddhist circles. She too had led a colourful life. Born and brought up among the English upper classes, she had scandalized society by marrying an Indian she had met at Oxford before returning to the subcontinent to live with him. She followed this by taking up arms against her own country

to fight the British in the independence movement, and was
duly imprisoned for her pains. On her release, a heroine to
her newly adopted country, her career took another dramatic
twist when she was dispatched by the Central Social Welfare
board to work with the newly arrived Tibetan refugees who
were pouring into India in the wake of the Dalai Lama's flight
in 1959. Once ensconced among them, Freda had been so
caught up by their plight and the potency of their message
that in middle age, married and with five children (one of
whom is Kabir Bedi, the famous Indian movie star), she had
become a nun, the first Western woman ever to do so, taking
the name Khechok Palmo.

'She was definitely a character – a strange mixture of
Indian and English county. She never completely shed her
roots. Everyone called her Mummy. I loved her very much,'
commented Tenzin Palmo. 'The thing was she was very good
at initiating ideas and excellent at getting money. At that time
Tibetans were not yet organized, did not know English or about
aid agencies and how to apply for help. Freda Bedi on the other
hand was extremely organized and excellent at presenting her
case. She got a lot of money. Her main fault, however, was
that instead of buying property, which was very cheap then,
and getting herself established, she dribbled the funds away
on buying things like bedlinen, towels and this and that. She
was not very practical. After a few years the land prices had
sky-rocketed and the aid agencies were giving to others and
she lost out. Still, the nunnery that she started is still going
and so many Tibetan teachers who came to the West, like
Trungpa, got their basic English at her school. So in fact she
contributed a lot.'

Dalhousie was a beautiful place, spread over a number of
hills covered in stately pine trees and inhabited by gangs of
raucous monkeys. It had been established as a hill station by
Lord Dalhousie in 1854, and by the time Tenzin Palmo got
there it was full of decaying officers' clubs, Anglican churches
and English brick houses with high ceilings, large verandas and
gardens filled with roses and dahlias – now relics from the
Raj. At 7,000 feet it not only provided blessed relief from the
searing summer sun, but also commanded breathtaking views

of the Indian plains on one side and the Himalayan foothills on the other.

Tenzin Palmo had managed to time her journey to arrive at an interesting moment in history – the point where some 5,000 Tibetans had congregated in Dalhousie, making it the major refugee centre in India. Later they decamped and went to Dharamsala, to southern India and other settlements, but in 1963 they were there in their masses, valiantly re-establishing replicas of the great monasteries that had flourished in their homeland, Sera and Drepung, and trying to resurrect at least the remnants of their unique culture. 'It was a lovely place then. There were no cars and it had a very special atmosphere. In the morning and the evening all the Tibetans would be out doing kora around the hills,' Tenzin Palmo remembered.

Interesting it may have been, easy it wasn't. The Tibetans had witnessed unspeakable atrocities. They had seen their mighty monasteries sacked, their monks and high lamas tortured; they had been traumatized by the dangerous journey out; they were destitute, displaced and in a pitiful state. 'They were desperately poor and the conditions they were living in were dreadful. They had tents made from flour sacks which of course were hopelessly inadequate and they were trying to make their butter tea from lard. The Indian heat was also terrible for them after the crisp coldness of Tibet. Many of them got sick and died.'

The situation that she found herself in was not much better. She was put first on to the covered veranda of the nunnery that Freda Bedi had started for Kargyu nuns, and then into a little room by herself. 'It was cold, freezing cold, and when it rained, it rained outside and in. It was so wet in fact that I had to sleep under the bed. And then there were the rats. They were everywhere. They were also enormous and would eat everything, including cloth and my prayer beads. They used to keep me awake at night by jumping on me. Actually I didn't mind the rats as much as the spiders. I remember there was one huge spider with little glassy eyes. That was far worse.'

Every day she walked round the hill from the nunnery to the quaintly named 'Young Lamas' Home School', which Freda Bedi had set up in one of the abandoned but magnificent former English houses. It had many rooms, was perched right on the edge of a hill and was surrounded by a beautiful garden. (The first of the Dharma Bums, the American poet Allen Ginsberg, had been there just before Tenzin Palmo, gathering the inspiration which would launch a cult.) Tenzin Palmo was given two jobs, acting as Freda Bedi's secretary and teaching the young lamas basic English. Her pupils were not ordinary lamas, however, they were the tulkus, the recognized reincarnations of previous high spiritual masters, in whose hands lay the future of Tibetan Buddhism itself. Choygam Trungpa was among the many future eminent teachers in the West who learnt their first lessons in rudimentary English here.

In spite of the spartan living conditions, Tenzin Palmo loved it, as her letter to her aunt back in England reveals:

My dear Auntie Joan,

Many, many thanks for your 2 letters, really I loved receiving them once I could decipher your handwriting – knowing Tibetan script helped! ...

I am now teaching some of the beginners' class all morning. There is the youngest lama of 12, a lama of 25 who is so sweet and a very good lama but rather hopeless at English, and also there is a lama of 22 who is really so gorgeous and was working on road-making for 2 years before coming to the school so his physique is wow! Added to this he is very intelligent and is learning very fast. It is like a village school with lots of classes going on in the same room – rather noisy but great fun.

We have 2 cats and a small Tibetan dog at the school and we also have a dog named Shu-shu whose mother and brother were both eaten by leopards. We love her very much but she is most definitely lacking in social graces having a marked appetite for cow dung and passing Indian shins. She sleeps on my bed and when asleep is a lovely dog. Anyway, she has character, we tell ourselves ...

At the moment the nuns are holding their evening puja. The storm has cut our electricity off so there is only the flickering lights of the butter-lamps for them to see by. It really looks like Tibet now. From my little room I can hear the sounds of the bells, drum and chanting very clearly. It

is very beautiful. We often go to the lamas' pujas because
it is really very good and their symbolic hand movements
are lovely and fascinating.

Thank you for offering to send me things, but really
there is nothing that I need and also customs duty on
everything is 100%. Give my love to Arthur, Graham,
Martin and Kim and you of course, Diane.

As her letter also revealed, Tenzin Palmo's eye was still very
much drawn to the attractions of the opposite sex. She was
twenty, attractive, vital, and the split between the two sides
of herself had not been resolved. As though to emphasize her
dilemma, one evening a nun brought her three letters. One was
from a former Sinhalese boyfriend lamenting the fact that she'd
gone away and beseeching her to return to England to marry
him. The second was from another Japanese boy who said he
had changed his mind about inter-racial marriages never working
and would she mind coming back to him. And the third was
from her Japanese 'fiancé', saying that the conditions she had
written about sounded so dreadful that she must immediately
fly to Japan – and that he was sending her a ticket.

'I laughed and laughed. The nun who'd delivered the post
asked what was going on. "Three men think I should marry
them," I told her. She asked me which one was I going to
accept. I paused for a moment and replied, "I'm not going to
marry any of them. I'm going to be a nun." None of those men
realized I was having the time of my life. They all thought that
because I wasn't with them I must be miserable. They didn't
understand at all. At that moment I remembered again what
I was there for.'

The fact was that some truly remarkable and interesting
new men were coming into Tenzin Palmo's life. The English
author John Blofeld, well known for his rendering of the Zen
masters and his translation of the *I Ching*, climbed the hill to
visit her. She had written to him after reading *The Wheel of
Life*, the account of his own journey into Buddhism written
with exquisite eloquence, expressing how much the book had
meant to her, and much to her surprise he had replied. A
long correspondence followed in which Tenzin Palmo spoke

of her plans and John Blofeld had replied offering guidance
and advice. He was to play an important part in her life right
up to his death in 1987.

'He was much older than me but we got along splendidly.
He was a lovely friend and such a wonderful person – kind,
intelligent. He was a very humble person who had a genuine
devotion to the dharma (Buddhist path) without any kind of
arrogance at all. Towards the end he wrote to me saying he
was becoming more and more involved in Chinese Buddhism,
was beginning to talk Mandarin like a Chinese, had grown a
white beard, and that when he looked in the mirror he reminded
himself of a Taoist sage. I replied that I'd hoped he'd grown his
hair too and was wearing it in a top knot with a jade clip because
if you're going to do something it's worth doing properly,' she
said, quoting her own personal lore. 'With him it was all very
natural – like rediscovering a personality that was very deep.

'But he also had a very strong connection with the Tibetans,
especially with Tara. He loathed, however, what they were giving
us to eat; dumplings one day, rice and lentils the next. Personally,
I couldn't see what was wrong with it!' she added.

Being one of the first Westerners on the scene, Tenzin Palmo
once again found herself in the unique position of meeting some
of the most eminent lamas in Tibetan Buddhism, figures such
as H.H. the Karmapa, head of the Kargyu lineage, whose
reincarnations can be traced back back further than the Dalai
Lama's. He was held in immense reverence by all Tibetans.

'It was a wonderful period. At that time if you were a
Westerner who was interested in the dharma everyone was
amazed and delighted and all the doors were open,' she recalled.
'I remember the first time I met the Karmapa, I was very afraid as
he looked so severe, rather like Napoleon. I went in and started
prostrating and heard this very high-pitched giggle. I looked up
and there he was with his big dimples giggling, pointing a finger
saying, "Who's this, who's this?" At that time we really got the
red carpet treatment, not like nowadays.'

One day in June, just three months after she had arrived in
Dalhousie, she met the Dalai Lama himself. She was wearing
traditional Tibetan costume – a floor-length wrap-around dress,
called a chuba, in dark blue with an underblouse of turquoise,

which had formerly belonged to a princess. It was warm and elegant. 'You look like a lady from Lhasa,' were the Dalai Lama's opening words. These were followed by the far more enigmatic phrase: '*Oh, Ani-la, tukdam gong phel?*' ('Oh, nun, is your practice progressing well?')

The interpreter turned to Tenzin Palmo in confusion. 'I don't know why he called you Ani-la, and that greeting is only used when two hermits meet,' he said. Had the Dalai Lama with his legendary clear-sightedness seen what was to come and maybe even what had gone before?

Tenzin Palmo looked at the Dalai Lama and heard herself saying: 'No, I'm not from Lhasa, I'm a Khampa,' meaning a person who originates from Kham, a region in eastern Tibet. She had no idea why she said it – having no particular knowledge of Kham or Khampas either.

'What are your plans?' inquired the Dalai Lama next.

'You should know that the best of all plans go astray,' replied Tenzin Palmo, with a boldness that was to surface on a much later date when she was to address the Dalai Lama again on a much more serious issue.

A week after this auspicious encounter Tenzin Palmo was to meet the most important man in her life – the man she had gone to India to find.

FIVE

The Guru

The eighth Khamtrul Rinpoche had come a long way.

He had left his monastery in Kham, East Tibet, one night, disguised as a merchant ready to make his daring escape. The Khampagar was a vast edifice as big as a palace, with bright yellow walls and a golden roof that glittered in the pristine Tibetan sun. It had been his world for almost thirty years, if you counted just this lifetime. If you took in all of his reincarnations, however, it had been his home, and the seat of his considerable power for the past 450 years ever since 1548, when the first of his reincarnations had been recognized. By the time the eighth Khamtrul Rinpoche was born, some time in the 1930s, the Khampagar had grown in size and influence, to encompass some 200 daughter monasteries, hundreds of thousands of monks, and an élite corps of yogis famed throughout all Tibet. This wasn't all. Like some enclave of Eastern Renaissance, over the centuries the Khampagar had simultaneously developed excellence in all fields of sacred art including painting and Lama dancing. In the face of the Chinese destruction, Khamtrul Rinpoche was leaving it all behind – the pomp, the privilege, the regalia, his retinue and an entire way of life.

The journey out had been treacherous. Travelling by horse with a small band of followers, they had crossed icy rivers in full flood, the horses swimming with just their nostrils above water, their meagre possessions transported on rafts. It was said that Khamtrul Rinpoche had calmed the waves by throwing sacred sand on them, but, whatever the reason, no life was lost and all their goods made it safely to the other side. After that there was a wide stretch of open land to traverse in full view of a road used by convoys of Chinese military trucks. Miraculously not one came into sight as the horseman rode on. The last and greatest obstacle was the Himalayas themselves, the highest mountain ranges in the world. Khamtrul Rinpoche had ridden over them and down into the safety of India.

For the past couple of years he had been in and around Dalhousie with the rest of the Tibetans, gathering together the few of his disciples who had also managed to escape, trying to resurrect the Khampagar way of life on this very foreign soil. On 30 June 1964 Khamtrul Rinpoche found himself at the Young Lamas' Home School visiting Freda Bedi.

Tenzin Palmo had her first premonition that her guru was about to appear one evening as she was checking the school's correspondence. In among all the letters she found one from a Tibetan craft community, enclosing a sample of hand-made paper which they hoped Mrs Bedi could market. It was signed by someone called Khamtrul Rinpoche. She had no idea who Khamtrul Rinpoche was, but as she later put it. 'The second I read that name faith arose.'

She turned to Mrs Bedi, heard his story and learnt that he was expected any day. 'The more I heard about him the more excited I became. I felt this was the person I wanted to take Refuge with,' Tenzin Palmo explained, referring to the ceremony where one commits officially to the Buddhist path.

It was Tenzin Palmo's twenty-first birthday, 30 June 1964, when he arrived. 'It was full moon and we were making preparations for some long-life initiations when the telephone rang. Mrs Bedi answered. "Your best birthday present has just arrived at the bus stop," she said. I was so excited and at the same time absolutely terrified. I knew my lama was here,' she recalled. 'I ran back to the nunnery to change into my Tibetan dress and to get a kata (the white scarf traditionally given in greeting), but by the time I had got back to the school Khamtrul Rinpoche had already come and gone inside. I nervously ventured after him. He was sitting on a couch with two young lamas, both of them recognized reincarnations. I was so scared I didn't even look at him. I just stared at the bottom of his robe and his brown shoes. I had no idea if he was young or old, fat or thin.'

Mrs Bedi introduced her, explaining that Tenzin Palmo was connected with the Buddhist Society in England and had recently travelled to India to work with her. 'I remember thinking that what was she was saying was extremely irrelevant but at the same time being so grateful that she was talking at all,' Tenzin Palmo continued.

Cutting across the small talk and still not knowing what Khamtrul actually looked like, she blurted out: 'Tell him I want to take Refuge,' she said, referring to the ceremony when one becomes officially a Buddhist.

'Oh yes. Of course,' Khamtrul Rinpoche replied. At that point she looked up.

She saw a tall, large man, about ten years older than herself, with a strong, round face, almost stern in expression and a strange knob on the top of his head. It was similar to that depicted on effigies of the Buddha. 'The feeling was two things at the same time. One was seeing somebody you knew extremely well whom you haven't seen for a very long time. A feeling of "Oh, how nice to see you again!" And at the same time it was as though an innermost part of my being had taken form in front of me. As though he'd always been there but now he was outside,' she explained.

Such is the meeting with a true guru – it happens rarely.

Within hours Tenzin Palmo had also stated she wanted to become a nun, and would he please ordain her. Again Khamtrul Rinpoche said, 'Yes, of course,' as though it were only natural. Three weeks later, on 24 July 1964, it was done. 'It took that long because Khamtrul Rinpoche said he wanted to take me back to his monastery in Banuri to perform the ceremonies there,' she said, without any trace of irony.

She had been in India only three months, but what seemed from the outside a recklessly hasty decision was to her mind utterly reasonable and completely logical.

'The point was I was searching for perfection. I knew that Tibetan Buddhism not only gave the most flawless description of that state but provided the most clear path to get there. That's why I became a nun. Because if one was going to follow that path one needed the least distractions possible,' she stated, single-minded as ever.

Back home in England, however, Lee was apprehensive. 'Take a little longer to think about it,' she wrote to her daughter. But by the time Tenzin Palmo received her letter it was too late. She had already put on the maroon and gold robes and shaved off her long curly hair. She sent a photograph to her mother of her new look, inscribed with these words on the back: 'You see? I look very healthy. I should have been laughing so then you would know that I am also happy.' Lee replied, 'My poor little shorn lamb!'

Her mother was not the only one who was distressed about Tenzin Palmo's bald pate. On the eve of her ordination, when the hair-cutting ceremony took place, some of the lamas who had grown to appreciate the attractive young woman begged her not to do it. 'Ask Khamtrul Rinpoche if you don't need to shave your head,' one of them implored. 'I'm not becoming a nun to please men,' she retorted. 'When I came out they gawped – they were horrified. But I felt wonderful. I loved it! I felt lighter, unburdened. From that day on I haven't had to think about my hair at all. I still get it shaved once a month,' she said.

The day of her ordination is etched indelibly on her mind: 'I was happy, extraordinarily happy,' she recalls. All did not go smoothly, however. Following the custom, she had bought some items in Dalhousie to give to Khamtrul Rinpoche as an offering but mysteriously when she went to get them she couldn't find them. They were completely lost and in fact she never found them again. Going empty-handed to your ordination was, she knew, an awful breach of spiritual etiquette. 'I felt terrible. When the time came to present my gifts I said to Khamtrul Rinpoche, "I'm sorry, I don't have anything to give you, but I offer my body, speech and mind." He laughed. "That's what I want," he said.'

Khamtrul Rinpoche then bestowed on her the name Drubgyu Tenzin Palmo, 'Glorious Lady who Upholds the Doctrine of the Practice Succession', and in doing so established her as only the second Western woman to become a Tibetan Buddhist nun – Freda Bedi being the first. She was to spearhead a movement, for shortly afterwards many women from all over Europe, North America, Australia and New Zealand followed in her footsteps, also shaving their heads and donning the robes, helping to formulate the newly emerging Western Buddhism.

Now established as part of Khamtrul Rinpoche's community, the true meaning of what lay behind their extraordinary first meeting began to be revealed. If Tenzin Palmo had somehow intuitively 'known' Khamtrul Rinpoche, he had certainly recognized her. And so had the monks of his monastery. Tenzin Palmo bore a remarkable resemblance to a figure depicted in a cloth painting that hung in the Khampagar monastery in Tibet, which had been in their possession for years. The figure had piercing blue eyes and a distinctive long nose. Furthermore, the figure was obviously someone of spiritual importance because, as others later testified, the monks immediately began to treat Tenzin Palmo with the deference afforded to a tulku, a recognized reincarnation. Khamtrul Rinpoche himself kept her closely by his side, unusual behaviour since he sent most Westerners away, not wanting to attract a following of foreign disciples, unlike other lamas of his time. This special closeness between Khamtrul Rinpoche and Tenzin Palmo was maintained all his life.

What exactly was going on in those unspoken exchanges about previous identities no one with ordinary perception could possibly tell, especially the average Westerner, to whom reincarnation remains largely an enigma. To the Tibetans, however, rebirth was a certainty. We are all born over and over again, they said, in many different forms and situations and to families with whom we have strong karmic connections. In the eyes of the Buddhist, therefore, your mother and father may well have been your parents in a previous life, or maybe even your son, daughter, uncle, cousin, close friend or enemy. The bond had been laid down some time back in 'beginningless time' and had been cemented in place through countless subsequent relationships. And so it went on, round and round on the wheel of life and death, the mind or consciousness being irrevocably drawn to its next existence by the propensities it had developed within itself.

If rebirth was a given, and quite ordinary, reincarnation was not. Only those who reached the highest level of spiritual development, it was said, could train their mind at the time of death to reincarnate consciously in the precise place and circumstances they wanted. And only reincarnations were sought for and recognized, under the elaborate Tibetan system developed over centuries. These were the tulkus, the rinpoches or Precious Ones, who had forsaken their place in the pure lands in order to fulfil their vow of returning to earth over and over again to release all sentient beings from their suffering.

Who Tenzin Palmo was, or had been, exactly, was difficult to establish, she being particularly vague on the subject. 'I think I had been a monk for many lifetimes and that my relationship with Khamtrul Rinpoche started a long time ago. That's why when we met again it was just a matter of taking up where we left off. I think I was his attendant monk, or something like that. Once a lama said to me in some amazement, "Don't you know who you were in your last lifetime?" and when I said "No" and would he mind telling me he replied, "If Khamtrul Rinpoche hasn't told you he must have his reasons." But I never asked,' she said.

'The thing is we met and we recognized each other, and that was enough,' she added. 'Khamtrul Rinpoche did say that we had been very close for many lifetimes. He also commented that because this time I had taken female form far away from him in the West it had been difficult for us to be together but that in spite of this he'd always held me in his heart.'

Later, more specific information of her past lives was revealed. Tenzin Palmo suspected that in one lifetime she had been a yogi, very close to the sixth Khamtrul Rinpoche, who lived earlier this century. The sixth Khamtrul Rinpoche had left the Khampagar monastery, got married and gone to live in a cave on the opposite side of the mountain to the monastery. He was a great yogi who boasted among his disciples the famous Shakya Shri, regarded as one of the greatest meditators of the century. It was said that Shakya Shri received teachings from Milarepa himself while in the clear light. Presumably Tenzin Palmo, in her past life, knew them both.

Here finally was the answer perhaps to many of the enigmas of Tenzin Palmo's life: why she had felt perpetually 'wrong' in London; her strange unfamiliarity with a female body as a child; her natural affinity with Tibetan Buddhism, especially the Kargyu sect; her spontaneous wish to become ordained; her announcement to the Dalai Lama that she was from Kham. If she had been a man, a monk and a meditator in eastern Tibet for many lifetimes it would all make sense.

Why she had been born a Westerner and a woman this time round was, however, a matter of speculation.

As she had said, she was now poised to take up the relationship with Khamtrul where she had left off, this time not as a monk or a lama but as a novice nun. She left Mrs Bedi's school and began work as Khamtrul Rinpoche's secretary, a position which meant she came into close contact with him on a regular basis. Again it was only the strangeness of the times which made such a thing possible. Had she been born back in Kham, as a woman he might have well recognized her but protocol and centuries of traditions would have demanded he send her off to one of his nunneries. In close proximity she got to know him again.

'He was a tall man, heavily built, but like many big people he was surprisingly light on his feet. He was an excellent "lama dancer" and a very accomplished painter as well. Quite famous among his own people. He was also a poet and a grammarian,' she began. 'His presence was also very big but he was extremely sweet and gentle, with a very soft little voice.' Her voice became soft itself in the memory. 'I was terrified of him. It's interesting that one felt this kind of awe. He was considered to be one of the fierce forms of Guru Rinpoche (also known as Padmasambhava, the man credited with bringing Buddhism to Tibet from India in the eighth century), and sometimes people would see him in that form. So I guess that's what it was. On the outside he was very sweet but you sensed this great force that was inside him.

'One evening I was typing when Khamtrul Rinpoche came in looking very tired. He glanced over at me, I looked at him and for a moment it was as if the mask had dropped and I was hit by a thunderbolt. I jumped and then I started shaking. It was as though an electric current had gone all the way through me. He immediately got up and came over. "I'm so sorry – I would never have done that for the world. I'm so sorry," he said. He got one of the monks to take me home and I spent the whole night just shaking. It was like that. He had this enormous power which all the time he was trying to keep in. But really he was extremely kind, funny and very loving. Some people found him remote and detached, but to me he was affectionate. He would hold my hand, stroke my face and was very nurturing – like a father and a mother combined.

'It was a beautiful relationship,' she continued. 'It was very simple, very uncomplicated. I never ever doubted who my lama was. He never doubted that I belonged to him. He always said, "You are my nun." Even when I became very connected to other lamas, the interrelationship was not there. I would sit with people like Sakya Trizin (head of the Sakya School) who became my second lama and suddenly get this great feeling of homesickness for Khamtrul Rinpoche. It's like with your mother – there may be other people who you admire and like but that special feeling you have with your mother you can't have with anyone else,' she said.

'You see, the relationship with your lama is so intimate, and on such a deep level, it's not like any other. How can it be? It's a relationship that has been going on for lifetime after lifetime. Your real lama is committed to you until Enlightenment is reached. What could be more intimate than that?'

Another person who knew Khamtrul Rinpoche intimately was Choegyal Rinpoche, one of his chief disciples, who had been with him in Kham. He threw more light on just who the guru was.

'He was amazing. His mind stayed the same whatever happened. I noticed that he was exactly the same here in India, as a refugee, as he was in Tibet when he had so much power and status. He'd didn't mind that he had to go and buy the cement and build the monastery himself. He'd throw his arm around the Indian shopkeepers, joke with all the locals, people really loved him. He was also very ecumenical, very broad. He would meet with Moslems and Hindus alike and discuss their religions with them,' he said.

Tenzin Palmo, aged twenty-one, had renounced a lot – her family, her country, her background, her hair and all aspirations of worldly accumulations, but there was one area of her being that had yet to be resolved. Shortly after her ordination she received a letter from John Blofeld, inviting her to his home in Thailand, to spend some time with his wife and himself. Tenzin Palmo thought it an excellent idea. Thailand was a Buddhist country, John was sympathetic, and the conditions in his house were bound to be more conducive to do a meditational retreat than those in Dalhousie. She asked Khamtrul Rinpoche's permission and he said, 'Yes, but come back quickly.'

When she arrived at John Blofeld's house she found her Japanese boyfriend there as well. She had written to him telling him she had become a nun and that therefore the engagement was off, but he had heard from a mutual friend that she was going to Thailand, and decided to try his chances yet again. Undeterred by her bald head and shapeless robes, he pressed her once again to marry him. Tenzin Palmo hesitated. She was only a novice nun and Khamtrul Rinpoche in his wisdom had only given her the one vow 'not to kill'. The Japanese boy was as attractive as ever.

'We got on just great. We felt completely at ease with each other, as though we'd known each other for always. It was a very mellow relationship. He was a lovely, lovely person,' she said. 'One time he swatted a mosquito. I said, "What are you doing?" I went on through this whole thing, how mosquitoes have feelings and that just as our life is precious to us, for a mosquito the most precious thing it has is its own life, and as we don't want anyone to squish us, so we shouldn't take the life of another being because while we could take it we could never give it back. By the end of it he was in tears. "Why has nobody ever said this to me before?" he said. He had such a kind heart. He never said a mean thing about anyone, ever. He was just so sweet and intelligent. He was exceptional, very very exceptional. I thought it unlikely I'd ever meet anyone like that again. And so the idea of giving him up was a renunciation,' she recalled.

He suggested that Tenzin Palmo go to Hong Kong for a couple of months, grow her hair and then proceed on to Japan. She was sorely tempted. 'I thought, I'm twenty-one and I'll never, ever be kissed again. I'm too young! I wanted the chance to take care of him, to please him, to be with him. To do that side of things. To have that sort of relationship, to be with someone, taking care – to express myself in that way. I wanted the opportunity to do that, not for ever, but for a time. Being a nun I felt thwarted,' she said frankly. 'I was very young. And again I had the thought that maybe we could live

together for a while until the relationship went sour and then
I could take up my role as a nun once more.'

There were other enticements. Back in Dalhousie conditions
were dreadful. Khamtrul Rinpoche's monastery was not yet
rebuilt and everybody was living in tents. It was frequently
knee-deep in mud, there were no toilets and no drinking water
on tap either. The Japanese boyfriend's parents, on the other
hand, had just moved into a new traditional house and had
extended an invitation for Tenzin Palmo to stay. She knew she
would love it. The inner struggle intensified. Slowly, however,
the decision was being made.

'I thought, in ten years' time which would I regret the most,
the chance of being with the guru and practising dharma or the
chance of a little samsaric happiness? And it was so obvious!
One has gone through worldly pleasures over and over again
and where has it got one? How could that compare to the
chance of being with the lama?' she said.

What finally decided her was the *I Ching*, the ancient Chinese
book of divination. John Blofeld had just finished translating
it and Tenzin Palmo was helping him proofread. During the
process he had taught her how to set up an I Ching shrine and
throw the yarrow sticks, seeing which way they fell to make the
hexagrams ready for the reading. She decided to ask the first
and only question she would ever ask of the *I Ching*: should
she go on to Japan or back to India? The answer was: 'Further
journey East not advisable. Return to the Sage.'

It could not have been clearer. Tenzin Palmo now knew what
course she was going to take. Still, forsaking earthly love was
not to be done without sorrow. That night as she was lying in
bed in tears thinking of what she had just given up, she prayed
to her guru to help her. He heard her call.

'As I was praying I felt my whole body fill with this golden
light coming from my head down to my feet and Khamtrul
Rinpoche's voice said, "Come back to India immediately!"
After that I was perfectly happy. I was filled with bliss,' she
explained.

The next day she went out and bought her ticket back to
India. She never saw the Japanese boy again.

SIX

Fear of the Feminine

Her decision made, her split resolved, Tenzin Palmo returned to Dalhousie ready to throw herself wholeheartedly into life as a nun and to follow the path to perfection. It was the only thing that she had really wanted all her life. She was dedicated, extraordinarily single-minded and spurred on by the highest of ideals. By rights it should have been the beginning of a glorious vocation, but as it turned out she now entered what was to prove the most miserable phase of her life. It lasted six years.

By some dint of fate (or force of karma) Tenzin Palmo, as Khamtrul Rinpoche's 'only nun', managed to find herself in the bizarre situation of being a lone woman among 100 monks. By absolute accident she had entered the mighty portals of Tibetan monasticism, barred to the opposite sex for centuries.

As the pyramids were to Egypt, so the monasteries were to Tibet. At their grandest they were vast institutions, stretching like towns over the mountain slopes and buzzing with the massed vitality of thousands of monks engaged in the pursuit of spiritual excellence. They had been in situ since the early part of the millennium, gaining steadily in stature and producing some of the finest mystics and scholar-saints the world has ever known. Here, in these academies of Enlightenment, the discipline was rigid, the curriculum impressive. Entering at boyhood, for some twenty-five years (the time necessary to get their Geshe degree) the monks studied such profound subjects as logic and reasoning, the identification of the different types of consciousness, methods for generating single-pointed concentration and 'formless absorption'. They examined the varying views of Emptiness, the perennial philosophy of the 'void' and, when they were developed enough, they were initiated into the esoteric realm of tantra, the secret way, deemed the fastest and therefore most dangerous path of all. And through it all they learnt about Bodhicitta, the altruistic heart without which none of the rest was truly viable. In short the monasteries of Tibet were magnificent, the pride of the nation, and exclusively male.

Into this unadulterated patriarchy marched Tenzin Palmo. Had she not been a Westerner, had she not been recognized as part of Khamtrul Rinpoche's entourage and had the Tibetans not been in disarray, it would never have happened. It was not, however, a comfortable position to be in. Whether it was simply because they didn't know what to do with her, or whether it was because since childhood they had been trained to view women with a wary eye (especially young, attractive women), the monks, usually so warm and affectionate, kept Tenzin Palmo at a distance. The effect on the young woman yearning for physical affection, who had just renounced her boyfriend, was devastating.

'It was terrible. There was this inner pain of loving people so much but not being able to reach out and touch them,' she explained. 'It was like having this glass partition down – you could see but you couldn't get near. It was very painful to be so alienated, especially at that age. It went on for ages and ages. The only person who ever came near me was Khamtrul Rinpoche, who would sometimes give me a big bear hug. I would cry every night, I was so unhappy,' she recalled.

Her feelings of isolation and rejection were compounded by the fact that, as a woman, she was barred from living with the rest of the community and sharing in their daily activities. Consequently by day she would work as Khamtrul Rinpoche's secretary in the monastery's office, and by night she would take herself back to the town, where she lived alone. She rented a quirky little room at the top of a dilapidated house, just big enough to hold a bed, a table and nothing else. Her bath was a cold standpipe, her toilet a bucket. There she ate by herself, slept by herself, belonging to neither the lay community nor the monks.

'Later people would ask me if I wasn't lonely in my cave. I never was. It was in the monastery where I was really alone,' she said.

Ironically, her emotional anguish and her longing for affection finally worked in her favour. She explained: 'One evening I looked inside and saw this grasping and attachment and how much suffering it was causing me. Seeing it so nakedly at that moment it all fell away. From that moment on I didn't need to reach out.'

Tenzin Palmo, it seemed, had learnt the lesson of detachment. It was a fundamental Buddhist tenet, deemed essential for getting anywhere on the path to perfection. For how can anyone feel compassion towards all living beings, the Buddha had argued, while in their heart they were dividing them into 'friend', 'enemy' and 'stranger'? Ideally sound it might have been, but detachment was also extremely difficult to attain, for in reality not many human beings actually want to live with that much equanimity. Later Tenzin Palmo was to remark pointedly: 'People are always asking me how they can give up anger, but no one has yet asked me how to give up desire.'

Before that breakthrough occurred, things in Dalhousie went from bad to worse. Of all the discrimination that Tenzin Palmo suffered, the hardest to bear was being refused the esoteric teachings and the sacred rituals – the very essence of Tibetan Buddhism, containing the methods that lead directly to Enlightenment. It was what she had become a nun to find. The path to perfection had come within her grasp and then been denied her. The reason, yet again, was solely because of her gender. Women, they said, had never been given access to these sacred truths. And so as the ceremonies and the ritual dances went on inside the temple, she sat literally outside looking in. And when she asked to be taught the secret texts she was refused. Instead she was delegated to Choegyal Rinpoche, one of her guru's closest disciples, who proceeded to tell her nice, simple Buddhist stories. It was the way they thought a woman, a Western woman, should begin.

Her frustration was enormous. 'It was like being at this huge banquet and being given a few little crumbs here and there. It drove me nuts. I could get absolutely nothing in depth,' she said. 'If I had been a man it would all have been so different. I could have joined in everything. Really, it was such a male-dominated situation. It was as though I had entered a big male club. The monks were very kind to me, but on a deeper level there was resentment. They regarded having a woman on their turf as a challenge!'

Tenzin Palmo had hit the spiritual glass ceiling – the one which all Buddhist nuns with spiritual aspirations crashed into. Over the centuries they had had a raw deal. While their male counterparts sported in the monastic universities, engrossed in profound scholarship and brilliant dialectical debate, the Tibetan nuns were relegated to small nunneries where, unable to read or write, they were reduced to doing simple rituals, saying prayers for the local community or, worse still, working in monastery kitchens serving the monks. This was why there were no female Dalai Lamas, no female lineage masters. Shut out from the Establishment, denied learning and status, they were not even starters in the spiritual selection stakes.

Their sisters in the southern schools of Buddhism had it worse. In Thailand the nuns had to shuffle backwards on their knees away from any monk and never allow any part of their body to touch his meditation mat. Those with big breasts were ordered to bind them up so as not to appear overtly female!

The root of the problem had gone back to the time of the Buddha (and even before that), when women were regarded as chattle with no rights of their own. In such a climate the Buddha is reputed to have refused women into his newly formed order. Probably, it is argued, because he felt the mendicant life would be too difficult and too dangerous for the 'weaker' sex. There were more insidious objections, too. Women, it was held, were lesser beings who were simply not capable of attaining enlightenment. Their bodies forbade it. They were defiled. Shariputra, one of the Buddha's main disciples, summed up the feelings of his day when he, on hearing of an eight-year-old girl who had reached Awakening, had exclaimed: 'This thing is hard to believe. Wherefore, because the body of a woman is filthy and not a vessel of the Law.'

This set the tone for the prejudice and discrimination which followed. In Tibet, where the word for woman is 'inferior born', it was written that 'on the basis of her body' a woman was lesser than a man. Consequently at any religious ceremony the nuns had to sit behind the monks, and in the offering of the butter tea the most senior nun would be served after a monk of one day's ordination. To compound it all, they were given a lesser ordination than the monks, thereby confirming them in the eyes of society as second-class spiritual citizens.

The effect of all this on the women, as Tenzin Palmo was now discovering for herself, was crushing. Their self-confidence in their ability to get anywhere on the spiritual path was reduced to virtually zero. 'Among Tibetan women their main prayer is to be reborn in a male body. They are looked down upon from all sides. It is so unfair,' Tenzin Palmo commented. 'I once visited to a nunnery where the nuns had just come back from hearing a high lama teach. He had told them women were impure and had an inferior body. They were so depressed. Their self-image was so low. How can you build a genuine spiritual practice when you're being told from all sides that you're worthless?

'At one point I asked a very high lama if he thought women could realize Buddhahood, and he replied that they could go all the way to the last second and then would have to change into a male body. And I said, "What is it about a penis that is so essential for becoming Enlightened?" What is it about the male body that is so incredible?' she asked, forthright as ever. 'And then I asked if there was any advantage in having a female form. He said he would go away and think about it. The next day he came back and said, "I have been thinking about it and the answer is 'no', there are no advantages whatsoever." I thought, one advantage is that we don't have a male ego.'

Urged on by her own unhappiness and the blatant unfairness of it all, Tenzin Palmo began to research the reasons for this loathing of the female body. Her findings were illuminating. 'The Buddha never denied that women could become Enlightened,' she said. 'In the early sutras the Buddha talked about thirty-two points of the body which were to be meditated on in depth. The meditator had to visualize peeling the skin off to examine what really was there – the guts, the blood, the pus, the waste matter. The Buddha's purpose was twofold: to create detachment from our obsession with our own body and to lessen our attraction to other people's bodies. The idea is that one is much less fascinated when one sees a skeleton stuffed with guts, blood and faeces! However, the writings later change. When you get to Nagajuna who wrote in the first century AD, and Shantideva, the object of contemplation has turned specifically to a woman's body! The meditator now has to see the woman's body as impure.

'The Buddha was truly Enlightened and saw things as they really were. Others, however, used the Buddha's insights to serve their own purposes. So, rather than looking at our identification and obsession with the physical, the Buddha's teachings were used as a means of arousing disgust towards women. If you have a monastic set-up, it is useful to view woman as "the enemy",' she added pointedly.

The idea that women were 'dangerous', wiling men away from sanctity and salvation by their seductiveness and rampant sexuality, was as old as the fable of Eve herself. Tenzin Palmo was having none of it: 'Really! It's not the woman who's creating the problem, it's the man's mental defilements. If the man didn't have desire and passion, nothing the woman could do would cause him any problem at all,' she said. 'Once a lama accused me of being seductive and causing him difficulty. I was aghast. "I'm not doing anything to you, it's your own mind," I protested. He laughed and admitted it was true.

'It's the man's problem and he blames it all on her!' she continued. 'Women are supposed to be these lustful, seductive creatures but when you look at it, it's absurd. Who has the harems? Do women have courts of men on hand to satisfy their sexual needs? Are men afraid to walk in the streets at night in case women will jump on them and rape them? Look at men in prison and the army, how they behave together! And how many male prostitutes are there? Even the male prostitutes that do exist are there to satisfy other men,' she said, warming to her theme. 'It's all unbelievable projection. Men have this big problem and they put it all on to women because females happen to have a shape which is sexually arousing to them. Women don't even have to wear seductive clothing for men to be turned on. When I was young and going through the phase of pulling my hair back and wearing big sweaters and no make-up I had just as many boyfriends and admirers as when I dressed up.'

Adding to her general misery was her challenging relationship with Choegyal Rinpoche, the monk put in charge of teaching her Buddhism. He was an interesting man. A few years younger than Tenzin Palmo, he had been closely associated with all the Khamtrul Rinpoches (and therefore by association with Tenzin Palmo too). Choegyal Rinpoche was not only an acknowledged lineage master, also in his eighth reincarnation, but was an acclaimed artist too. He had had a particularly traumatic escape out of Tibet aged just thirteen, having been captured and then released by a Tibetan 'Red Guard' who happened to recognize him beneath his disguise. This experience together with the trauma of seeing his monastery with its works of art destroyed made him highly strung and difficult for Tenzin Palmo to deal with.

'Our relationship was both close and exceedingly fraught. Actually I saw him as a Taoist sage living on a mountain painting the moon,' she said. 'I got affected by his temperament. He was quite erratic and neurotic, so that I never knew where I stood with him. Frankly, it was one of the most difficult relationships that I have ever had. I felt it had to be karmic, something that had to be resolved in this lifetime.' She begged Khamtrul Rinpoche to give her someone else to instruct her, but he declined. 'No, Choegyal Rinpoche is your teacher,' he insisted.

Her alienation was exacerbated by the fact that she could neither speak the language well nor read the texts, Snellgrove's lessons back in London being very rudimentary. 'I would have to look up every word in the page. It took ages. And nobody spoke English. Choegyal and I would communicate in "Tiblish". That was the thing with Khamtrul Rinpoche. He wasn't a hip lama who wanted to attract a large group of Western followers. If you wanted to be with him you had to learn Tibetan and do it his way.'

Eventually she would be able to hold prolonged conversations in Tibetan and read the texts fluently, actually preferring them to the translations, which, she said, lost nearly all of the poetry and the soaring inspirational flavour of the originals. But for now gaining meaning from the unfamiliar script was a decided ordeal.

Tenzin Palmo went along with it all for a long time – the discrimination, the prejudice, the put-downs. There was no one to advise her otherwise. She had never heard of women's lib, never seen any bra-burning, had never read Germaine Greer's revolutionary words in the *Female Eunuch*: 'Women have very little idea of how much men hate them.' She had left England long before all that had happened. More specifically, there were no women gurus to turn to for help.

'It was only gradually that I began to think, no, wait a minute, this isn't right, and to feel very sad,' she said. It all reached a crescendo at one significant point in time. It was then that Tenzin Palmo made the vow that was to inspire hundreds of women across the world when they later heard of it. The vow to attain Enlightenment as a woman.

'It was a moment of sheer frustration after I'd been rejected yet again on account of being female. I made this heartfelt pledge: I'm going to continue to take female form and achieve Enlightenment!' she said, puffing with indignation. 'I was so exasperated by this terrible male chauvinism that was all around me. I thought, "Forget it! I don't want to be born in a male body under these circumstances." And so I made this strong prayer; even if I can't do that much in this lifetime, in the future may this stream of consciousness go forward and take on the transitory form of a female rather than a male.'

She was not being particularly militant about it. It was simply that the balance of power on the spiritual front had to be redressed. 'Of course being male or female is all relative, but at this moment we are living on a relative plane and the point is that there is such a great dearth of female spiritual teachers. So at this time being a female is more helpful,' she said simply.

The gloom was punctuated by small moments of light. About a year after Tenzin Palmo had been living in Dalhousie, the indomitable Lee travelled out to see her daughter. 'I wish I could do something meaningful with my life,' she had written to her. 'Well, in that case why don't you sell your house and come and meet the lamas?' Tenzin Palmo had replied. Lee did just that and duly arrived in Dalhousie, carrying tapes of Bob Dylan in an effort to update Tenzin Palmo with Western culture. She loved everything about India, the way of life, the Tibetans, the Buddhist doctrine, and decided to take Refuge with Khamtrul Rinpoche, thereby committing herself officially to the Buddhist path, as her daughter had done. On the morning of the ceremony, while she was still in bed, she had a vision of Tara, the female Buddha of compassionate action, smiling beatifically at her and handing her a flower.

'She had a wonderful time and wanted to live in India permanently,' said Tenzin Palmo, 'but she couldn't take the food, the climate and the lack of comfort so after ten months she went back to England.'

Life went on. There was the Saturday night excursion to the Bengali sweet shop for the syrupy gulab jamuns and the occasional picnic, which in typical Tibetan style sometimes went on for days and days. There was one famous picnic which started off at three days, went on for ten, and then stretched to twenty. The food might have been very poor but the Tibetans' capacity for fun was still intact.

When, one day in 1967, she suddenly got an unexpected windfall of 400 rupees (about £8), Tenzin Palmo made the journey to Sikkim, on the other side of India, to receive her full ordination from the Karmapa, head of the Kargyu sect and a close friend of Khamtrul Rinpoche. It was the formal admittance into the monastic assembly, poetically called 'The Going Forth' – referring to the going forth into homelessness, which in Tenzin Palmo's case had already been enacted. She would have liked Khamtrul Rinpoche to perform the ritual, but he had not been formally ordained himself for the prerequisite ten years and she didn't want to wait any longer.

The ceremony itself was memorable. During the proceedings the Karmapa leant down and whispered in her ear: 'You're the first Western nun that I've ordained. You've never been married, you've never had children, therefore there is more temptation for you to fall. You must be very strong and very careful. We Tibetans believe the founding of any movement or institution is of great importance for the future. In the years to come there will be many, many who will ordain. Whatever happens, you must never give up your ordination.' The responsibility really struck home.

When it was all over Tenzin Palmo returned to her room and collapsed into bed. It had been a long day; the ceremony had lasted almost three hours and had been conducted entirely in

Tibetan. She immediately fell asleep, only to be awoken by a loud banging on the door and a voice shouting, 'Usha coming, Usha coming.'

'I leapt out of bed and dashed back to the monastery, thinking someone important was about to arrive. When I got there I found the Karmapa in a side room, sitting on a high throne with a hat box in front of him. At that moment I realized that "Usha" was the honorific name for "hat" and that the Karmapa was going to perform the black hat ceremony.'

Tenzin Palmo was about to be privy to one of the most mystic and powerful rituals that existed in Tibetan Buddhism. Said to be made from the hair of 100,000 Dakinis (powerful female spirits), the black hat or crown was regarded as a mystic object of awesome power. It was believed to be self-existent over the head of all the Karmapas, visible to those whose sight was pure enough to see it, and was held to be capable of liberating on sight.

Now the Karmapa took the earthly replica out of its box, held it up in the air, and placed it on his head. Simultaneously he built up in his mind the true black hat while reciting the mantra of Chenrezig, the Buddha of compassion, 'Om Mani Padme Hung'. Tenzin Palmo, sitting at the Karmapa's feet, was suddenly overcome. 'I was already worked up emotionally and now tears of absolute devotion began streaming down my face. When it was over everyone went up for a blessing but I couldn't move. I was empty. People left and I still sat there. The Karmapa put his hands out to me, I got up and went to him. He put both hands on my head and gave me his blessing.'

The next day she went to look at the old Rumtek monastery, once belonging to the Karmapa, now deserted. In one room there was a hole in the bricks and for some reason, totally unwise in a subtropical place like Sikkim, Tenzin Palmo had an urge to plunge her hand into it. She pulled out a bone artefact made of beautifully carved pieces, strung together like a net. It was identical to the garment worn by the powerful female tantric deity Vajrayogini. Having taken the vow 'not to take anything that was not freely given', however, Tenzin Palmo dutifully put it back. Later, when she told Khamtrul Rinpoche about it, he told her that she should have kept it. 'It was for you,' he said.

Undoubtedly the greatest highlight of all during those dark days in Dalhousie was meeting the Togdens. They were fascinating characters. With their dreadlocks and scruffy white skirts they looked like Eastern Rastafarians. In reality, however, they were ordained monks, the élite yogis of Khamtrul Rinpoche's community. Traditionally, they always numbered thirteen, although in Dalhousie there were only seven. Selected from childhood for the purity of their intention, they were removed from the rest of the monks to undergo the most rigorous and most secret of trainings. Their mystic feats were legendary. One of their forebears, called Amkha Dechen Dorje, who happened to be married with children, managed to dematerialize not just himself but his entire family as well, plus his yaks, sheep, goats and dogs – an assembly of some sixty-two individuals. According to the story, Amkha went first to the Pure Land playing his damaru, followed by his wife, his children and finally his animals.

Among the present community there were still some remarkable men. Back in Tibet one old Togden, Atrin, had meditated on the edge of a precipice to stop himself from falling asleep. He had lived for years on just water and tsampa, and when that ran out had salvaged what was left over from a leopard's kill. One day the leopard caught him picking up the bits of a deer and had chased him. Atrin, realizing how attached he still was to food, had dropped the meat and returned to his cave to continue meditating on an empty stomach.

For a year Tenzin Palmo lived with these remarkable men in her own room in one of the houses of their compound. At night they would sit out in the cold, damp air, their bodies wrapped in wet sheets, learning to dry them through the force of raising the mystic inner heat, tumo. She heard them leaping in the air and crossing their legs in the full lotus position before landing in the ground. She heard their chants. Out of all the monks, the Togdens alone treated Tenzin Palmo as one of their own.

'Once I went to look for them and found them together in a room completely naked, preparing for some ritual. "Come in! Come in, Ani-la!" they called, completely unabashed. I backed out quickly and closed the door. On another rare occasion when I was invited to join an intiation I was making my way

to the back of the temple when one of the Togdens called me
to the front row to sit next to him on his tigerskin rug. I sat
there for hours not moving, trying to be like the Togdens, but
getting very cold. Suddenly I felt this warmth – the Togden
next to me had put his long dreadlocks over my lap, covering
me in a blanket of his hair.

'I used to worry about their hair – thinking it must have been
full of lice. When I said that to one of them they bent down and
let me look at it – it was completely clean! When they used to
go swimming in the river it would fall like ropes to their feet
and the little monks would get hold of it and swing round on
it, playing with it like maypoles.'

'They told me that in Tibet when they were chosen to be
Togdens and taken up to the caves they were so excited because
they felt that now they were going to become yogis. But for the
first three years they were instructed to do nothing but watch
their mind and practice Bodhicitta, the altruistic mind. They
did that and nothing else for three years! They said it was
in those three years that their minds transformed. After that,
all the many practices they did were just building up on that
foundation. One time one of them said to me: "You think we
yogis are doing some very high, fantastic, esoteric practice and
if only you had the teachings you also could really take off! Let
me tell you, however, that there is nothing I am doing that you
have not been taught. The only difference is that I am doing it
and you aren't," ' she recalled.

'The amazing thing about these yogis is that they are so
ordinary,' Tenzin Palmo continued. 'There's no ego there.
They are wonderful people, totally unjudgemental, totally
unpretentious, absolutely un-self-regarding and the easiest
people in the world to be with. Their minds are so vast.
One time someone had sent me a tape of Gregorian chants
and I put it on very softly so as not to disturb them. After
ten minutes there was a knock on the door. It was one of
the Togdens. "Could you turn it up because I can't hear it,"
he said. And then after he'd listened for a while he asked, "Is
that Christian puja?" When I replied that it was he commented
rather wistfully, "We don't sound like that, do we?" After that
he used to come in and play it by himself.'

Living in close and intimate proximity with the Togdens, the natural instinct to look after a man that she had surpressed after declining her Japanese boyfriend's proposal now resurfaced. 'I picked up their clothes, washed them and tried to mend them. I was so badly wanting to serve and their clothes were in such a dreadful state. They had no money and didn't own anything. But they were having none of it. They were horrified at the amount of time it took and wouldn't let me continue.'

It was, however, the first lesson the Togdens taught Tenzin Palmo that left the strongest impression on her. 'If anyone asks you what realizations you have gained you reply "Nothing", because compared to the Buddhas it is nothing. And, in any case, the more you realize the more you realize there is nothing to realize,' they told her. It was advice she was to remember always.

One day Tenzin Palmo heard of Togdenmas, the women equivalent of the Togdens, and her heart rose. She learnt that there had been a community of Togdenmas associated with the Khamtrul Rinpoches in Kham, who lived in secret places practising their spiritual skills with outstanding success. It was said that even when they were old they looked like women in their early thirties, a sign of their spiritual powers. Sadly, like most of the treasures of Tibet, the Togdenmas had disappeared in the revolutionary zeal of the Cultural Revolution, no one knowing what had become of them. But what Tenzin Palmo did learn excited her greatly.

'I heard that they had this long hair which they used to hang over ropes when they assembled together to do their pujas. The men were not allowed to join them and could only look at them from a gallery above. They were extremely powerful. The Togdens said that if I had seen the Togdenmas I wouldn't even look at them,' Tenzin Palmo said. 'I knew that was what I wanted to be. I rushed to Khamtrul Rinpoche to ask him. He was delighted. "In Tibet I had many Togdenmas," he said, "but now I don't have even one. I pray that you will become an instrument in re-establishing the Togdenma lineage."'

Like all Tenzin Palmo's desires to progress on the spiritual path, this one too was thwarted by opposition from the community. She continued to be given the most elementary of teachings. Finally, one day she cracked. She packed her bags and prepared to say farewell to Khamtrul Rinpoche, the man who had guided her for hundreds of years and whom in this life it had been so difficult to meet.

'Leaving? You're not leaving! Where do you think you're going?' Khamtrul Rinpoche exclaimed.

'You'll always be my lama in my heart but it seems that I have to go elsewhere to get the teachings – otherwise I could die and still not have received any dharma,' she replied.

'One thing I can assure you, you will not die before you have all the teachings you need,' he promised, and organized for her to be taught by one of the of Togdens. It helped but not enough. The situation to her mind was still far from satisfactory. And then one day Khamtrul Rinpoche turned to her and announced: 'Now it is time for you to go away and practise.'

Her probation was over. She looked at her guru and suggested Nepal. Khamtrul Rinpoche shook his head. 'You go to Lahoul,' he said, referring to the remote mountainous region in the very northernmost part of Himachal Pradesh, bordering on to Tibet. It was renowned for its meditators and Buddhist monasteries, especially those started by a disciple of the sixth Khamtrul Rinpoche, the yogi whom Tenzin Palmo had been close to in a previous life.

This time happily following her guru's wishes, Tenzin Palmo packed up her few belongings and set off. A gompa (monastic community) had been found to accommodate her. It was 1970, she was twenty-seven years old, and another entirely new way of life lay in store.

SEVEN

Lahoul

Like all journeys taken with a spiritual goal in mind, the way into Lahoul was strewn with difficulties and dangers, as if such obstacles were deliberately set in place by the heavenly powers in order to test the resolve of the spiritual seeker. For one thing, the remote Himalayan valley was totally cut off from the rest of the world for eight months of the year by an impenetrable barrier of snow and ice. There were only a few short summer weeks when Tenzin Palmo could get through and she had to time it correctly. For another, the way into this secret land was guarded by the treacherous Rhotang Pass. At 3,978 metres, it had claimed many a life, rightly earning its name, 'Plane of Corpses'. As if this was not enough, Tenzin Palmo had to make the journey on foot, for when she first went there Lahoul and its more inaccessible neighbour Spitti had not been discovered by the tourists and there were no nicely constructed roads carrying busloads of adventurers clutching their Lonely Planet Guides, no young men making romantic journeys on motorbikes, as there are today.

She began the climb before dawn. It was essential she cross the Rhotang before noon. After midday the notorious winds would rise, whipping up the snow that still remained at the very top even in the height of summer, blinding unwary travellers, disorientating them, causing them to lose their way. A night spent lost on the Rhotang meant exposure and inevitable death. Knowing this, the authorities insisted that before she set off Tenzin Palmo supply them with a letter absolving them of all responsibility should she meet her doom. She happily complied.

As she climbed she left far behind the lush, soft greenness of

Manali, with its heavily laden orchards and chaotic bazaars full of its famous woven shawls. The picturesque town in the Kulu valley had been her last stop from Tashi Jong, and she had taken the opportunity to stay with an eminent lama, Apho Rinpoche (a descendant of the famous Sakya Shri from her own Drugpa Kargyu sect), in his small, charming monastery surrounded by roses and dahlias. He had welcomed her, impressed by the spiritual fervour of the Western nun, a sentiment which would be reinforced over the coming years as he and his family got to know her better. Now she headed for the Rhotang Pass, climbing beyond the treeline, the land growing more rugged and desolate with every step. Here and there she saw the occasional shaggy-haired yak, small herds of stocky wild horses, and in the distance a huge solitary vulture perched imperiously on a rock. At this altitude the slopes were no longer friendly and pine-covered but austere, jagged and bare, scarred by the heavy weight of near-perpetual snow and the run-off from the summer melt. Crossing her path were slow-moving glaciers, and 'streams' of loose rock from recent landslides. Even in the height of summer the wind was icy. Undeterred, she continued climbing until she reached the pinnacle. Then, as if to reward her for her considerable effort, she was greeted by a remarkable sight.

'At the top was this large piece of flat ground, about a mile long, with snow mountains all around. It was incredible. The sky was deep blue, flawless. I met a lama up there with his hand drum and human thigh bone, which he used as a ritual trumpet to remind him of death, and I walked along with him. We crossed the pass together and virtually slid all the way down the other side,' she said.

When she got to the bottom she found she had entered another world. 'It was like arriving in Shangri-la. I had gone from an Indian culture to a Tibetan one. The houses all had flat roofs, there were Buddhist monasteries dotted over the mountainsides, it was full of prayer wheels and stupas and the people had high cheekbones, almond-shaped eyes and spoke Tibetan,' she recalled.

Tenzin Palmo had stumbled upon one of the oldest and most potent strongholds of Buddhism in the world. It had been in existence for centuries – first fed by the influx of refugees fleeing the Islamic invasion (which sacked the great monastic universities existing in India at that time) and then nourished by a constant stream of accomplished yogis from both neighbouring Ladakh and Tibet. Secreted away in these vast mountains and narrow valleys, Buddhism had flourished, spurred on by the efforts of the many mystical hermits who took to the caves in the area to practise in solitude. Over the years their spiritual prowess had grown to legendary proportions, so that, it was said, the very air of Lahoul was ionized with spirituality. And just setting foot on the soil there was guaranteed to shift any sincere spiritual aspirant into a higher gear.

In 1970, when Tenzin Palmo got there, the Lahoulis had seen little of the outside world. They were a good-looking, simple people steeped in their faith, who spent their lives cultivating their potato and barley crops and tending their animals. Twentieth-century inventions such as electricity and television had yet to be seen, as had many white faces. Tenzin Palmo's arrival, in maroon and gold Buddhist robes no less, caused flurries of excitement and distrust. What was such a strange-looking person doing there? How could a Westerner be a Buddhist nun? Rumour hurriedly went round that the only possible explanation was that she was a government spy! It was only when they witnessed the sincerity of her spiritual life and her complete dedication that they relaxed and accepted her as one of their own. She became known as 'Saab Chomo' (European nun), and after her long retreat in the cave was hailed as a saint.

Her destination was Tayul Gompa, meaning 'chosen place' in Tibetan. It was an impressive building some 300 years old, situated among the trees a few miles away from the capital, Keylong. It contained an excellent library, a fine collection of religious cloth paintings and a large statue of Padmasambhava, the powerful saint accredited with bringing Buddhism to Tibet. In many Buddhists' eyes he was regarded as a Buddha. Now Tenzin Palmo's living conditions improved. After years of moving from rented room to rented room she was finally given her own home, one of the small stone and mud houses on the hill behind the temple where all the individual monks and nuns lived. She liked the people of the district enormously and over the years befriended many of them, becoming especially close to one man, Tshering Dorje, whom she called 'my Lahouli brother'. He was a big, craggy man of aristocratic descent, who came from one of Lahoul's oldest and most famous families. He had made his name as a scholar, amassing a collection of fine books from all over the world, and later becoming a guide and friend to several trekking dignitaries including the publisher Rayner Unwin.

Tshering Dorje had his own view on Saab Chomo: 'She used to come to my house for a few days in the summer when she was not in strict retreat and join in the family activities. I remember her as always laughing and kind-hearted. She wanted to give everything away, but of course she had so little. She only wanted to talk about Buddhism, nothing else. She was always very strict about dharma matters. I think of her not as holy, but hallowed, because of her practice and her karma. I believe her past life exerted an extremely strong influence on this present one. Sometimes I used to compare her with Alexandra David-Neel,' he said, referring to the renowned Frenchwoman who, earlier this century, disguised herself as a man and smuggled herself into Tibet when it was banned to outsiders. She wrote about 'the magic and mystery' of 'the forbidden country', whetting the public's appetite for the ancient, esoteric wisdom which Tibet contained. She even took the title 'lama'.

'I went through all David-Neel's books looking for similarities,' Tsering Dorje continued. 'Both were brave, women, adventurers and drawn to Tibetan Buddhism. But Tenzin Palmo was much deeper into the spiritual path than Alexandra David-Neel. When she went to live in the cave I used to worry about her greatly. She is not a strong woman, although her willpower is stronger than any man's.'

Tenzin Palmo now entered an extremely pleasant phase of her life. She was content at last. Finally she was left alone to practise. The long snow-bound winter months provided the most perfect opportunity to enter prolonged retreat – the absolutely necessary prerequisite for spiritual advancement. That was what she intended. Her dedication, however, was not shared by the rest of the community.

'You will need eighteen cups and plates,' instructed an old nun who greeted her on her arrival.

'Whatever for?' asked Tenzin Palmo, puzzled.

'You see, dear, in the winter we all get together and have dinner parties. There are eighteen of us so when we come to your house you'll need eighteen cups and plates,' the nun replied.

'Well, for one thing if anyone comes they can bring their own eating utensils, and for another I'm intending to spend the winter meditating,' responded the Western convert, single-minded and forthright as ever. She proceeded to do just that, following the prescribed meditational practices advised by Khamtrul Rinpoche that would provide the essential foundation for the long retreats that were to follow in the cave. Much of them consisted of the 'Preliminary Practices' – a series of ritual acts such as performing prostrations, and making mandala offerings, which had to be done literally hundreds of thousands of times. Such repetition was said to be necessary to make the mind pliable for the more complex and esoteric meditations which were to follow. She did them diligently, as well as studying the sacred texts and refining her knowledge of the Buddhist canon. Here, in Lahoul, with no one speaking English, her Tibetan took a quantum leap.

During the summer and autumn months she rested and prepared for winter – gathering fuel and getting in stocks to see her through the long, cold months ahead. Now she allowed herself fun, sociability and a certain amount of bingeing: 'In the autumn, after the harvest, there was a special period when we did the traditional alms rounds in the surrounding villages,' she recalled. 'You go to each house. Outside you say a blessing prayer and then someone leans out and calls you in. They get out their best carpet, their best china and silver and lay it out on their special little Tibetan tables. You'd go in and sit down and recite the best loved prayers such as the Twenty-one Praises to Tara – to bring them blessings and protection. They'd give you salt tea, sweet tea and their home-brewed bean *chang* to drink. If there was any food they'd give that too. Then they told you all the local gossip. After that they'd put barley grain and vegetables into the sack you were carrying.

'Then you'd go to the next house and the next. When you first started it was great. You'd have been walking for an hour or two through the pre-dawn and you'd be numb with the cold by the time you got to the first house. The hot tea they offered was wonderful. But by the end of the day the sack and the stomach is getting bigger and bigger, and you're feeling completely nauseous and you beg them not to give you any more. But the villagers really loved it. At the end of it all you had about fifty to eighty kilos of barley. It was more than enough for me,' she said. The process didn't stop there. After amassing the barley, Tenzin Palmo had to get it roasted before going to the local mill to grind it into flour, ready for it to be mixed with tea and rolled into balls to make the ubiquitous tsampa, staple food of all Tibetans. Tenzin Palmo developed a genuine taste for it.

Life went on in this manner for six years. Occasionally she ventured out of her valley. Every year during the summer she went back to Tashi Jong to see Khamtrul Rinpoche, to report on her spiritual progress and to receive further instruction. It was imperative. The guru was the guide who, knowing his disciple's mind more intimately than anyone else on earth, could steer her course and tailor-make her path to ensure maximum progress towards Enlightenment in her lifetime.

Once, in 1973, she made her way back to England to see her mother. It was her first visit to her homeland in ten years, and was to prove an eye-opener. Lee had moved from Bethnal Green to fashionable Knightsbridge, in the heart of London's West End, where she had taken a job as housekeeper to a wealthy Canadian who had an opulent apartment there. From living in a little stone house and fetching her own water, Tenzin Palmo now found herself just a few steps away from Harrods, the exclusive department store, and from the manicured splendour of Hyde Park, steeped in luxury. She had a soft bed to sleep in, wall-to-wall carpets, central heating, two colour television sets, and every modern convenience Western civilization had thought of. Far from revelling in the unaccustomed comfort as one might expect, she hated it.

'I was so bored. The London water I found undrinkable. I had to drink fruit juices all the time, I couldn't even drink tea. It made me sick. The food was so rich it made my head feel as if it was stuffed with black cotton wool. I got electric shocks from everything I touched and I felt tired all the time.

"If ever you think that happiness depends on external factors, remember this," I told myself.'

Finding absolutely nothing in her former life to attract her, she was eager to get back to her stone house in Lahoul, but there was a problem. She did not have the plane fare back. As was so often the case, she was completely out of cash. Over the years Tenzin Palmo had developed an interesting, if highly unusual relationship with money. Like all religious in the Tibetan Buddhist tradition, she was not funded by a common fund or central government body – being left to her own devices to find a living allowance. As such she was at the mercy of whatever people found it in their hearts to offer her. Since she made it a personal policy never to ask, this frequently made for a precarious and astonishingly lean existence indeed. With remarkable equanimity she learnt to let go – and somehow managed to survive.

'From time to time people would give, usually small amounts,' she explained. 'For the first few years when I was a nun in Dalhousie my mother sent me £5 a month. Sometimes that managed to feed two of us. A couple of rupees would get you a plate of rice and dhal (lentils), which is what I lived on. The most expensive item was milk powder for tea. Everything could be bought in small amounts according to your need. When I went back to London I was staggered when I went to buy butter being asked if I wanted New Zealand, Australian, Devon, Danish, salted, unsalted. The choice and quantities were so enormous!'

When her mother could no longer afford the allowance, John Blofeld suddenly wrote saying that he and his friend, a Thai princess called Mom Smoe, had decided they both wanted to support her.

'I wrote back thanking him and saying I could live on half the amount he was suggesting. He replied that if he took a Thai farmer out to a 10-baht meal it would seem an enormous amount to the farmer but little to him and that likewise I should accept. When Mom Smoe died John took over her share until his own death. He used to put the money, about £50 a year, into a bank account and I would take it out when I needed it. His donations were extremely helpful when I was living at

Tayul Gompa and not going out and meeting anybody to give me donations,' she said.

Still, £5 or less a month is little to live on, even in India. Sometimes there was not even that. It taught her, the hard way, the fundamental principle of being non-attached to the material, and the rare lesson of trust: 'There have been times when I have had no money, not even for a cup of tea. I can remember one time in Dalhousie when I didn't have anything left. Not a single rupee. I had nowhere to live, and nothing to buy food with. I stood on the top of a hill with waves of isolation and insecurity running over me. And then I thought, if you really take refuge in the Buddha, Dharma and Sangha (the monastic community), as we all do at our ordination, and sincerely practise, then you really shouldn't be concerned. Since that time I have stopped worrying,' she said nonchalantly.

'I have learnt not to be scared. It's not important. The money appears from somewhere, usually the exact amount I need, and nothing more. For example, one time I needed £80 for a train fare to visit friends. I had arrived with just £10 in my purse. On the day I was leaving the woman I was staying with handed me an envelope with a donation of just £80 in it. I thanked her and laughed. It was such a strange amount to give, but precisely what I required. So it's like that.

'Actually, as ordained Buddhists we shouldn't care about money – be it big or small,' she went on. 'I always travel third class in Asia and sleep on the floor of pilgrims' rest houses, but I'm not adverse to travelling first class and staying in beautiful places if they're offered. We also have to learn not to be attached to simplicity and poverty. Wherever one is one should feel at home and at ease, be it an old chai shop or a five star hotel. The Buddha was entertained by kings and lepers. It was all the same to him. And Milarepa said, "I live in caves for the practitioners of the future. For me, at this stage, it's irrelevant."'

But for the Englishwoman wanting to get out of London and back to Lahoul money was definitely needed. True to form, her faithful friend and sponsor John Blofeld offered her a plane ticket but this time Tenzin Palmo refused. Her principles wouldn't allow it. 'I said I could not possibly accept donations as I had not been doing any dharma activity in the West to earn them,' she said crisply.

There was nothing for it but to get a job. So, dressed in her robes, with her severely short hair-do, Tenzin Palmo fronted up to the Department of Employment to ask for work. Unfazed by her unorthodox appearance, or perhaps intrigued by it, they listened to her curriculum vitae (librarian skills, office work, teaching experience) and promptly hired her themselves. She was just the person they were looking for to set up panels of different professionals to interview applicants for vocational training. In spite of being out of the workforce for ten years, Tenzin Palmo was so efficient at her job they begged her to stay on to co-ordinate the whole project.

She politely but hastily declined. If ever she had any doubts about her vocation, her two and a half months at the Department of Employment soon banished them. 'I felt very sad. There were all these middle-aged guys saying, "What have I done with my life?" and young married people with mortgages, already trapped. All they talked about was what was on TV. I was in my robes and because of that they opened up. They told me about their lives and used to ask me all sorts of questions – they were very interested in my way of life and what it meant,' she said.

Her appearance, still extremely unusual in the early seventies, in fact drew people to her everywhere. They were fascinated by the phenomenon of an English Buddhist nun and hungry for the values that she had embraced. More than once she was approached in social gatherings and told she looked like St Francis of Assisi. One well-dressed man stopped her in Hyde Park and told her she looked so chic that she must be French. There was also the time when she was travelling by train to Wales to visit her brother who was living there and she was joined by two policemen, a detective inspector and a sergeant. Conversation started up and they explained that they were on their way to arrest a man in a Welsh village for murder.

'Can you tell me anything that will help me make sense of my life?' asked the Inspector, obviously depressed by his mission.

Tenzin Palmo answered by telling him about karma, the law which decrees that every action of body, speech and mind, when accompanied by intention, brings about a correlating reaction. In short, she said, we are all ultimately responsible for our lives and as such can actively influence the future. It was a long lucid discourse and the policemen listened attentively. When it was over the Inspector leaned across and said in appreciation: 'I think it is the custom to make offerings to Buddhist monks and nuns,' and handed her £5. The sergeant did likewise. These were gratefully added to her escape fund.

Finally she had earned enough money and was off, back to her beloved India. *En route* she stopped over in Thailand to visit John Blofeld, who attempted once again to give her a donation. 'Since you are too proud to take my offerings for secular purposes, here is some money for you to go to Hong Kong to take the Bhikshuni ordination,' he said.

This was an offer she couldn't refuse. The Bhikshuni ordination meant nothing less than official and full admittance into the Buddhist order with all the authority and prestige that that entailed. It was a gem all Buddhist nuns yearned for, and few ever received. For complicated reasons steeped in tradition and the patriarchy, no Buddhist country other than China allowed their nuns the honour and respect of full ordination, thereby relegating them to inferior standing in the community. And since few nuns had the money or means to travel to Taiwan or Hong Kong (the only places it was available), that was where they stayed.

Arriving in Hong Kong, Tenzin Palmo duly donned the black and brown robes of the Chinese Buddhist nun and with head bowed and hands together stood through the long ceremonies which formally accepted her as a full member of the Buddhist monastic community. As she did so camera lights flashed and reporters scribbled furiously. Tenzin Palmo made the headlines. Once again she was the first Western woman to take such a step and the Chinese occupants of the former British colony were mesmerized. What the photographers did not pick up, however, were the little stumps of incense which, as part of the ritual, had been placed on the nuns' heads and left to burn slowly down on to the freshly shaven scalps, leaving a small scar to remind them for ever of their commitment. Tenzin Palmo cried, but not from pain.

'I was absolutely blissed out,' she said. Later, when she showed a photograph of the event to H. H. Sakya Trizin, her second guru, he took one look at her white beatific face silhouetted against the black cloth and remarked: 'You look like a bald-headed Virgin Mary.'

After all these delays and detours she finally reached Lahoul and resumed her way of life with renewed determination: getting in supplies during the summer weeks, strict meditational practice during the winter. Her mind and heart were still set on Enlightenment. But for all her enthusiasm, and the strength of her will, the conditions at Tayul Gompa for the sort of spiritual advancement that Tenzin Palmo was seeking were still far from satisfactory.

'Getting water was a problem. When you are in retreat you should not be seen by anyone, which meant that I had to collect water at night. The path was full of snow and very icy. I didn't have any wellingtons so I used to wrap my straw sandals in plastic bags which made it even more slippery. I used to go out once a week after dark with a hurricane lamp, a big tin on my back and a bucket and would carry back thirty litres of water. It was very difficult. I learnt to be very frugal with water.'

And then there was the noise. Just as the elderly nun who had greeted Tenzin Palmo on her arrival had intimated, the winter months for the majority of the community were set aside for serious partying. 'While I was trying to be in retreat, the others would sweep all the snow from the top of their houses, take their mats up there, and have these great conversations, yelling at each other across the rooftops in the sun. In the evening they held these dinner parties with their eighteen plates and cups. It was very sociable! It was also very difficult to meditate.' Actually, they gathered to card and spin fleece for their families. One person would provide food and drink while their guests would spin their wool for them. They would rotate so everyone's work was completed as a team.

After six years she had had enough. 'I had gone to Lahoul to meditate, not to have a swinging social life!' she said. 'I decided I had to move out, to find somewhere quieter. So I went up above the monastery to look for a place where I could build a small house.' Up in the mountains she called upon the dakinis, those ethereal female Buddhist spirits, known for their wildness, their power and their willingness to assist spiritual practitioners, to come to her aid. She had always had a particularly intimate relationship with them. Now she addressed them in her own inimitable way: 'Look here – if you find me a suitable place to do a retreat, then on my side I promise I will try to practise,' she prayed. 'I felt very positive about it, very happy. I was sure something was going to happen,' she commented.

She came down the mountain and the next morning went to see one of the nuns. 'I'm thinking of building a house above the monastery,' she remarked.

'How can you do that? You need money for building materials and labour and you don't have any. Why don't you live in a cave?' the nun replied.

'A cave is out of the question. To begin with there are very few caves in Lahoul, and where there are caves there isn't any water, and where there is water there are people,' Tenzin Palmo pointed out.

'That's true,' the nun replied, 'but last night I suddenly remembered an old nun who told me about a cave up on the mountain which has water nearby as well as trees and a meadow outside. Why don't we go and look for it?'

The moment the words were out Tenzin Palmo knew.

'That's it!' she said.

The next day she gathered together a group of people, including the head lama of the monastery, and set off up the mountain in search of the cave the nun had heard about.

EIGHT

The Cave

Tenzin Palmo, with her small band of companions, began to climb the mountain which stood behind Tayul Gompa in the direction in which they had been told the cave lay. They trudged up and up in a steep ascent, leaving the habitations of human beings far behind. Higher and higher they went, across the sweet-smelling grasses which gave off aromatic scents as they brushed by, climbing more than 1,000 feet beyond the Gompa, their chests bursting with the effort and the altitude. This was not a trek for either the faint-hearted or the short-winded. The way was perilously steep and treacherous. There was no path to follow and the drop beside them was sheer. At various points the way was made more hazardous by wide streams of loose scree – boulders and stones that the mountain rising over them habitually shrugged off as though irritated by their presence. They had to be traversed if the cave was to be found, but one false foothold on those slippery stones meant likely death.

Undaunted, they carried on. After two hours of climbing they suddenly came across it. It was so well blended in with the mountain, so 'camouflaged', that until they were almost upon it they had no idea it was there. It was certainly not the archetypal cave of one's imagination or of Hollywood movies. Here was no deep hollow in the mountainside with a neat round entrance and a smooth dirt floor, offering a cosy, self-contained, if primitive living space. It was less, much less than that. This 'cave' was nothing more than an overhang on a natural ledge of the mountain with three sides open to the elements. It had a craggy roof which you had to stoop to stand under, a jagged, slanting back wall and beyond the ledge outside a sheer drop into the steep V of the Lahouli valley. At best it was a flimsy shelter. At worst a mere indentation in a rock. It was also inconceivably small: a space measuring at most ten feet wide by six feet deep. It was a cupboard of a cave. A cell for solitary confinement.

Tenzin Palmo stood on the tiny ledge and surveyed the scene. The view was sensational. How could it be otherwise? In front of her, stretching in a 180 degree arc, was a vast range of mountains. She was almost eye to eye with their peaks. Right now, in summer, only the tops were covered with snow but in the long eight-month winter they would constitute a massive wall of whiteness soaring into the pristine, pollution-free, azure-blue sky above. The light was crystalline, imbuing everything with a shimmering luminosity, the air sparkling and crisp. The silence was profound. Only the rushing grey-green waters of the Bhaga river below, the whistle of the wind and the occasional flap of a bird's wing broke the quietness. To her right was a small juniper forest, which could provide fuel. To her left, about a quarter of a mile away, was a spring, gurgling out from between some rocks, a vital source of fresh, clean water. And behind her was yet more mountain towering over her like a sentinel. For all the awesome power of her surroundings, and the extreme isolation, the cave and its surroundings felt peaceful and benign, as though the mighty mountains offered security by their sheer size and solidity, although this, of course, was an illusion – mountains being as impermanent as everything else made of 'compounded phenomena'.

She was 13,200 feet above sea level – a dizzying height. At this altitude it was like contemplating living just below the peak of Mount Whitney in the the Rockies or not far short of the top of Mont Blanc. In comparison Britain's highest mountain, Ben Nevis, at 4,402 feet, was a pygmy. It would have to be stacked three times on top of itself to approach the spot where Tenzin Palmo now stood. Up here the eye was forced upwards and outwards, bringing the mind automatically with it, forcing both beyond the confined boundaries of the earthbound mortals below. It was no wonder that the highest peaks had always been the favoured haunts of solitary meditators.

Tenzin Palmo took all this in, and in spite of the minute size and condition of the overhang was sold. 'I knew instantly. This was it,' she said. It had everything she needed. Here, perched like an eagle on the top of the world, she would most definitely not be bothered by the clamour and clutter of human commerce. She would have the absolute silence she yearned for. The silence that was so necessary to her inner search, for she knew, like all meditators, that it was only in the depth of silence that the voice of the Absolute could be heard. She could bury herself in the confines of her cave to pursue her spiritual practices without interruption. She could go out and look at the mountains and the infinite sky. She would see no one. No one would see her.

There were other attractions. Fortuitously, considering her quest to attain enlightenment as a women, she had landed in the midst of a vortex of female spiritual energy. On the summit of the mountain opposite was a curious black rock called by the locals 'The Lady of Keylong'. Even in the midst of winter the shape remained inexplicably free of snow. On closer inspection one could make out the silhouette of a kneeling woman draped in a mantle with a baby at her breast and one hand outstretched feeding a small bird. To the Western eye it bore an uncanny resemblance to the Madonna and child, although to the Lahoulis she was Tara, the female Buddha of Compassion. High on a precipice nearby could be found a faded blue and gold painting of the same goddess. It had apparently appeared there spontaneously several centuries earlier, having moved itself from the opposite side of the valley, its form still clearly visible to the perceptive eye. And down the way, not far from the cave, was a spot said to be inhabited by the powerful Buddhist protectress Palden Lhamo, traditionally depicted riding on a mule. One day several years later Tenzin Palmo was to see footprints of a mule embedded in the snow at this very spot. Strangely there were no other footprints leading to or from it.

All in all it was perfect. Here she could finally devote her entire energy and time to profound and prolonged meditation. She could begin to unravel the secrets of the inner world – the world that was said to contain the vastness and the wonder of the entire universe.

If she was happy at her discovery of the cave, her companions were not. They proceeded to throw at her all the objections and discouragements that had been hurled at women who wanted to engage in serious meditation in total isolation down the ages. Tenzin Palmo deftly fielded each one.

'It's too high! Nobody, let alone a woman, can survive at this altitude. You will die,' they chorused.

'But caves are warmer than houses. They are thermostatically controlled. My house in Tayul is freezing in winter and I survive that. This cave will be better,' she replied.

'Well, living so far away from any living person you will be a sitting duck for thieves who will break in and rob you,' they retorted.

'There are no thieves in Lahoul. You can see for yourself how the Lahouli women walk around wearing all their jewellery quite openly and no one tries to rob them,' she argued.

'Men from the army camp will come up and rape you,' they tried again.

'By the time they have climbed this high they will be so exhausted all they will want is a cup of tea,' she responded.

'What about the ghosts? These places are haunted, don't you know? You will be terrified,' they continued.

At this point Tenzin Palmo's Tibetan failed her. Believing they were talking about snakes instead of ghosts (the word being similar in Tibetan), she blithely replied, 'Oh I don't mind them at all.' This nonchalant declaration impressed her detractors almost to silence, but not quite.

'Well, we're not going to help you move up here because if we do we will only be aiding you in your own death. And we are not going to be party to that.' They were adamant.

'If I get permission from my guru, Khamtrul Rinpoche, will you agree and help?' she asked. They finally nodded their heads. A letter was duly dispatched to Tashi Jong, and after asking her several searching questions about the position and condition of the cave Khamtrul Rinpoche gave his permission. The objections were at last quelled.

In that one brief argument Tenzin Palmo overturned centuries of tradition, which decreed that women were not capable of doing extensive retreats in totally isolated places in order to advance themselves to higher spiritual levels. In doing so she also became the first Western woman to follow in the footsteps of the Eastern yogis of old and enter a Himalayan cave to seek Enlightenment.

Before she could begin her great work, however, the cave had to be made habitable. With the help from her Lahouli friends she employed labourers to brick up the front and side of the cave with walls made especially thick to keep out the ferocious cold. A small area inside was partitioned off to use as a storeroom for her supplies of food. It was essential, but reduced her living space still further, to a minuscule area of six feet wide by six feet deep. The floor also had to be scooped out to give her room to stand up, then baked earth was put on top of it, then flagstones, then more earth. They put in a window and a door, which Tshering Dorje insisted open inwards – an insight which was to prove invaluable in the drama that was to follow. Then they slapped mud and cow-dung on the floor and walls. After that they levelled off the ledge outside, making it into a patio where Tenzin Palmo could sit and bask in that breathtaking view. Finally they constructed a stone wall around the perimeter of the cave to keep the wild animals at bay and to establish a boundary for her retreat area.

Into the cave Tenzin Palmo put her furniture: a small wood-burning stove (a legacy of the Moravian missionaries who had once tried to convert the Lahoulis) with a flue pipe that thrust out of the front wall; a wooden box for a table covered with a flowery tablecloth; a bucket. On the walls she hung pictures of Buddhist deities in their various manifestations. A handy depression in the wall became her bookshelf holding her precious dharma texts, carefully wrapped in yellow cloth to keep the loose pages together, bookbinding never having made it to Tibet. On a natural ledge she placed her ritual implements of dorje and bell, the mystic thunderbolt signifying compassion, the bell Emptiness or wisdom. These were the two 'wings' of Tibetan Buddhism which, when realized, were said to fly you all the way to Enlightenment. And against the back wall was her altar, holding the images of her personal meditational deities, a miniature stupa (representing the Buddha Mind) and a text (representing the dharma). In front of this she set up seven small offering bowls which she filled with water. They represented the seven gifts offered to any distinguished visitor who graced your house with his or her presence: water for drinking, water for washing the feet, flowers, food, perfume, light and music.

And then there was the most unusual object of all, a traditional meditation box. This was a square wooden structure measuring 2ft 6in by 2ft 6in and raised slightly off the ground to insulate the meditator from rising damp. It was where she would spend the greater part of her life. Over the years she developed a remarkably close attachment to it: 'I loved my meditation box. I'd wrap myself in my cloak and be perfectly snug there, out of the way of draughts,' she said enthusiastically.

When it was finished the gaping, jagged hole in the mountain had been transformed into a pretty little house with a crooked rocky roof, so quaint it could have come out of the pages of a fairytale book. It instantly dispelled any notion of clichéd cave-living.

'It was a very pukka cave,' Tenzin Palmo admitted. 'The few people who saw it were always very surprised how neat and cosy it was. It was small, certainly. There was no room to dance! Although when I did my long retreat I did do Hatha yoga there. Yoga was great in counteracting all the sitting I did and in helping with the problems with my spine,' she said, referring to the back problems which had plagued her since birth. 'But the cave was so small I had to do different postures in different parts of the cave, depending on where there was room.'

Didi Contractor was one person who witnessed the cave. A large, grey-haired woman now in her late sixties, she had come to India from California many decades earlier and had led a colourful life in an extended family with her Indian husband. She had met Tenzin Palmo during one of her visits to Khamtrul Rinpoche and had stayed in touch. As an interior designer (responsible for such famous landmarks as the Lake Palace in Udaipur), she wanted to throw a professional eye over Tenzin Palmo's unorthodox living arrangements to make sure she was safe: 'The climb up was horrific, especially over the loose scree. I looked down on the tiny houses in the valley below and thought, "If I fall I'm strawberry jam." Tenzin Palmo, who escorted me, however, bounded up like an antelope. When I finally got there I was reassured. The cave was very secure and safe. The walls were thick – although I did arrange for her to have double glazing put on the windows. Most importantly, it was south-facing, which meant it got the sun for the whole day which was essential in winter. My God, it was tiny though. There was just room for me to lay my sleeping bag down beside her meditation box. That was it,' she said, from the mud-brick house which she had built herself just below Dharamsala, home of the Dalai Lama and his government in exile.

With the cave finished, Tenzin Palmo moved in and began her extraordinary way of life. She was thirty-three years old. This was to be her home until she was forty-five.

Her quest may have been purely spiritual but before she could get down to grappling with the immaterial she first had to conquer the eminently mundane business of simply staying alive. For the bookish, other-worldly and decidedly un-robust woman this was a challenge.

'I was never practical. Now I had to learn to do umpteen physical things for myself. In the end I surprised even myself at how well I managed and how self-sufficient I became,' she admitted.

The first priority was water.

'Initially I had to get my water from the spring, which was about a quarter of a mile away. In summer I'd have to make several trips, carrying it to my cave in buckets on my back. In the winter, when I couldn't get out, I melted snow. And if you've ever tried to melt snow you would know how difficult that is! A vast amount of snow only gives you a tiny amount of water. Fortunately in the winter you don't need a lot because you're not really washing either yourself or your clothes and so you can be very economical with the water you use. Later, when I did my three-year retreat, and could not venture beyond my boundary, someone paid for a water-pipe to be laid right into the cave's compound. It was an enormous help,' she explained.

Next was food.

There was of course nothing to eat on that sparse mountain-side. No handy bushes bearing berries. No fruit trees. No pastures of rippling golden wheat. Instead she arranged for supplies to be brought up from the village in the summer, but as often as not they would not arrive and Tenzin Palmo would be reduced to running up and down the mountain herself carrying gigantic loads. 'It took a lot of time and effort,' she said. For the bigger task of stocking up for her three-year retreat Tshering Dorje was put in charge:

'I would hire coolies and donkeys to carry up all that she needed,' he recalled. 'There would be kerosene, tsampa, rice, lentils flour, dried vegetables, ghee [clarified butter], cooking- oil, salt, soap, milk powder, tea, sugar, apples and the ingredients for ritual offerings such as sweets and incense. On top of that I employed wood-choppers to cut logs and these were carried up as well.'

To supplement these basic provisions with a source of fresh food Tenzin Palmo made a garden. Just below the ledge outside her cave she created two garden beds in which she grew vegetables and flowers. Food to feed her body, flowers to feed her soul. Over the coming years she experimented to see what would survive in that rocky soil. 'I tried growing all sorts of vegetables like cabbages and peas but the rodents ate them. The only things they wouldn't touch were turnips and potatoes. Over the years I truly discovered the joy of turnips! I am now ever ready to promote the turnip,' she enthused. 'I discovered that turnips are a dual-purpose vegetable. You have the wonderful turnip greens, which are in fact the most nutritious of all vegetable greens and absolutely delicious, especially when young,' she waxed. 'No gourmet meal in the world is comparable to your first mouthful of fresh turnip greens after the long winter. And then you've got the bulb, which is also very good for you. Both of them can be cut up and dried, so that right through the winter you've got these wonderful vegetables. Actually I was waiting for the book *One Hundred and Eight Ways to Cook Turnips* but it never showed up,' she joked.

She ate once a day at midday, as is the way with Buddhist nuns and monks. Her menu was simple, healthy and to ordinary palates excruciatingly monotonous. Every day she ate the same meal: rice, dhal (lentils) and vegetables, brewed up together in a pressure-cooker. 'My pressure cooker was my one luxury. It would have taken me hours to cook lentils at that altitude without it,' she said. This meagre fare she supplemented with sour-dough bread (which she baked) and tsampa. Her only drink was ordinary tea with powdered milk. (Interestingly, the traditional tea made with churned butter and salt was one of the few Tibetan customs she did not like.) For desert she had a small piece of fruit. Manali was renowned for its apples and Tshering Dorje would deliver a box of them. 'I'd eat half an apple a day and sometimes some dried apricot.'

For twelve years this was how it was. There was no variation, no culinary treats like cakes, chocolates, ice creams – the foods which most people turn to to relieve monotony, depression or hard work. She professed she did not mind and as she logically pointed out: 'I couldn't pop down to Sainsbury's if I wanted anything anyway. Actually, I got so used to eating small quantities that when I left the cave people would laugh seeing me eat only half an apple, half a slice of toast, half a quantity of jam. Anything more seemed so wasteful and extravagant.'

And then there was the cold. That tremendous unremitting, penetrating cold that went on for month after month on end. In the valley below the temperature would regularly plunge to –35 degrees in winter. Up on that exposed mountain it was even bleaker. There were huge snowdrifts that piled up against her cave and howling winds to contend with too. Once again, Tenzin Palmo made light of it. 'Just as I suspected, the cave proved to be much warmer than a house. The water offering bowls in front of my altar never froze over in the cave as they did in my house in Tayul Gompa. Even in my store-room, which was never heated, the water never froze. The thing about caves is that the colder it is on the outside the warmer it is on the inside and the warmer it is outside the cooler it is inside. Nobody believed this when I told them, but the yogis had told me and I trusted them,' she insisted.

For all her avowed indifference, the cold must have been intense. She lit her stove only once a day at noon and then only to cook lunch. This meant in effect that when the sun went down she was left in her cave without any source of heat at all. Somehow she survived. 'Sure I was cold, but so what?' she stated, almost defiantly, before adding in a somewhat conciliatory tone, 'When you're doing your practice you can't keep jumping up to light the stove. Besides, if you are really concentrating you get hot anyway.' And her comment begged the further question of how far she had got in her ability to raise the mystic heat, like Milarepa had done in his freezing cave all those centuries ago and the Togdens, who had practised drying wet sheets on their naked bodies on cold winter nights in Dalhousie. 'Tumo wasn't really my practice,' was all she would say.

Endurance was one thing, however, comfort another. The pleasure of a hot bath, a fluffy towel, scented soap, a soft bed, crisp sheets, an easy chair, a clean lavatory – the soft touches that most women appreciate and need – she had none of. This desire for physical ease was said, by men, to be one of the biggest obstacles to women gaining Enlightenment. How could they withstand the rigours of isolated places necessary to spiritual progress, they argued, when by nature they wanted to curl up cat-like in front of a warm fire? In this, as in many things, Tenzin Palmo was to prove them wrong.

Her bath was a bucket. She washed sparingly, especially in winter when water was scarce and temperatures reduced body odours to zero. Her lavatory in summer was the great outdoors – her privacy was guaranteed. 'In the winter I'd use a tin and later bury it.' None of this bothered her. 'To be honest I didn't miss a flushing toilet or a hot shower because I'd already been so long without those things,' she said.

Compounding her asceticisms was the total absence of any form of entertainment. Up in that cave she had no TV, no radio, no music, no novel, in fact no book which spoke of anything but religion. 'There was no "luxury" I missed. Life in Dalhousie had prepared me admirably. I had everything I needed,' she repeated.

Arguably, the most radical of all her deprivations was the absence of a bed. It was not that the cave was too small, it was simply that Tenzin Palmo did not want one. She intended to follow in the tradition of all serious meditators and train herself to do without sleep. According to the sages, sleep was nothing but a tragic waste of precious time. If we spent eight hours of every day asleep, that amounted to a third of our life which, they calculated, if we lived until we were seventy added up to some twenty-four years of voluntary unconsciousness. Time which could be spent striving for spiritual betterment in order to help all living beings. Knowing this the yogis disciplined themselves not to fall asleep but to use the refined levels of consciousness induced by meditation to bring about both mental and physical refreshment. It was agreed that the quietness and solitude of a cave was the perfect place to practise such a feat, for even the best of them would have been hard-put enduring sleeplessness while living in the midst of a busy town. But sitting up all night in their remote hideaways they learnt to see that whatever images arose from the subconscious, be they in the waking, semi-waking, or sleeping state (should they nod off), were nothing but projections, 'mere appearances' from their own minds. It was, they said, an invaluable exercise.

In actuality this meant that for as long as Tenzin Palmo was in the cave she never fully lay down. Instead she spent the night, every night, sitting upright in her meditation box. 'The idea is that you're meant to stay sitting up in order to meditate. It's good for the awareness,' was all she would say on the matter. 'If I really felt I had to I would curl up inside my meditation box, or flop my legs over the side.'

And at such moments you wondered how much of Tenzin Palmo's capacity to endure these prolonged physical hardships was due to her unadorned childhood in the East End of London, her mother's stoical genes, or some innate predisposition for high-altitude cave dwelling – as the Tashi Jong lamas had recognized.

Not least of all her austerities was the isolation. As she had anticipated, even longed for, she was quite alone. Occasionally during the summer she would see a shepherd or yak-herder. Sometimes the nuns from Tayul Gompa or a friend would visit for a day or two. Following the pattern she had established she would ensure that every year she saw Khamtrul Rinpoche for further guidance on her retreat. Very rarely she would leave for a few weeks to attend some teachings. But mostly she was completely by herself for months every year, cut off by the snows and for the last three years she saw and spoke to literally no one.

Tenzin Palmo more than coped: 'I was never lonely, not for a minute. It was nice if someone visited, but I was perfectly happy not seeing anybody. In that cave I felt completely safe.

And that's a wonderful feeling for a woman to have. I never used to lock my door or window. There was no need. The cave was on the road to nowhere,' she said. Interestingly, however, a male friend she lent the cave to once while she away on a summer errand did not find the cave experience so easy. He left after two days, spooked by the solitude. 'Me, I found it the easiest thing in the world,' she said.

If human company was rare, animals were everywhere.

Any woman of fainter heart or flabbier backbone might well have been unnerved at the array of beasts which prowled around and even entered her cave. But Tenzin Palmo was never frightened of any animal and they, in turn, were never afraid of her. It was yet another unusual facet of an already unusual woman. 'Animals are drawn to Tenzin Palmo – but what is interesting is that whereas usually, when there is that kind of attraction, the feeling is reciprocal, with Tenzin Palmo she is completely detached,' commented Didi Contractor, the friend who had visited her cave when Tenzin Palmo first moved in.

'I like animals and I respect them but I am not St Francis,' Tenzin Palmo said crisply. Nevertheless, her encounters with the animals around her cave bore a strong resemblance to the tales told of the brown-robed friar in his cave in Assisi.

Like St Francis, she too had her 'brother wolves'.

At night she could hear them on the roof above her head making their long, mournful sounds. They roamed around the mountains, looking for food, seeking their mate, baying at the moon. Tenzin Palmo, sitting in her cave, knew they were very close and did not stir an inch.

'I love wolves,' she said simply. 'For a long time I listened to them howling, which was wonderful. In the mornings after it had snowed I used to see their paw marks around the cave, but I never saw them. Then one day I was sitting outside on the patio, soaking up the sun, and five of them came by. They stood very close, just a few yards away. They were beautiful, not mangy or bedraggled as I had imagined. I thought they would look rather like jackals, but they were extremely handsome with those strange yellow eyes and sleek brown coats. They seemed very well fed, though heaven knows what they found up there to live on. They just stayed there and gazed at me very peacefully. I was so happy to see them. I smiled back and sent them lots of love. They stood there for a few minutes more and then left,' she reported.

She also came close to encountering the rarest and most beautiful of the wild cats, the snow leopard. When Peter Mathiessen wrote his haunting book *The Snow Leopard* about this near mythic beast only two Westerners were ever thought to have seen one.

'I once saw its prints outside the cave and on the window- sill,' Tenzin Palmo said, her voice rising with excitement at the memory. 'There were these big pug marks, very strange with a kind of hole in the middle. I drew it and later showed it to two zoologists and they both immediately said it was snow leopard, which apparently has a distinctive paw.' While the elusive snow leopard might well have seen Tenzin Palmo, much to her sorrow she did not ever see it.

More exotic and enticing still were the completely bizarre set of footprints that she found one morning in the snow running along the boundary wall. She looked at them in puzzlement:

'Everyone says there are no bears in Lahoul but the first year that I was there I discovered these huge footprints outside the fence. They were much bigger than a man's but looked similar to a human's with an instep. You could see all the toes but they also had claws. It looked like a human print with claws. And these footprints came all the way down from the mountain and had got to where the boundary was and the creature was obviously very confused. I think this must have been its cave. You could see from the tracks the prints made, it was wandering around and then it went up again.'

Could it possibly have been the mythical Yeti? Had Tenzin Palmo inadvertently moved into a Yeti's den?

'I don't know – I never saw the footprints again. But the Tibetans are familiar enough with the creature, whatever it is, to have a name for it, and tell stories about it. Lamas also talk about it so I don't see why it should not exist,' she said. Further support for the actual existence of the Yeti came in 1997 when Agence France Press reported that 'bigfoot' tracks had been found in Shennonija National Nature Reserve, in Hubei province, by China's Researchers for Strange and Rare

Creatures: 'The head of the committee said a research team found
hundreds of footprints 2600 metres above sea level. The biggest
footprint is thirty-seven centimetres long, very similar to that
of a man but larger than that of a man's, and is different from
the footprint of a bear or any other identified animals,' the
story read.

Much more familiar were the rodents – the same rodents that
ate the cabbages and peas Tenzin Palmo attempted to grow in
her garden. They came into her store-room trying to get at her
grains and dried vegetables and again Tenzin Palmo adopted a
curiously friendly attitude towards these intruders.

'They were mostly mice and hamsters and in the autumn there
were an awful lot of them. They were terribly sweet. Sometimes
I used to trap them in a cage and then take them outside and let
them go. It was very interesting watching them because each
one you trapped had a different response,' she said, hinting
at the Buddhist belief that animals, since they possess minds,
are subject to reincarnation like the rest of us. In this respect
it was perfectly logical that animals could well be former or
future human beings in the endless stream of becoming and
unbecoming.

'Some of them were frightened and would cower in the corner
of the cage. Others would be very angry and roar and try and
rip the cage trying to get out. Others would put their little
paws on the bars and push their noses through and look at
you and allow you to pet them. They'd be so friendly. Each
one had completely different reaction,' she went on.

'Then there were the martens, which look a bit like weasels
only prettier. They were grey with a white front, huge eyes
and a big bushy tail. There was one that used to slide open the
window get inside my store-room and head for the saucepan
which had my bread inside wrapped in a cloth. This marten
would take off the saucepan lid, unwrap the cloth and then eat
the bread. It wasn't like a rat, which would just gnaw through
the cloth. Then it would proceed to unscrew the plastic lids of
the containers holding the fat, pull off the zinc covering then
eat it. It was amazing. Everything I had it would undo. I tried
putting food outside for it but this would often get frozen and
the marten would look so let down. I read somewhere that if

you can catch one when they're young they make excellent pets because they're so intelligent.'

Another visitor was the little stoat which she caught sight of in her garden. It was about to run away when it obviously thought better of it and bravely decided to approach Tenzin Palmo instead.

'It came trotting all the way up to me, stood there and looked up. It was so small and I must have been enormous to it. It just stood there looking at me. Then it suddenly became excited. It ran back to the fence and began swinging on it, hanging upside down and looking at me all the time to see if I was still watching – like a child.'

If the animals never frightened her, there was an occasion, just one, when man did. Then it seemed that her breezy optimism that no male would bother to climb that high to harm her was sadly misplaced.

'It was during a summer when a young boy about fifteen or sixteen years old came by with his flock of sheep. He was extremely strange. He would sit on this big boulder near the cave and look down on me. If I smiled at him he would just glare back. One morning I discovered the pole with my prayer flag on it had been thrown down. Another time the stones in my spring had been moved so the water no longer flowed. Then the window to my store-room was smashed, although nothing had been taken. I was certain it was this boy and worried because he had an infinite amount of time to sit there thinking up mischief. He could do anything he wanted! I felt very vulnerable,' she recalled.

She was so worried, in fact, that she called on her old friends the Dakinis, praying to them in her familiar way:

'Look here,' she said, 'this boy has obviously got a lot of psychological problems, so please do something to change his mind and help him,' she prayed.

As usual the Dakinis took up Tenzin Palmo's challenge.

'A couple of days later I found on my gate a bunch of wild flowers. Then, when I went to my spring not only had it been repaired but it had been put back together so much nicer. After that, when I saw the boy he gave me a nice smile. He was completely transformed. Dakinis are very powerful,' she added.

And so Tenzin Palmo, the girl from Bethnal Green, learnt to live in her cave watching the seasons come and go. As the years went by life took on its own rhythms.

'In winter, which lasted from November to May, the blizzards made it particularly difficult. There would be these great big snow drifts which I had to clear from above the cave with a shovel. That meant I had to walk through it. It was very physical work and not very good for the back. I had to throw the snow over the top of the cave. It took days sometimes. I would just finish and then it would snow again. I would do it over and over again. It had to be done for me to be able to get to my wood pile. The first snow was nice but after months and months of it I'd be saying "Oh no, not again."

'The first signs that spring was on its way were these little rockflowers, very delicate, which would appear usually while it was still snowing. I could spend hours looking at them. Actually, spring was for me the most difficult time. The snow would thaw and come seeping through the cracks of the cave, flooding it. I could actually watch streams of water running down the walls soaking everything. I had sacks to mop it all up, which I would then have to dry and use again. I used to have to lay everything out in the sun to dry out. Even my meditation box, which was above the ground and lined with layers of cloth, would get damp. It was a real nuisance. You'd dry everything out, put it back and then it would flood again. Outside, everything got really muddy. One of the questions which Khamtrul Rinpoche had asked me when he was vetting the cave was whether it was wet. I said "no" because I honestly thought it wasn't. If he had known how damp and musty it got he might never have agreed to let me live there,' she conceded.

By the end of May Tenzin Palmo could begin to garden, planting her vegetables and flowers – cornflowers, marigolds, calendulas. She enjoyed gardening even though it demanded much fetching and carrying of water. For the last three years of her solitary retreat someone sent her a packet of flower seeds from England and her much to her amazement they flourished in that foreign soil, transforming her Lahouli Cave into a cottage garden.

'There were dahlias and night-scented stock. So beautiful!

But I was the only one to see them,' she said. By full summer the entire landscape had turned green – the fields, the valleys, and the willow trees planted by the Moravian missionaries to halt the erosion of the landslides. 'Now, you could burn sitting in the sun while the part of you in the shade would still feel chilly,' she said.

In summer the birds started coming back: the choughs, a red-legged crow, were regular visitors. She would watch them perform the beautiful aerial dances for which they are famous, and would sometimes cut pieces off a mat to provide nest furnishings for them. Once, one evening when she was coming back from a rare visit to the village, she came across an extraordinary scene.

'As I turned a corner I saw hundreds upon hundreds of vultures sitting in circles. They were grouped on the boulders, on the ground, all around. It was as though they had come together for a meeting. I had to walk through the middle of them! There was nowhere else for me to pass. Now these birds are big, about three feet high, with hooded eyes and strong, curved beaks. I took a deep breath, started saying the "Om Mani Padme Hung" mantra and walked right through them. They didn't even move. They just watched me out of the corner of their eyes. Later I remembered that Milarepa had had a dream in which he was a vulture and that among Tibetans these birds are regarded as extremely auspicious,' she recalled.

With autumn the world around her was transformed into a blaze of brilliant colour. It was spectacular. 'The mountains in front of me turned blood red crossed with lines of dazzling yellow – the willow trees whose leaves had turned. Above these were the snow mountains soaring into the bright blue sky. This was the time when the villagers would harvest their crops. I could hear them from my cave singing in the valleys below as they worked their yaks.'

A letter home to her mother dated 8 May 1985 when she had just begun her long three year retreat revealed how easily she was managing with her difficult situation, and how, inspite of her extreme isolation and singular way of life, others were not forgotten:

Dearest Amala [Tibetan for 'mother'],

How are you? I hope that you are very well. Did you have a nice stay in Saudi?

No doubt you have written but Tshering Dorje hasn't been up so there has been no mail. He is rather late and I hope that this is only because of being busy with ploughing and other field work. He did come up in early March as the SP [Superintendent of Police] had brought new forms to be filled out for the visa. Fortunately this year there was not too much snow and February was so mild that most of the snow at that time had melted (it snowed again later, of course). However, poor Tshering Dorje has now developed arthritis in both knees and can only hobble around painfully with a stick – so imagine having to come all the way up to the cave through the snow just so I could sign some papers! He should have forged my signature. Anyway I do hope that his bad knees are not the reason for his not coming now. Lahaul is all up and down and also TD earns his living by leading trekking parties in Ladakh and Zanskar so this is really a big problem for him.

Here everything is well. This morning I planted out potatoes and more turnips. The weather is still rather cold and it snows from time to time but my cave is not as wet as usual because there was never a really heavy snowfall at one time. My water supply happily kept running all through the winter though it got covered in a canopy of ice every night. What a joy to have water so close by and not to have to bother with melting snow. This also saved on wood.

So the winter was quiet and pleasant and February so mild and gorgeous that in Keylong they had rain! (The weather made up for it in March and April!)

My hair is getting long and falling out all over the place. A great nuisance – no wonder the yogis just mat it.

Because of being in retreat and Tshering Dorje only coming up twice a year you must not worry if there are long intervals between my letters. I can no longer go down to Keylong to post them. Tell May that I wore her sweater

(and yours) all winter and indeed still have them on. They
have been very useful so many thanks. Stay very well, All
my love, Tenzin Palmo.

For all the physical hardships she endured, the misgivings of
others and the prejudice against her gender attempting such
a feat the truth remained that Tenzin Palmo in her cave was
sublimely happy.

'There was nowhere else I wanted to be, nothing else I wanted
to be doing. Sometimes I would stand at the edge of my patio
and look out across the mountains and think, "If you could be
any place in the whole world, where would you want to be?"
And there was nowhere else. Being in the cave was completely
satisfying. I had all the conditions I needed to practise. It was
a unique opportunity and I was very, very grateful.'

NINE

Facing Death

For all her easy dismissal of her friends' concerns and her own genuine disinterest in her own safety and physical well-being, the dangers that Tenzin Palmo faced in her cave were real. Calamity struck more than once and as had been feared there was no rescue service, no doctor, no telephone, no friend to come to her aid. Tenzin Palmo faced each crisis head-on and alone. It was what she had bargained for when she had decided to enter the cave.

'When you go into retreat you make a vow for how long you are going to go in and you stick to it. It's considered part of the practice. Even if you are sick you pledge that you will not come out. If necessary you have to be prepared to die in retreat. Actually, if you do die it's considered auspicious,' she explained.

Extraordinarily, considering her medical history, in those extreme conditions she was never as ill as she had been as a child. She did not break a leg, get appendicitis nor contract any of the diseases Westerners often get in Asia like cholera and hepatitis. But she was often sick. In that damp cave she got frequent chills, which brought with them high fevers. She simply lived through them. 'You cope because you have to. The Tibetans have a saying: "If you're sick you're sick. If you die, you die." So that takes care of the problem,' she said pragmatically. Once she discovered a lump under her arm, but carried on meditating regardless. 'I forgot all about it and at the end of the retreat I suddenly remembered it but it had gone.'

There was also an eye infection which brought with it excruciating pain. 'I had to have the cave in darkness because

I couldn't bear the light. I couldn't move, not even flicker my eyelid. That meant I couldn't get to my stove to cook, so I didn't eat,' she reported. 'I couldn't even meditate because the eye would go down. I couldn't do anything. I just had to wait, to sit there and watch it. If I tried to lay down it got worse. Actually, it was quite fascinating. I'd sit there and observe the pain. It was like a symphony. You'd have the drums, the trumpets, the strings, all these very different types of pain playing on the eye,' she said in a detached voice.

'When I counted up how long it lasted it was forty-nine days, which was interesting because that is said to be the duration of the Bardo, the period of transition between death and rebirth. In fact it was really like a kind of Bardo, I was having to wait. Then it gradually got a little better. What I learnt from that was that the exhaustion that pain brings arises because we resist it. The thing is to learn to go with the pain, to ride it.'

Although she never fell off her roof while shovelling snow (as many imagined she would) there were near accidents whose consequences could have been fatal. 'I was outside my cave stacking the wood when I heard this voice inside me saying "Get up and move away",' she recounted. 'I took no notice. I thought "I'm busy doing my wood and I'm not interested in what you are saying," and I carried on. Then the voice said in a really imperious tone, "Move Immediately!". So I did. About two minutes later there was a huge thud and this big boulder landed just where I had been sitting. If I'd been caught under it or if a limb had been crushed I'd have been in a lot of trouble,' she conceded.

Danger came even closer during the period when Tenzin Palmo almost starved. One year when she was in total seclusion Tshering Dorje did not make the arranged delivery of food to the cave. She waited and waited, the supplies in her store-room getting smaller and smaller. When it was apparent he was not coming she had no alternative but to eke out what she had left. It was a pitiful amount of food, which became increasingly reduced as the months went by. Somehow, it kept her alive, but only just.

'I did get extremely thin,' was all she would say of the experience. She never asked Tshering Dorje why had not come, nor berated him. 'He must have had his reasons,' she said with equanimity.

These incidents were eclipsed, however, by a far greater drama. It was March 1979 and Tenzin Palmo was sitting as usual in her meditation box in her cave. Outside a blizzard was raging, as it had been for seven days and seven nights. Tenzin Palmo was well used to storms but this one was particularly strong. The snow piled higher and higher, gradually rising above her window, above her door. On it went without abating, getting thicker and thicker, heavier and heavier. Suddenly the awful truth dawned on her. She was buried alive.

The memory is indelibly etched on her mind:

'I was plunged into total blackness and cold. I couldn't light my fire because the snow had broken the pipe of my wood stove, which jutted out of the cave, so there was no way of keeping warm or cooking. I didn't dare light candles either because I thought they would use up oxygen. When I looked out of the window it was nothing but a sheet of ice. When I opened the door it was just blackness. It was completely dark,' she recalled

As the days wore on with no rescue in sight and no relief in the weather, Tenzin Palmo, entombed in her cold, dark cave, faced the very real possibility that she was going to die. With her stove pipe broken, her window and door completely sealed with snow, she was convinced she was going to be asphyxiated.

From the very beginning she had been taught like every good Buddhist to look death squarely in the face. 'Death is definite' but 'the time of death is indefinite,' the Buddha had said. With this fundamental but often much ignored truth placed firmly in mind she had meditated over and over again on the inescapable fact of her own demise – bringing the reality home by visualizing in graphic detail her body decomposing in the earth or melting in the heat of the funeral pyre, her possessions being dispersed and her friends and loved-ones left behind. The results were said to be twofold: to lessen the shock when Death was upon you and to sort out your priorities for whatever time you may have left.

As a tantric practitoner, however, Tenzin Palmo knew she could go even further using the moment of death as her final and greatest meditation. Steering her mind through the various stages of death she could, if she were skilful enough, arrive fully aware at the Blissful Clear Light, the most subtle mind of all, and in that sublime state transform her consciousness into a Buddha. As such, for the yogi death was never to be feared but grabbed as the golden opportunity of a lifetime of endeavour.

That, at least was the theory. Tenzin Palmo was now faced with the reality.

'I really thought I was going to die. I had a lot of time to think about it,' she said. 'It was interesting. I wasn't worried. I figured "OK, if I'm going to die, I'm going to die." I was not afraid. I thought it would be fascinating to see what would happen. Since a small child I felt the body was really temporary – that we'd all had so many roles in many different lifetimes. So on some deep level I'd never really identified with it,' she said. 'I got all my little Blessed Pills* ready for if and when it happened. I reviewed my life to try to think of anything wrong that I'd done and what I'd done right. I felt I had been so lucky. I'd met so many great lamas and received so many wonderful teachings. There were few regrets. One thing became crystal clear at that point – I was very happy that I was still a nun,' she declared. Her difficult decisions to renounce the comfort and passion of an intimate relationship that had been made more than once in her life were finally validated. The 'other side' of Tenzin Palmo, the one drawn to the fun and frivolity of mainstream life, had, it seemed, finally disappeared.

Tenzin Palmo now found herself spontaneously turning to the one man who had remained constant in her life.

'I felt such devotion to Khamtrul Rinpoche, the real tear-gushing kind. I really knew at that point what was essential and what was irrelevant. I understood first hand that when you are going to die, the only thing that matters is the Lama. From my heart I prayed to Rinpoche to take care of me in the Bardo and in my future life. I could see that ultimately he was the only refuge.'

---

* Blessed Pills are specialities of Tibetan medicine. Made from various relics, special ingredients, herbs and ground jewels, they are potentized by months of prayers and mantras being said over them. At death specific Blessed Pills are believed to facilitate the transference of consciousness to a higher realm.

Thoughts of what might happen to her once she'd crossed the great divide flashed across her mind. They were reassuringly positive, upholding the general Buddhist view that one dies as one has lived. 'Personally, I think anybody who is making efforts in this life will continue to make efforts in the next life. I don't see why we should change. I believe you find yourself among like-minded people – that consciousness just goes on', she said. 'I was certainly hoping that my personal meditation deity would come and greet me,' she added, referring to the particular form of the Enlightened Mind that had been selected as best suiting her own inclinations and dispositions. For many a Westerner being greeted by most of the Tibetan deities, with their fangs and multitude of arms and heads, could be a terrifying prospect. Tenzin Palmo had no such qualms. 'Of course whichever deity it is would appear in a form which was reassuring and appropriate,' she said.

She pondered on the possibility of going to a Pure Land, the Buddhist Heaven, although with her belief in rebirth and the Bodhisattva ideal it had radically different connotations from the Christian abode: 'There are many advantages to going to a Pure Land. For one thing it is very enjoyable. It's the highest joy apart from Nirvana,' she said.

'But one doesn't cling even to that. High lamas stay there a while and then return here. You see, a Pure Land is not like a holiday camp, it's like a pressure-cooker which brings on rapid advancement. You evolve very quickly there because there are no obstacles. There one's realization of Emptiness (the ultimate wisdom that nothing is inherently existing) gets developed and refined. And that is essential if you are to come back and live among all the suffering, because it is only when you understand non-duality that you are not overwhelmed by it all and have the genuine ability to help. The Buddhas and Bodhisattvas go everywhere to help, even to the hell realms. You can't do that if you are paranoid like all the beings in the hell realm. That is the vow of the Bodhisattva, which in Tibetan means spiritual hero,' she explained.

Tenzin Palmo did not get the chance to see what death would be like. As she sat there meditating, preparing to make the transition, she heard her voice once more. It said one word:

'Dig!' She opened the door to her cave, which with Tsering Dorje's foresight opened inwards, and using one of the lids from her saucepans tins began to dig her way out. She dug up and up, piling the snow back into her cave which made the place even colder and wetter. She dug for an hour or more, not knowing which way she was going, for she was in total darkness and was disorientated, crawling along on her stomach, tunnelling her way through the cold blackness to where she hoped the outside and oxygen lay. Suddenly she came out into the open air and was free. The relief was enormous.

'To see light and breathe fresh air again was wonderful,' she said. 'However, the blizzard was still raging so I had to crawl back inside the cave again! Once I was there I realized that the air inside was not stale but fresh. I knew then that caves could "breathe", that snow "breathes" and I was not going to die,' she said.

However, the tunnel that Tenzin Palmo had made quickly filled up with snow again. All in all she had to dig herself out three times. When the blizzard finally abated, she stood outside almost blinded by the light and looked around. An extraordinary sight met her eyes. Everything, including the trees, was totally buried in snow. It was a featureless white landscape. A helicopter flew overhead, bringing supplies to the devastated area, and someone inside waved. The villagers now knew that their prayers for the safe passing of 'Saab Chomo' in her cave had not been necessary, but nobody thought she could have possibly survived.

A letter written to an English friend who had visited the area reveals the full extent of the disaster that almost overtook her.

The cause of all the trouble was an avalanche which swept down at just before midday in early March. It started at about 19,000 feet and came down carrying everything in its wake. Many houses in Gungrang (above Yornath) were also destroyed. The avalanche was estimated to have been almost 2 km in width. In all Lahoul about 200 people died especially in the Udaipur area. That stream we have to cross to get to Keylong is at present a glacier several metres thick

so one just strolls across it with no water in sight. Tayul
Gompa was made level with the snow and everyone there
also had to tunnel their way out. It reached higher than
their roofs.

Yornath (a nearby village) looks as if it had been hit
by a tornado. Four houses there completely destroyed
(including that big one near the road next to Sonam
Ngoedup's shop). About 35 people there were killed,
whole families wiped out. All the garrie families were
killed, so no more blacksmiths at Yornath. One house at
Guskiar had the top blown off from air pressure as the
avalanche roared past at 350km an hour! Practically all the
trees from Yornath to Guskiar are completely uprooted –
all those lovely old willows, many about 200 years old. The
place is a wilderness. As one girl from Guskiar remarked,
one can hardly recognize it any longer. Tseten has spent
about 6 back-breaking weeks just removing stones, trees
and other debris from her fields which are mostly in the
Yornath area.

Anyway, it was naturally rather a lot of work to clear
away all that heavy white stuff and my face was like Dorje
Phagmo (a fierce red protector deity with puffed-out cheeks
and bulging eyes). My eyes were also crimson, no whites at
all, and swollen so that I gazed through slits. The pain! I
fixed a khatag (white offering scarf) around the brim of
my floppy hat as a veil and that worked quite well.

Tenzin Palmo may have had a reprieve but death, as the
Buddha pointed out, was all around her. Lee Perry, optimist
and spiritual seeker herself, passed away in 1985 without her
daughter knowing. It was a high price to pay for spiritual
aspiration. Tenzin Palmo had received a letter, several months
late, informing her that Lee was very sick with cancer and to
please 'come home'. But Tenzin Palmo had already started her
three-year retreat and nothing could or would break it. It was
the condition. 'I wrote back explaining why I could not come.
It was the hardest letter I had ever written. Even if I had had
cancer myself I could not have left that cave,' she explained.

The next time the post arrived, a year later, there was a

note from a friend telling her that Lee had died, peacefully, aged seventy-eight. Tenzin Palmo said prayers for her mother's well-being and consoled herself with the thought that Lee, like herself, had not been afraid of death. 'She viewed death as merely the shaking off of an old body in order to start again refreshed and energized. I knew she was looking forward to seeing her spirit guides, who she believed would meet her and look after her,' she said.

Tenzin Palmo's mind was not entirely at ease, however. She had made a brief second visit to London to visit her mother in 1984, a year before she died. It had been eleven years since she'd last been to her homeland and she was urged to see her mother before she disappeared into her cave for her three-year retreat. Although she was grateful for the time they'd spent together, she now looked back on the visit with some feelings of regret and reproached herself for things 'that could have been', as one often does after a death of a loved one.

'I think I was rather cold to my mother, and now I always feel very sad about that. She took it well, believing "that's how nuns are". But I had been in the cave for a long time and was not used to relating closely to people. We were friendly but on reflection I feel I was quite judgemental and I'm really sorry,' she confessed. 'Now I think I would be able to be much warmer towards her than I was then.'

When the time had come to say goodbye, Lee had turned to her daughter and said: 'I feel this is the last time I am going to see you in this life.' Then she added: 'I pray that I may be reborn as your mother in future lives so that I can help you continue your spiritual path.' It was the greatest act of love and approbation of her daughter that she could have made.

For all Tenzin Palmo's training, however, nothing could prepare her for the death of her lama, Khamtrul Rinpoche. Even though she had been physically separated from him for several years, first by moving to the Gompa in Lahoul and then by retreating further to her cave, the bond between them had remained as close as ever. 'Whenever I felt I needed him I would pray to him. I would have significant dreams in which he would appear,' she said enigmatically. And her annual visits back to Tashi Jong remained an integral part of her life. Then she'd sit with him feeling the reassurance of his physical presence and receive personalized, tailor-made instructions on her spiritual path.

'I'd go back with questions. During my meditations I would always have paper nearby so that I could jot down queries as they came up. I'd walk in and Khamtrul Rinpoche would lean back and say, "OK, where's your list?" And I'd bring out this long list of questions,' she recalled. 'His answers were absolutely right. He answered from both his scholastic expertise and from his own experience. "According to the books it says this, but from my own experience it is like this," he used to say. He was always spot on. And I could always discuss things with him. Sometimes I would go to him with an idea of a practice I wanted to do and he would suggest something else that hadn't occurred to me. Immediately he had said it I knew he was right. That is the beauty of a real guru – he knows your mind and can steer your spiritual progress in the direction that is best for you,' she said.

It was in 1981 while she was in Nepal, receiving some teachings and slowly making her way to Bhutan to meet up with Khamtrul Rinpoche, when she heard the news.

'One day I was summoned to the monastery. I thought I was being called for some special teaching or something. On the way I met someone who said, "You look very happy, you couldn't have heard." And then they told me. I nearly fainted. It was awful. Absolutely devastating.' Her world had fallen apart. In her words: 'The sun had set and there was only darkness. I felt as though I was in this vast desert and the guide had left – completely lost.'

The strong, sturdy, sociable Khamtrul Rinpoche, who had led such an extraordinary life, from powerful regional monarch to penniless refugee, had died of diabetes aged just forty-nine. He had been ill for only an hour before his death. If his passing had been completely unexpected to his followers, he must have been exceptionally well prepared himself, for in the manner of his dying he demonstrated the full extent of his spiritual mastery and proved to Western eyes exactly what could be achieved.

Those who were present reported that Khamtrul Rinpoche stayed in tukdam, the 'clear light' of death, for some weeks after physiological death had occurred – his body not collapsing but remaining youthful-looking and pleasant-smelling. More surprising still, when the time came for his cremation the mourners noticed that his large and formerly bulky body had mysteriously shrunk to the size of an eight-year-old child's. The coffin that they had originally made for him was now redundant and another smaller one had to be hastily constructed. The shrinking of the body in this manner was not unknown among Tibetan high lamas. To those who looked on, it was proof that Khamtrul Rinpoche had indeed reached a high level of spiritual attainment, one only surpassed by the ultimate triumph of achieving the 'rainbow body' whereby at death the whole body is de-materialized, leaving nothing behind but the nails and hair. Such things could well be dismissed as spiritual science fiction were it not for the plethora of eye-witnesses and factual documentation to back them up.

Rilbur Rinpoche, a venerable high lama and historian who was imprisoned for many years by the Chinese, tells of several adepts who managed to eject their consciousness at will (the practice of powa) while imprisoned with him. 'I saw many people who sat down in the corner of their cell and deliberately passed away to another realm. They weren't ill and there was nothing wrong with them. The guards could never believe it!' he said.

In his recent best-selling book *The Tibetan Book of Living and Dying*, Sogyal Rinpoche explains precisely what the rainbow body is and how it is achieved:

Through these advanced practices of Dzogchen, accomplished practitioners can bring their lives to an extraordinary and triumphant end. As they die they enable their body to be reabsorbed back into the light essence of the light elements that created it, and consequently their material body dissolves into light and then disappears completely. This process is known as the 'rainbow body' or 'body of light' because the dissolution is often accompanied by spontaneous manifestations of light and rainbows. The ancient Tantras of Dzogchen, and the writings of the great masters, distinguish different categories of this amazing otherworldly phenomenon, for at one time, if at least not normal, it was reasonably frequent.

Sogyal Rinpoche goes on to quote a case of Sonam Namgyal, a man who actually achieved the rainbow body in East Tibet in 1952.

> He was a very simple, humble person, who made his way as an itinerant stone carver, carving mantras and sacred texts. Some say he had been a hunter in his youth and had received teaching from a great master. No one really knew he was a practitioner; he was truly what was called a 'hidden yogin'. Some time before his death, he would be seen to go up into the mountains and just sit, silhouetted against the skyline, gazing up into space. He composed his own songs and chants and sang them instead of the traditional ones. No one had any idea what he was doing. He then fell ill, or seemed to, but became, strangely, increasingly happy. When the illness got worse, his family called in masters and doctors. His son told him he should remember all the teachings he had heard, and he smiled and said: 'I've forgotten them all and anyway, there's nothing to remember. Everything is illusion, but I am confident that all is well.'
>
> Just before his death at seventy-nine, he said, 'All I ask is that when I die, don't move my body for a week.' When he died his family wrapped his body and invited lamas and monks to come and practise for him. They placed the body in a small room in the house, and they could not help noticing that although he had been a tall person, they had no trouble getting it in, as if he were becoming smaller. At the same time an extraordinary display of rainbow-coloured light was seen all around the house. When they looked into the room on the sixth day, they saw that the body was getting smaller and smaller. On the eighth day after his death, the morning on which the funeral had been arranged, the undertakers arrived to collect his body. When they undid its coverings, they found nothing inside but his nails and hair.

My master Jamyang Kyentse asked for these to be brought to him and verified that this was a case of the rainbow body.

Tenzin Palmo had her own stories: 'It's well known that the third Khamtrul Rinpoche's body shrank to eighteen inches,' she said. 'It's not a first-class rainbow body, where everything disappears, but it's pretty good. Actually these feats can be achieved even by Westerners. A lama called Khunnu Rinpoche told me that once back in Kham all these rainbows appeared above the monastery. At the time there was an American staying there and he rushed to get him to show him the fantastic light show that was appearing in the sky. When he opened the American's door he found nothing there except his clothes, his nails and his hair. Often it is said to happen like this to seemingly "ordinary" people, like old Norbu down the street, who nobody knows is an accomplished practitioner.'

But in 1981 Tenzin Palmo was caught up in the drama of her own guru's death and the fascinating series of events that were to follow. Immediately after hearing the news she had gone into retreat. But she emerged to return to Tashi Jong for the cremation. The occasion is etched deeply on her mind.

'It was an incredible time. There was this very strong sense of being together and sharing. The weather had been extremely rainy and cloudy and the night before cremation there was this terrific storm. They'd been building this beautiful stupa (funeral reliquary) and I thought everything was going to be washed away. All the banners would be soaked, including the wood for the funeral pyre. But the morning of the funeral dawned incredibly clear. There was this translucent, blue sky and everything looked washed and clean. Nothing was amiss at all. It was wonderful. Interestingly, the following day it clouded over again and began to pour with rain.'

Khamtrul Rinpoche's remains were duly placed in the stupa that had been erected next to the very temple that he had designed and helped to build with his own hands. It was a tall, impressive structure, gleaming white, built according to the laws of sacred geometry and containing a small glass window behind which sat a statue of the Buddha. Strangely a bodhi seed implanted itself behind the glass and over the years a bodhi tree forced its way out of the very centre of the container. It had grown from the heart of the Buddha. No one knew how it had got there, nor how it had grown without any soil. Coincidence maybe. To the believers, however, it was further evidence of the awakened state of Khamtrul Rinpoche's mind.

According to the Bodhisattva rule, masters of Khamtrul Rinpoche's calibre are not meant to stay away for long, however. Consequently immediately after his cremation his disciples began to look for clues as to where his future rebirth might be found. Like trackers following spoor, they examined any sign that the eighth Khamtrul Rinpoche might have left behind indicating in which direction he was planning to make his re-entry into this world. They discovered a poem he had written just before he passed away and, scrutinizing it, realized that the names of his future parents were concealed as anagrams at the end of each line. They were now hot on the trail. At the same time two eminent lamas, Dilgo Kheyntse Rinpoche and the Karmapa, who were both extremely close to Khamtrul Rinpoche, each had significant dreams.

Tenzin Palmo took up the story: 'Dilgo Kheyntse Rinpoche dreamt he was going up a hill when he came across a temple from which came Khamtrul Rinpoche's voice. He went in and found all these monks inside and Khamtrul Rinpoche sitting on a throne teaching. Dilgo Khentse Rinpoche went up to him and said, "What are you doing here, you're supposed to be dead?" And Khamtrul Rinpoche replied, "I am beyond birth and death." Dilgo Kheyntse Rinpoche then asked, "Out of compassion for beings where have you chosen to be reborn?" and Khamtrul Rinpoche gave him the name of his parents. The Karmapa also received the parents' name in a dream. They also discovered that the rebirth had taken place "in the cradle of Buddhism", which meant India. This was a relief – at least it was not Tibet, which would have been impossible to search!'

India, however, is a vast country in which to find one small if special baby. More specific clues were needed. Finally the Karmapa, on his deathbed in Chicago, gave the vital missing piece of jigsaw – the name of the place where Khamtrul Rinpoche had been reborn – Bomdila, in Arunachal Pradesh, a Himalayan town close to Bhutan. Although it was the other side of India from Tashi Jong and the Kangra valley, relatively speaking, the discovery of the ninth Khamtrul Rinpoche was in the bag. The child was found, recognized, and reinstated in Tashi Jong to take up his spiritual duties where his predecessor (himself) had left off.

The ninth Khamtrul Rinpoche was a quiet boy, as introverted and small as the eighth Khamtrul Rinpoche had been large and outgoing. In Tenzin Palmo's mind he was still her guru – the reincarnation of the man whom she had loved so deeply. He was three years old when she first saw him. She approached the meeting with some trepidation, anxious that the rapport she had shared with his predecessor would not be the same.

'I was afraid. I wondered what he'd think of this "strange looking Westerner". I thought he'd probably burst into tears,' she admitted. It did not turn out as she had anticipated. 'I went in, started prostrating and this small child began laughing. "Oh look, that's my nun, that's my nun," he burst out. He was so excited. His monk attendant turned to him and said, "Yes, that's your nun, she's been your disciple for so long." The young Khamtrul Rinpoche was laughing and smiling at me and giving me his toys. We spent the whole morning playing and running around together. The monk said such behaviour was very unusual, as he was generally very shy and withdrawn with strangers.'

If the young tulku had instantly recognized 'his nun', Tenzin Palmo had to look a little longer to find similarities with the former Khamtrul Rinpoche. 'He is and he isn't like the past Khamtrul Rinpoche. For a start this one is so much younger than I am, whereas the other one was like a father to me, so there is a different type of relationship. I'm also told that the previous Khamtrul Rinpoche had been a real terror when he was a child, while this one is very sweet, gentle and delicate. But he looks at me – right through my eyes – exactly the way the other Rinpoche did, for minutes at a time. And sometimes when I am with him, not thinking of anything in particular, this incredible devotion wells up from my heart. It's so strong and spontaneous I burst into tears.'

But the memory of the beloved eighth Khamtrul Rinpoche

was still fresh in her mind. She rushed back to her cave even more determined to continue with her quest. 'I felt that the only thing that I could really do to repay my kind lama was practise, practise, practise,' she said.

TEN

Yogini

The scenery outside her cave may have been awesome, but what of Tenzin Palmo's inner world? This, after all, was what she had gone to the cave to discover. What was she seeing on that long journey inwards? Was she sitting there having visions, like watching TV? Was she being bathed in golden light? Hearing celestial voices? Experiencing waves of transcendent bliss? Or was she perhaps being tormented by the devils of her psyche, disturbed from the depths of her subconscious by those penetrating tools of meditation designed to dig deep beneath the surface?

According to the legends of solitary mediators, this was what cave-dwelling was really all about. Up in his icy, barren cave the great yogi Milarepa, founder of Tenzin Palmo's own lineage, after years of terrible deprivation and unwavering endeavour, found himself in a realm of surreal splendour. The walls and floor of his cave melted with the imprint of his hands, feet, buttocks where he pressed them into the rock. Goddesses appeared bringing him delicious morsels to stave off his hunger. His emaciated body, turned green from eating only nettle soup, was filled with intense ecstasy. In his dreams he could turn his body into any shape he wished, traversing the universe in any direction unimpeded. In his waking state he learnt to fly, crossing the valleys of his homeland at great speed, much to the consternation of the farmers ploughing the fields in the valley below.

Was the fishmonger's daughter from Bethnal Green experiencing any of this?

No one will ever know exactly what Tenzin Palmo went through in all those years of solitary retreat, the moments of dazzling insight she might have had, the times of darkness she may have endured. She had learnt well from the Togdens, those humble yogis whose qualities had touched her so deeply, that one never reveals, let alone boasts, of one's spiritual prowess. Getting rid of the ego, not enhancing it, was the name of the game. Besides, her tantric vows forbade her to divulge any progress she may have made. It was a long-held tradition, ever since the Buddha himself had defrocked a monk for performing a miracle in public, declaring the transformation of the human heart was the only miracle that really counted.

'Frankly I don't like discussing it. It's like your sexual experiences. Some people like talking about them, others don't. Personally I find it terribly intimate,' she said.

When pressed, she conceded the barest essentials: 'Of course when you do prolonged retreats you are going to have experiences of great intensity – times when your body completely melts away, or when you feel the body is flying. You get states of incredible awareness and clarity when everything becomes very vivid.'

There were visions too – occasions when her guru Khamtrul Rinpoche appeared to her to advise her on her meditations. Other holy beings manifested in her cave as well. But these signs, normally taken as indications of supreme spiritual accomplishment, she dismissed as events of little true significance.

'The whole point is not to get visions but to get realizations,' she said sharply, referring to the stage when a truth stops being a mental or intellectual construct and becomes real. Only when the meditation dropped from the head to the heart, and was felt, could transformation begin to take place. 'And realizations are quite bare,' she continued. 'They are not accompanied by lights and music. We're trying to see things as they really are. A realization is non-conceptual. It's not a product of the thinking process or the emotions – unlike visions which come from that level. A realization is the white transparent light at the centre of the prism, not the rainbow colours around it.'

As for the bliss, that most attractive of all meditational states, did Tenzin Palmo know this? To the average lay person, sitting at home in her house reading about the heroic meditators, it was the bliss that made it all worthwhile – all the terrible hardships and deprivations, the lack of comfort and human companionship. Bliss, in short, was the reward. Certainly the one or two photographs taken of Tenzin Palmo at this time show a face suffused with happiness.

'There are states of incredible bliss. Bliss is the fuel of retreat,' she confirmed in her matter-of-fact voice. 'You can't do any long-term practice seriously unless there is inner joy, because the joy and enthusiasm is what carries you along. It's like anything, if you don't really like it you will have this inner resistance and everything is going to be very slow. That is why the Buddha named Joy as a main factor on the path.

'The only problem with bliss is that because it arouses such enormous pleasure, beyond anything on a worldly level, including sexual bliss, people cling to it and really want it and then it becomes another obstacle,' she added, before launching on a story to illustrate her point.

'Once when I was with the Togdens in Dalhousie there were two monks who were training to be yogis.' One day they were standing outside shaking a blanket and they were so blissed out they could hardly stand up. You could actually feel these waves of bliss hitting you. The Togdens turned to me and said, "You know, when you start, this is what happens. You get completely overwhelmed by bliss and you don't know what to do. After a while you learn how to control it and bring it down to manageable levels." And it's true. When you meet more mature practitioners they're not completely speechless with all this great bliss, because they've learnt how to deal with it. And of course they see into its empty nature.

'You see, bliss in itself is useless,' she continued. 'It's only useful when it is used as a state of mind for understanding Emptiness – when that blissful mind is able to look into its own nature. Otherwise it is just another subject of Samsara. You can understand emptiness on one level but to understand it on a very subtle level requires this complement of bliss. The blissful mind is a very subtle mind and that kind of mind looking at Emptiness is a very different thing from the gross mind looking at emptiness. And that is why one cultivates bliss.

'You go through bliss. It marks just a stage on the journey. The ultimate goal is to realize the nature of the mind,' she insisted.

The nature of the mind, she said, was unconditioned, non-dual consciousness. It was Emptiness and bliss. It was the state of Knowing without the Knower. And when it was realized it wasn't very dramatic at all. There was no cosmic explosion, no fanfare of celestial trumpets. 'It's like waking up for first time – surfacing out of a dream and then realizing that you have been dreaming. That is why the sages talk about all things being an illusion. Our normal way of being is muffled – it's not vivid. It's like breathing in stale air. Waking up is not sensational. It's ordinary. But it's extremely real.'

Nor apparently does the real thing happen in a Big Bang. 'At first you get just a glimpse of it. That is actually only the beginning of the path. People often think when they get that glimpse that it is the whole thing, that they've reached the goal. Once you begin to see the nature of the mind then you can begin to meditate. Then after that you have to stabilize it until the nature of the mind becomes more and more familiar. And when that is done you integrate it into everyday life.'

At other times Tenzin Palmo's revelations were decidedly more ordinary, although in her eyes equally valuable. There was the occasion one spring when the thaw of the winter snows had begun and her cave was being systematically flooded. 'The walls and the floor were getting wetter and wetter and for some reason I was also not very well,' she related. 'I was beginning to think, "Oh dear, what they say about caves is really true," and started to feel very down.'

Suddenly the Buddha's First Noble Truth which she had learnt when she first encountered Buddhism struck her with renewed force. 'I thought, "Why are you still looking for happiness in Samsara? and my mind just changed around. It was like: That's right – Samsara is Dukka [the fundamental unsatisfactory nature of life]. It's OK that it's snowing. It's OK that I'm sick because that is the nature of Samsara. There's nothing to worry about. If it goes well that's nice. If it doesn't go well that's also nice. It doesn't make any difference. Although it sounds very elementary, at the time it was quite a breakthrough. Since then I have never really cared about external circumstances. In that way the cave was a great teaching because it was not too perfect,' she said.

If the results of meditation could be sensational, the path to

Enlightenment was plodding and exceedingly hard work. There was a lot to do and an inconceivably long way to go. The lamas said if you reached there in three lifetimes you were moving incredibly quickly, for the task at hand was the transformation of the body, speech and mind into that of a Buddha. No less. Understanding this, the Tibetans had developed the Way into a science. Anyone could do it, given the texts which held the instructions, the initiations which conferred the empowerment and the right motivation which ensured the seeker did not fall into the abyss of self-interest. There were clear-cut paths to take, detailed directions to follow, delineated levels to reach each marked with their own characteristics so that you knew precisely where you were. There were specific landmarks to watch out for, special yogic exercises to do, and a myriad aids harnessing all the senses to propel the seeker forward. This was the mind working on the mind, consciousness working on consciousness, the task at hand unlocking the secrets of that three-pound universe contained within our own heads. In short, what Tenzin Palmo was engaging in was arguably the most important and significant adventure of all time – the exploration of inner space.

Dr Robert Thurman, Professor of Indo-Tibetan Studies at Columbia University, New York, one of the world's most lucid and entertaining exponents of Buddhism, put it this way: 'What the meditator is doing in those long retreats is a very technical thing. He's not just sitting there communing with the Great Oneness. He's technically going down, pulling apart his own nervous system to become self-aware from out of his own cells. It's like you are using Word Perfect and you are in the chip. And you are self-aware of being in the chip. The way you have done that is by stabilizing your mind where you can go down to the dots and dashes, and you've gone down and down even into that.

'In other words the Mahayana Buddhist, filled with the technical understanding of tantra, has become a quantum physicist of inner reality,' he continued. 'What he has done is disidentified from the coarse conceptual and perceptual process. He's gone down to the neuronal level, and from inside the neuronal level he's gone down to the most subtle neuronal level, or supra-neuronal level and he's become where it is like the computer is self-consciously aware of itself. The yogi goes right down to below machine language – below the sub atomic level.

'When you have done this what you have achieved is not some kind of mystical thing but some very concrete, evolutionary thing. It's the highest level of evolution. That's what the Buddha is defined as. The highest level of evolution.'

Personally Tenzin Palmo had never doubted the efficacy of the methods she was following. 'Tibet had been producing Enlightened beings like an assembly line for centuries. For such a small population it was extraordinary,' she said.

Being a methodical and highly conscientious person, she had started at the beginning with the preliminary practices, which she had begun in Dalhousie and Lahoul long before she went into the cave. These consisted of certain rites such as mandala offerings, where the practitioner builds up a symbolic universe on small silver trays decorated with 'precious' items and offers it to all the Buddhas, or doing full-length prostrations, or mantra recitation. These are then performed literally hundreds of thousands of times in order to prepare and soften the mind for the esoteric tantric meditations that were to follow. In the cave Tenzin Palmo did them all again. At one point she fasted completely (although she would not reveal for how long). At another she conducted a partial fast while simultaneously doing prostrations and singing praises to Chenrezig, the thousand-armed Buddha of compassion. Always an extremely arduous exercise both physically and mentally, this time it was made even more difficult by the extreme conditions in which she was living.

'It was winter and I didn't have the right food. What I was eating was too heavy. When you fast it's much better if you have light, nourishing food. So, physically it was quite tough. I got digestive problems and became very weak,' she said, while refusing to amplify any further.

Mentally, however, it worked. 'The mind does become purified. The prayers are very beautiful and the mind grows extremely clear and light, very devoted and open,' she confirmed.

After she had done six months of purification practice, Tenzin

Palmo had a dream. Arguably it revealed more than anything she said, the level of spiritual development she had reached.

'I was in a prison, a vast prison composed of many different levels,' she began. 'On the top floor people were living in luxury, in penthouse type splendour, while in the basement others were undergoing terrible torture. In the intermediate floors the rest of the inhabitants were engaged in various activities in diverse conditions. Suddenly I realized that no matter what level people were on, we were all nevertheless trapped in a prison. With that I found a boat and decided to escape taking as many people as I could with me. I went all over the prison telling people of their predicament and urging them to break free. But no matter how hard I tried, they all seemed to be locked in an awful inertia and in the end only two people had the will and the courage to come with me.

'We got into the boat, and even though there were prison guards around, nobody stopped us as we sailed out of the prison to the world outside. Once we were there we started to run alongside the prison. As I looked over at it I could still see all the people in the windows busily engaged in their different activities, not the least concerned about the truth of their situation. We ran for miles and miles on a path parallel to the prison which seemed never-ending. I became increasingly exhausted and dispirited. I felt I was never going to get beyond the prison and that we might as well return and go back in. I was about to give up when I realized that the two other people who had followed me out had their hopes pinned on me and that if I gave up they would be doomed as well. I couldn't let them down, so I kept going.

'Immediately we came to a T-junction beyond which was a completely different landscape. It was like suburbia. There were these neat houses with flowery borders and trees. We came to the first house and knocked at the door. A nice middle-aged woman opened it, looked at us and said, "Oh, you've come from that place. Not many people get out. You'll be OK now, but you must change your clothes. To go back would be dangerous, but you must try to help others also to get out." At that point I had a great surge of aspiration. "I have tried but no one wants to come," I told the woman. She replied, "Those in power will be helping you." At that I said, "I dedicate myself to working with them so that I can help free all beings."

'I woke up at that point – and giggled at the image of the middle-aged lady in suburbia,' she said.

The dream was clear. In her subconscious Tenzin Palmo had pledged herself to lead the great escape out of the prison of Samsara, the realms of suffering existence we're condemned to until we reach the eternal freedom of Enlightenment. She had also internalized, it seemed, the Bodhisattva ideal of unconditioned altruism.

When she was not doing her preliminary practices she worked on her Single Pointed Concentration – the meditative discipline which trains the mind to focus single-pointedly on one subject without interruption. Yogis were said to be able to stay in this state for days, weeks, months even, without moving, their mind totally absorbed on the wonders of their inner reality. Single Pointed Concentration, or Samadhi, was essential for penetrating the nature of reality and discovering absolute truth. It was also exceedingly difficult, the mind habitually wanting to dance all over the place flitting from one random thought to another, from fantasy to fantasy, perpetually chattering away to itself, expending vast quantities of energy in an endless stream of trivia. The mind was like a wild horse, they said, that needed to be reined in and trained. When the mind's energy was harnessed and channelled like a laser beam on a single subject, its power was said to be tremendous. Ultimately this was the high-voltage power-tool needed to dig down into the farthest reaches of the mind, unlocking the greatest treasures buried there.

'For any practice to work,' said Tenzin Palmo, 'the mind which is meditating and the object of meditation must merge. Often they are facing each other. One has to become completely absorbed, then the transformation will occur. The awareness naturally drops from the head to the heart – and when that happens the heart opens and there is no "I". And that is the relief. When one can learn to live from that centre rather than up in the head, whatever one does is spontaneous and appropriate. It also immediately releases a great flow of energy because it is not at all obstructed as it usually is by our own intervention. One becomes more joyful and light, in both senses of the word,

A young Tenzin Palmo (centre), then known as Diane Perry, in her home town, London. 'Three times a bridesmaid, never a bride – I better do it and make sure,' she had said.

Gerald York (editor of a Buddhist magazine), a youthful Chogyam Trungpa (Tenzin Palmo's first meditation teacher), and author John Blofeld (Tenzin Palmo's future sponsor), at the Buddhist Society Summer School, Hertfordshire, 1962.

Aged twenty-one in 1964, just after her novice ordination. Tenzin Palmo wrote to her mother on the back: 'You see? I look healthy! I should have been laughing then you would know that I am also happy!'

'Kailash', the former British hill station house in Dalhousie which Freda Bedi turned into her Young Lama's Home School. Tenzin Palmo's first port of call in India, 1964.

A class of young Tulkus (reincarnated lamas) whom Tenzin Palmo taught at Kailash, Dalhousie, 1964.

Early days in Dalhousie, 1966. Choegyal Rinpoche (who taught Tenzin Palmo Buddhist stories), Khamtrul Rinpoche (Tenzin Palmo's guru), Lee Perry (Tenzin Palmo's mother) and Togden Anjam.

Tenzin Palmo, one of the first Western women to receive full Bhikshuni ordination, Hong Kong, 1973. Sakya Trizin, Tenzin Palmo's 'second' guru, remarked, 'You look like a bald-headed Virgin Mary!'

Some of the monks whom Tenzin Palmo befriended during her six-year stay at Tayul monastery, Lahoul, between 1970 and 1976.

Houses of the monks and nuns of Tayul monastery. The flat roofs provided perfect venues for winter parties.

Still close: renowned artist Choegyal Rinpoche and Tenzin Palmo with the late 8th Khamtrul Rinpoche in the background. Tashi Jong monastery, Kangra Valley, 1997.

Tenzin Palmo with the 'new' 9th Khamtrul Rinpoche, Tashi Jong, 1997.

Togden Cholo, one of the elite meditators of Tashi Jong and a close friend of Tenzin Palmo.

The young 8th Khamtrul Rinpoche in Tibet, circa 1958, surrounded by the regalia of his unique status. Shortly afterwards he was a refugee.

The stupa (reliquary) Tenzin Palmo built on a ledge outside her cave as an act of religious devotion.

Inside Tenzin Palmo's cave, showing the wood-burning stove, table, bookcase with cloth-wrapped texts, pictures of Buddhas, and the meditation box. 'People were surprised how neat and tidy it was. It was a very pukka cave,' she said.

Outside the cave, drying out her soaked possessions after the spring thaw – the cave leaked dreadfully. Note the size of her meditation box (upright to the left of the cave), her 'bed' for twelve years.

Tenzin Palmo's garden in which she grew turnips and potatoes (her only source of fresh food) and flowers.

13,200 feet above sea level, a cave with a view! During the eight-month-long winter Tenzin Palmo was presented with a solid wall of white.

because it's going back to the source, the heart, rather than being in exile in the head. Our modern scientific approach has thrown such emphasis on the brain, we're all so cut off. That is why so many people feel life is meaningless and sterile.'

When she had finished all her preparations she got down to the core of her practice, tantra – the alchemical process which promised the transformation to full awakening. If the end result was magical, the business of getting there was infinitely prosaic and, some would say, horribly tedious. Every day for the months and years she was in formal retreat inside her cave she got into her meditation box and followed the same gruelling, utterly repetitive routine: Up at 3 a.m. for the first three-hour meditation session; 6 a.m. breakfast (tea and tsampa); 8 a.m. back into the box for the second three-hour meditation session; 11 a.m. lunch and a break; 3 p.m. return to the box for the third three-hour meditation session; 6 p.m. tea; 7 p.m. the fourth three-hour session; 10 p.m. 'bed' – in the meditation box! All in all that amounted to twelve hours of meditation a day – day in, day out, for weeks, months and years on end. Ironically for a woman who left the world, she had a clock to time all her sessions and was living a life as disciplined and structured as any worker on the factory floor.

For all the mind-numbing monotony she was never bored. 'Sometimes I would think that if I were having to watch the same TV programme four times a day I'd have gone up the wall,' she said candidly. 'But in retreat there's a pattern that emerges. At first it is very interesting. Then you hit a period when it's excruciatingly boring. And then you get a second wind after which it becomes more and more fascinating until at the end it's much more fascinating and interesting than it was in the beginning. That's how it is even if you're doing the same thing four times a day for three years. It's because the material begins to open up its real meaning and you discover level after level of inner significance. So, at the end you are much more involved in it and totally identified with it than you were at the beginning,' she said.

She remained deliberately vague about the precise nature of the material she was working with. 'I was doing very old traditional practices ascribed to the Buddha himself. He revealed them to various great masters who then wrote them down after having realized them themselves. They involve a lot of visualization and internal yogic practices,' she hinted. 'Basically, you use the creative imaginative faculty of the mind to transform everything, both internally and externally. The creative imagination in itself is an incredibly powerful force. If you channel it in the right way it can reach very deep levels of mind which can't be accessed through verbal means or mere analysis. This is because on a very deep level we think in pictures. If you are using pictures which have arisen in an Enlightened mind, somehow that unlocks very deep levels in our own minds.

'What you are dealing with are images which are a reflection of the deepest qualities within oneself,' she continued. 'They are reflections of one's Buddha mind, therefore they are a skilful means for leading you back to who one really is. That's why, when you practise, things occur and experiences happen.'

Maybe it was her Cockney upbringing which taught her to be cheerful in adversity and gave her resilience, maybe it was her psychological make-up, which was unusually well-balanced and unneurotic, or perhaps it was that for some reason she was predisposed to be up in the mountains meditating all alone, but Tenzin Palmo claims that for her there was no dark night of the soul. There was never a moment when those legendary demons confronted by other recluses rose up to torment and taunt. She suffered no moments of madness, no paranoia, no agonizing periods of doubt or depression. And not for a second was she prey to the barbs of lust that seemed to attack the most 'holy' of male hermits. 'I found myself surrounded by bands of dancing girls. My face was pale with fasting but though my limbs were cold as ice my mind was burning with desire and the forces of lust kept bubbling up before me when my flesh was as good as dead,' cried St Jerome before going off to flagellate himself in repentance.

None of this happened to Tenzin Palmo. 'I didn't encounter anything that was particularly awful – maybe because I didn't have a traumatic childhood. I was very lucky in that respect,' she suggested.

While she may not have hit the spiritual wall in any dramatic fashion, she claims she did not get off scot-free. The pitfalls were there, lethal just the same. It was inevitable. With no social life to distract her, no roles to fulfil, no other person to deflect her feelings on to, the masks all fell away. Now the mirror was held up to herself. It was not always a comfortable sight. 'In retreat you see your nature in the raw, and you have to deal with it,' she said.

'I may not have heavy negative karma but that does not mean my problems don't exist. They are just not so transparent and therefore more difficult to catch,' she said. She elaborated: 'When you get into the practice you begin to see how it should be done, and when it is not you begin to ask yourself "why?" In my case it came down to laziness, a fundamental inertia. That's my main problem. It's tricky. It's not like facing the tigers and wolves of anger and desire. Those sort of problems you can grapple with. My failings are much more insidious – they hide in the undergrowth so that they are more difficult to see,' she confessed.

The laziness she was referring to was not the idleness of sitting around doing nothing, of being slothful, of engaging in frivolous tasks. Tenzin Palmo could never be accused of that. Instead it was laziness of a much more subtle kind. 'One knows how to practise, and of that one is perfectly capable. But one settles for second or third best. It is like getting the progress prize at school – one is not really doing one's best. It's a very low grade of effort and it is much more serious than having a bad temper. The times when I have genuinely put my whole self into something, the results have surprised even me.'

Inside her cave she was doing more than just sit in her meditation box. During her break she painted – beautiful pictures of Buddhas and Bodhisattvas. She copied out texts for her monastery in the elegant calligraphy that she had taught herself. And as she had done all her life, she read prolifically and deeply all the works she could get her hands on about the Buddha and about teachings, including works belonging to other traditions. It was highly unusual – most Tibetan Buddhists never stepped outside their own literature. This learning was to hold in her good stead later on (in a way she could hardly imagine), when she would draw on it time and time again to back up a point she was making.

'I think it's very important for Westerners who come from such a totally different background to really study the foundations of Buddhism – what the Buddha taught. If you read the very early sutras, the early Theravadin tradition is the foundation for everything which came after it. Without having really understood what the foundation was you cannot really appreciate what comes after. As Western Buddhists I think we have a responsibility to the Buddhist dharma,' she reasoned.

Curiously in amongst this plethora of Buddhism there was one token of Christianity – the autobiography of St Teresa of Lisieux. In spite of Tenzin Palmo's antipathy to the Christian religion in general, she was drawn to the French saint who had entered a Carmelite nunnery when she was just fifteen and who had died at the age of twenty-four. She read her story several times and could quote from it at will.

'The ironic thing is that the "little way" that she wrote about had nothing to do with the Way that I practised. What I liked about her, however, was that she was very sensible. She sometimes slept through the church services and it did not worry her that she slept. God would have to accept her as she was! She never worried about her faults so long as her aspiration was right! She had this thing that she was like a small bird scratching around looking for seeds, glancing at the sun but not flying near it. She reasoned that she didn't have to because the sun was shining even on a small being like a bird. Her whole attitude was very nice. She described herself as "a little flower" by the wayside which nobody sees but in its own self is very perfect as it is. And to me that is her primary message – that even in small, little ways we can be fulfilling our purpose and that in little things we can accomplish much.'

She went on: 'St Teresa was interesting because from the outside she didn't do anything. She performed no miracles, saw no visions, yet she was extremely devout. However, she must have been special because her Mother Superior made her write her story, which was completely unusual. A photograph taken of her at her death shows how beatific she looked. She had said that she wanted to spend her heaven doing good on

earth. That's a Bodhisattva aspiration – you don't loll around
in heaven singing praises, you get on and do something good,'
she said.

Tenzin Palmo may have removed herself from the world
but others were certainly not forgotten. Over the years she
had developed a lengthy correspondence with a wide variety
of people, some of whom she had not seen for years. When
she was not in strict retreat she would faithfully answer all
of their letters, which were delivered by Tshering Dorje along
with her supplies. Sometimes there were as many as sixty. She
looked upon these friendships as 'treasures' in her life. 'I have
met some truly wonderful people – and I am always grateful
for that,' she said.

Her friends, family and the multitude of sentient beings she
did not know were also included in her prayers and meditations.
'You automatically visualize all beings around you. In that way
they partake of whatever benefits may occur,' she said. It was
part of her Bodhisattva vow, for true Enlightenment could not
be reached without bringing all living beings to that state.
How could one be sincerely happy anyway, knowing countless
others were enduring untold miseries throughout every realm
of existence?

Albert Einstein, arguably the West's greatest guru, knew this
too: 'A human being is a part of the whole called by us universe,
a part limited in time and space. He experiences himself, his
thoughts and feelings as something separated from the rest, a
kind of optical delusion of his consciousness. This delusion is
a kind of prison for us, restricting us to our personal desires
and to affection for a few persons nearest us. Our task must
be to free ourselves from this prison by widening our circle of
compassion to embrace all living creatures and the whole of
nature in its beauty,' he had said, using the same metaphor of
a prison that had occured in Tenzin Palmo's dream.

Tenzin Palmo was a firm believer in the efficacy of prayer.
'Actually one doesn't have to be a great yogi to help others
– the practices in themselves have great power and blessing,'
she commented. 'I believe there are infinite beings embodying
intelligence and love, always beaming in, always trying to help.
We just have to open up. So you can definitely pray to the

Buddhas and Bodhisattvas, but it's better not to pray for a bicycle at Christmas. Rather pray for spiritual growth that can flower in the mind. Pray to lesser beings for a bicycle. Just as if you wanted to get a tax return you wouldn't write to the Prime Minister but to some semi-minor official. If you wanted to stop war you'd write to the Prime Minister,' she said.

After all those hours of meditating, those twelve years of sitting in her box looking inwards in her cave, did she improve?

'Like anything else, if you practise long enough it gets easier. For example, if you are learning to play the piano, in the beginning your fingers are very stiff and you hit many wrong notes, and it is very awkward. But if you continually practise it gets easier and easier. But even so, although a concert pianist is very skilled at playing, still his difficulties are there. They may be at a higher level and not apparent to other people but he sees his own problems,' she said, modest as always.

In the end had it all been worth it? After that protracted extraordinary effort, the hardships, the self-discipline, the renunciation, what had she gained? The answer came back quick as a flash.

'It's not what you gain but what you lose. It's like unpeeling the layers of an onion, that's what you have to do. My quest was to understand what perfection meant. Now, I realize that on one level we have never moved away from it. It is only our deluded perception which prevents our seeing what we already have. The more you realize, the more you realize there is nothing to realize. The idea that there's somewhere we have got to get to, and something we have to attain, is our basic delusion. Who is there to attain it anyway?'

ELEVEN

Woman's Way

Tenzin Palmo was proving them wrong. Against all odds the frail, blue-eyed woman from Bethnal Green was surviving in a cave in the most extreme conditions, heroically meditating her way to Enlightenment in the body of a woman. Her heart may have been strong, her will iron-clad, but in actuality there was woefully little to encourage her in her quest. The problem was that she was on her own, treading uncharted territory. There were no living examples of female spiritual excellence for her to emulate, no woman guru who had trodden the path before her whom she could turn to for advice and support. There was no map plotting the way specifically to female Enlightenment with all the pitfalls and joys it may contain. There was no glowing female Dalai Lama to give her an idea even of what supreme feminine spirituality looked like.

What did she have to go on? Certainly there were a multitude of images of female Buddhas, all paying homage to the notion of women's Enlightenment. Beloved Tara, serenely smiling, with one leg outstretched ever-ready to race to those in need. Tenzin Palmo had sung her praises many times to the villagers in Lahoul on her alms rounds in return for barley flour. How the people loved her! It was Tara they turned to in their moments of greatest distress because Tara, as a woman, heard and acted quickly. She was compassion in action, said to have been born out of the tears of the male Buddha Chenrezig, who saw the suffering of all sentient beings but was unable to do anything about it. Tara, it was said, had the distinction of being the first woman to attain Enlightenment. Like Tenzin Palmo, she had been spurred on by the total dearth of females in the vast pantheon of male Buddhas. 'As there are many who have reached Buddhahood in a masculine form but very few who have done so in a woman's body, and as I have embodied Bodhicitta, may I continue along the Way to Enlightenment with a woman's body and become Buddha in a feminine form!' she had reputedly proclaimed – somewhat defiantly.

There was powerful Vajrayogini, bright red and standing proudly naked in a circle of fire, firm breasts thrust out, legs apart in her mystic dance. Here was a feisty female to whom all modern women could relate. Vajrayogini was queen of her own realm and interceder for no one – an unusual accolade for a woman in her position. (The Christian Queen of Heaven, the Virgin Mary, being hailed as the arch interceder.) Alone of all the tantric deities, Vajrayogini was so independent that she was depicted without a consort. Instead she carried her mystic lover around with her as a ritual implement slung over her shoulder, like a handbag, transforming it into a living man whenever the divine occasion demanded.

There was the exquisite Kwan Yin, labelled Regarder of the Cries of the World for her all-embracing compassionate heart. There was the mighty Prajnaparamita, the Mother of All Buddhas, sitting strong and solid on her lotus throne, embodying absolute wisdom, out of which all things arose. There were these and there were many, many more.

Loved and worshipped though these female Buddhas were, however, there was no evidence that they ever existed in human form. As a result they stayed on the level of archetypes. Idealized figures, female icons, forever perfect and perpetually out of reach.

Then there were stories – fabulous tales of derring-do and remarkable spiritual achievements carried out by just a few women who had lived in the Land of Snows and who had risen to eminence in that overtly patriarchal culture. These were the heroines who had all the prerequisites necessary for their role. They were high-spirited, fiercely independent, outrageously brave in combating the social mores of their culture, and most especially relentlessly single-minded in their determination to reach Enlightenment. The accounts of their deeds had become woven into the national folklore, standing as beacons of inspiration, telling of what might be possible.

The most famous by far was Yeshe Tsogyel, also known as the Sky Dancer. Born in 757 AD to a noble family, Yeshe Tsogyel from an early age showed all the signs of spiritual precociousness. Her one avowed intent was, she declared, to become a Buddha in one lifetime. With this in mind, she refused her arranged marriage on the grounds that she had better things to do with her 'precious human body' than romp in the conjugal bed, thereby bringing the wrath of her outraged suitors and disgraced parents down on her head. After many vicissitudes she eventually met the man who saved her life, Padma Sambhava, the man credited with bringing Buddhism to Tibet from India and hailed as a Buddha in his own right by his many followers. Padma Sambhava became not only Yeshe Tsogyel's mentor and guru, but her mystic lover as well. Yeshe Tsogyel loved Padma Sambhava passionately, reverently, and with an exquisite lack of inhibition. The details of their divine union are poetically explicit and shrouded in tantric metaphor:

Then without shame or in the manner of the world, gladly and with devotion, I, Tsogyel, prepared the mystic mandala and offered it to my Guru. The radiance of his smile of compassion shone in five-fold rays of light so that the microcosmic universes were pervaded by clear light, before again the beams of light concentrated in his face. Invoking the deity with the ejaculations DZA! and HUNG! the light descended through his body and his mystical vajra arose in wrath and as Vajra Krodha he united with the serene lotus in absolute harmony.

Even in the midst of her ecstasy, however, Yeshe Tsogyel, never having lost sight of her own purpose, implored her lover to teach her the 'sacred word which transcends cause and effect'. Padma Sambhava complied, but as the Sky Dancer was to discover, a woman harbouring the ultimate ambition was to be tested as severely as any man. Going to a series of caves in order to undergo her training, she suffered the most extreme asceticisms: she sat naked in blizzards until her skin blistered with the cold in her attempts to raise the mystic inner heat; she forsook all gross food until she learnt to 'eat air'; she prostrated until the bones of her forehead stuck out through her skin. Often she came close to death but she persevered. In the end her tenacity was rewarded.

Her own words, written by her biographer Taksham Nuden Dorje, and translated by Keith Dowman in his evocative book *Sky Dancer*, reveal the sublime state her austerities brought her to: 'I was transformed into the Pure Being that functions to imbue all creatures of the infinite universe with the value and meaning of existence, and I gained the innate ability to understand and employ any of the qualities of the Buddha at will.'

From then on the glory of Yeshe Tsogyel's achievements were displayed to the full. Everywhere she went (and the records show she travelled extensively throughout Tibet and Nepal), people were dazzled by her wisdom, compassion, and supernatural powers. She could walk through solid objects, ride on sunbeams, levitate, and on one occasion she raised the son of a Nepalese merchant from the dead by pointing her index finger at his heart until it began to glow and the blood began coursing through his veins once more. But it was at the spiritual show-down with the followers of Tibet's old religion, Bon, that Yeshe Tsogyel really showed what she was made of. Levitating in the full lotus position before the multitude, she spun wheels of fire from the tip of each finger, shattering a massive boulder nearby and then moulding it 'like butter' into various images. As a final flourish she then hurled thunderbolts at the black magicians, flattening their settlement once and for all. The disbelievers were converted, reasoning that if a woman could perform such supreme feats then the power of the Buddha must be mighty indeed.

More than a mistress of spiritual pyrotechnics, Yeshe Tsogyel was a woman of wisdom. She was accredited with organizing the writing of all of Padma Sambhava's teachings, many of which were hidden for future generations to find and benefit from. It was a vast undertaking, consisting of thousands of tomes, and an extraordinary accomplishment for a woman of her time, when female illiteracy was the norm.

On a personal level her influence was equally enormous, the beauty and power of her words reaching not only kings, queens and ministers, the crowds who thronged to hear her, but also those who wished her harm. On one momentous occasion she turned and faced her seven rapists and sang them the following song:

My sons you have met a sublime consort, the Great Mother,
And by virtue of your resources of accumulated merit,
Fortuitously, you have received the four empowerments,
Concentrate upon the evolution of the four levels of joy.

Needless to say her attackers were completely disarmed by her reaction to their violence and immediately became her disciples.

Yeshe Tsogyel gave food to the hungry, clothes to the poor, medicine to the sick and her body to whoever might need it. At one point she married a leper out of compassion for his lonely, hopeless state. But it is in the description of her attainment of Buddhahood that the real power and persuasiveness of the Yeshe Tsogyel story lies. For in this one instance all gender bias is suspended and woman is afforded equal supreme spiritual status to man. It is a glorious moment. Interestingly the tale contains remarkable parallels to the sequence of events related in Buddha Shakyamuni's Enlightenment. Just as the Buddha sat under the bodhi tree in Bodhgaya while Mara, the great illusionist, threw all manner of obstructions at him in a last-ditch attempt to prevent his Awakening, so the Sky Dancer sat in a cave in Tibet rapt in meditative equipoise while demons posed an all-out attack on her. In Yeshe Tsogyel's version, however, there is a distinctive feminist twist. While the Buddha was tempted by voluptuous maidens, Yeshe Tsogyel was lured by 'charming youths, handsome, with fine complexions, glowing with desire, strong and capable, young men at whom a girl need only glance to feel excited'. She resolutely resisted them all – of course – as did the Buddha his female sirens. Finally she reached her goal.

At that moment Padma Sambhava heaped praises upon her. His words not only reflected the glory of Yeshe Tsogyel's accomplishment, but surprisingly revealed the superiority of female capacity to reach such an exalted state:

Oh yogini who has mastered the Tantra,
The gross bodies of men and women are equally suited,
But if a woman has strong aspiration, she has higher
  potential.
From beginningless time you have accrued merit from
  virtue and awareness,
And now, faultless, endowed with a Buddha's Qualities,
Superior woman, you are a human Bodhisattva.
This is you I am speaking of, happy girl, is it not?
Now that you have achieved your own enlightenment,
Work for others, for the sake of other beings.
Such a marvellous woman as you
Never existed in the world before
Not in the past, not at present,
Not in the future – of this I am certain.

Yeshe Tsogyel left this earth at Zapu Peak in central Tibet on a palanquin of light shaped like an eight-petalled lotus. As she dissolved into radiant light her disembodied voice could be heard pouring forth final words of wisdom and exaltations of joy.

For all its inspiration and soaring heights of poetry, the Yeshe Tsogyel story took place 1,300 years ago. How much of it was believable? Over the centuries it had inevitably been embossed with symbolism and exaggeration, so that to most Westerners the Sky Dancer represented more metaphor than real woman. Certainly to Tenzin Palmo, Yeshe Tsogyel was no help at all. 'She never meant anything to me,' she declared.

More plausible was the other great heroine of Tibetan Buddhism, Machig Lapdron. Although she also belonged to an entirely different age, having lived from 1055 to 1145 AD, she was responsible for founding one of the most important and widespread rituals still practised to this day. At a purely external level Chod is blood-curdling stuff. In essence it involves the practitioner taking him or herself off to a charnel ground or cemetery in the dead of night and there, surrounded by decomposing corpses and the stench of death, visualizing the systematic dismemberment of his or her own body right down to the eyes, brain and entrails. When it is done all the pieces are visualized being put into a pot, boiled up and offered to all beings to satisfy their every craving. While the Tibetans may have been a wild, unruly bunch with a love of swashbuckling stories, Chod contains meaning of profound significance. By these seemingly gruesome visualizations, what the meditator is doing is giving up the object of greatest attachment – the body. Chopping it up and putting it into a sacred cauldron to transform into nectar before offering it to all sentient beings thus becomes the ultimate exercise in relinquishing the ego – the supreme act of selflessness.

In her day Machig Lapdron's exceptional talents inevitably caught the attention of the patriarchs who, roused by jealousy and fear, thought to discredit her once and for all by challenging her in the very public arena of spiritual debate. This was a speciality of Tibetan Buddhism, the platform on which all the scholar-saints had to prove themselves. Their plan dramatically backfired. The story tells how Machig Lapdron made intellectual and spiritual mincemeat of her male opponents, thereby establishing her permanently as one of Tibet's most important spiritual figures.

To the modern woman, however, Machig Lapdron is particularly interesting for the fact that she combined her spiritual career with marriage and children. Unlike most women with these appendages, however, she was not attached to them, nor did she demonstrate any particular sense of responsibility towards their upbringing. She happily wandered off to meditate in caves whenever the will for spiritual advancement took her, leaving them with their father for months on end. Among her many claims to fame is that she started her own lineage, using her children as her lineage holders. She died aged ninety-nine, passing on, as legend has it, to the land of the Dakinis.

More typical of the fate of women mystics was what befell Jomo Menmo, a simple young girl of the thirteenth century. Legend has it that she suddenly acquired profound wisdom from Yeshe Tsogyel, the Sky Dancer, in a dream, which she then imparted to all who asked her. As usual this raised the ire of the lamas, who branded her insane. Devastated, Jomo wandered the country refusing to speak but benefiting countless people in 'the secret way' i.e. by the sheer force of her physical presence. It was success by stealth, a ploy much used by women of all cultures.

Weighty though such characters as Machig Lapdron and Jomo Menmo were, they were too distant to have any real impact on Tenzin Palmo's life, or to help her in her own mission for female Enlightenment. There was, however, one woman who did offer some inspiration. A-Yu Khadro was a woman of her own time. The major details of her extraordinary life were taken down from the woman herself by a very living lama, Namkhai Norbu, now based in Italy. He in turn related them to Tsultrim Allione, who included A-Yu Khadro's story in her ground-breaking book *Women of Wisdom*. A-Yu Khadro was a youthful-looking 113 when Namkhai Norbu met her, with long hair still black at the tips. She was also still giving teachings and conferring secret initiations.

Aside from her unusual dedication to the life of the spirit (and the fact that marriage literally made her sick), A-Yu Khadro's story is noteworthy because of her 'egg-shaped rock'. Apparently this object was first revealed to her in a dream, but when, after months of searching for it, she finally saw it, access was barred by a raging river in full flood. Camping on the bank, looking at the rock on the opposite side, A-Yu Khadro determined to wait until the river subsided. On the third night she dreamt that a bridge had materialized over the turbulent waters, allowing her to cross over. When she awoke she inexplicably found herself on the other side.

This most mysterious occurrence was overshadowed, however, by what happened next. Having reached her 'egg-shaped rock', A-Yu Khadro proceeded to enter it via a cave and there, in total darkness, lived and meditated for seven years. Paradoxically the complete black-out was necessary to practise attaining the famous 'body of light'.

Her efforts must have paid off because when she died in 1954 aged 115 (without any signs of illness), she reportedly stayed in the meditation posture for two weeks after her external breath had stopped. Her body had not decayed – it had just become very tiny. Like Tenzin Palmo's guru, Khamtrul Rinpoche, she had demonstrated in death that she had reached an exceptionally high level of spiritual development.

But these few women, inspirational though they may have been, were of little help to Tenzin Palmo. They lived far away and long ago. When it came to finding out what female spiritual qualities looked like she was having to make her own journey of discovery. Over the years in her cave she came to a few conclusions about women's strengths and weaknesses:

'To me the special female quality (which of course many men have as well) is first of all a sharpness, a clarity. It cuts through – especially intellectual ossification. It's very sharp and gets to the point. To me the Dakini principle stands for the intuitive force. Women get it in a flash – they're not interested in intellectual discussion which they normally find dry and cold with minimum appeal. To women that's the long way of going about it. They go through the back door! This reveals itself as women being more practical in their approach, less abstract and idealistic than men. They want to know, "What can we do?" They're not entranced by theories and ideas – they want to be able to crunch it between their teeth,' she said. 'Of course, Prajnaparamita is female,' she added, referring to the Mother of All Buddhas. 'She's the Perfection of Wisdom which cuts away all our concepts and desires to make something very stable and settled. We build up our ideas. We try to make them concrete. She cuts away, cutting, cutting, cutting. She cuts things back to the bare essentials.

'At the same time women have a nurturing, a softness, a gentleness. Women tend to be more into feeling than men, which makes it easier to develop Bodhicitta. Loving kindness is innate in women, because of the mothering factor. A mother is prepared to die for her child. That impulse can be developed towards all beings. Again it's a matter of feeling, not intellect. These are not just useful qualities – they're essential.'

'Female spiritual energy is also very quick. Like Tara. You don't have to be a great yogi to communicate with Tara. She's there! Like a mother she has to be very quick because she can't wait until her child has reached a certain level before she gives it her attention and compassion. She has to be right there with it – from the moment it's born – a little wriggling worm. Whether it's a good child or a bad child she's there to help.

'And then women can often attain the experience of tumo

often more swiftly than men,' she said, talking about the famous
inner 'mystic heat' that can be raised through meditation. 'It's
something to do with our physiology. Milarepa had a lot of
trouble getting heat and bliss whereas his woman disciple
Rechungma got all the experience in three days. So many
lamas have said that women are especially good at tumo.
Not only can they generate the bliss, they're able to handle
it better as well. For myself, however, I cannot claim to be a
tumo yogini. It wasn't my main practice.'

If women had their strong points it followed that they should
also have their failings. The biggest and most insidious stigma
attributed to women on the spiritual path was their menstrual
cycle. The Curse! This, in the eyes of the male priests in most
religions throughout the world, was what rendered women
unclean and therefore unsuitable canditates for higher spiritual
office. Consequently, at the time when her period was upon
her it was decreed in many parts of the world that a woman
may not enter the sanctity of the temple. Nor may any priest
touch her! This reproachment was certainly an obstacle to be
overcome if her body was to incarnate the Divine. On a more
profound and serious level, to the serious female practitioner
her period was said to create havoc with her meditations –
bringing with it 'irritability', 'irrationality', 'pain' and PMT
– all of which supposedly disturbed her concentration and
peace of mind. Her period thus became one of her greatest
hinderances to full spiritual development.

Tenzin Palmo, having trod the path, was having none of it.
'Hormones were no obstacle to me! Personally I've never been
affected by my periods and I think that all this talk about
menopause and PMT is just making an issue of it. Besides,
I've noticed that men are often more moody than women. All
humans fluctuate in their moods, that doesn't mean you have
to cling to it,' she said in her usual pragmatic way.

'One lama did tell me, however, that women's main problem
is that they have a volatile mind. It swings up and down, which
makes it more difficult to attain steadiness in meditation. But
he also added that when a woman learns to check that energy
she can go very fast in her practice – much quicker than
men because there's this fund of energy which has not been

dissipated. In fact many, many lamas have said that once women get going on meditation their experiences are much more rapid and higher than most men's. But again, because women weren't into writing books or publicizing it you don't hear about them.'

That additional major drawback, women's craving for physical comfort, didn't apply to Tenzin Palmo either. But she was unusual. The grim living conditions which seem an inescapable part of all advanced spiritual trainings had blighted many women seekers. Irina Tweedie, the great Sufi teacher and author of *Chasm of Fire* (the diary of her own spiritual path), admits to being constantly crushed by the searing heat, the noise, and the dust of the Indian village where her guru lived. He had made her give up everything she owned, including her money, which only exacerbated her misery and the discomfort-factor further.

'We women need comfort, we need security, we need love, we need this and that. We women need, need, need. In Western society for a man to give up everything is much easier than for a woman. I know it because I did it myself, so I can speak,' she said from her home in north London just before she died. 'You see, the training for a woman is different. The man has to learn to control his sexuality. The woman has to overcome attachment to worldly objects. Ours is the way of detachment. A woman's awakening will lead her to complete detachment. One of the reasons why we are so attached, of course, is because our bodies are made to have children and for that you need comfort, security and love. It is a great thing to have children but if you reach the stage where you love the whole world exactly like your children, that's something. You don't love your children less, oh no. But you love the whole world more.'

But Tenzin Palmo had never wanted children and was able to withstand the cold, the absence of a bed, the lack of hot water and every other creature comfort with disarming ease. She had also conquered the most insuperable difficulty of all – living in an isolated place in absolute solitude. What then were her chances, or any woman's, of becoming another Yeshe Tsogyel? What were the odds of her ever attaining her goal? What, for that matter, were the chances of anyone, male or female, reaching the stage of omniscience, given the limitations that a human body automatically imposes?

Tenzin Palmo had no doubt on either score. 'The Buddha proved that Enlightenment was possible,' she said. 'When he finally broke through all the veils of delusion his mind became vast – he remembered all of his past lives stretching back eons and eons, which he dictated to his disciples. At one point he picked up some leaves from the forest floor and asked his followers: "Which is greater – the leaves in my hand or those on the trees of the forest?" When his disciples replied: "The leaves on the trees," the Buddha said: "The leaves in my hand represent the amount of knowledge that I can give to you." But that didn't mean that he didn't get toothache. He had his personal physician for the times when he did get sick,' she said.

'As to the continuing controversy about whether women can get Enlightened, most of that is only due to cultural discrimination and on-going male chauvinism. Personally I have no doubts. And the benefits of having women up there among the men are obvious. For one thing women are half of the human race. So women who have got a lot of genuine practice and understanding are necessarily going to raise the level of humanity because there are so many of them,' Tenzin Palmo stated.

Irina Tweedie agreed: 'I personally feel that we women can reach exactly the same heights as men – providing we keep our femininity. We are all created in the image of God – God is masculine and feminine both, so we have all capacities, all abilities in us. It is in the female nature to be powerful. The problem is that men are afraid of powerful women, it's the competition! But I don't think women are! Thousands of years ago there was a matriarchal society then the pendulum swung back (too much in my opinion) – now women are ascending once more. The result will be a world which is more balanced, more full of love. There will not be so much hardness in it.'

Contemporary male Buddhists in high places were beginning to change their minds as well. 'Of course a woman can become a Buddha,' announced the Dalai Lama recently, before substantiating his statement with references to the scriptures.

'In the texts of the Vehicles of Perfection, and those of the first three classes of the tantras, it has been said that Buddhahood is generally attained in the masculine form. But according to the fourth class of tantras there is no distinction between masculine and feminine; Enlightenment may come about just as easily in a woman's body as in a man's.'

Another eminent and much-loved lama, the late Kalu Rinpoche, who established a centre in France after the Tibetan diaspora, echoed the Dalai Lama's words: 'Regardless of whether you are a man or a woman, if you have faith, confidence and diligence, if you have compassion and wisdom, you can become Enlightened. The reason for this total equality of opportunity is the nature of mind itself, which is neither male nor female. There is no such thing as the intrinsic nature of one person's mind being better than someone else's, on the ultimate level the empty clear and unimpeded nature of mind exhibits no limiting qualities such as maleness or femaleness, superiority or inferiority.

'On a relative level, however, there are differences, including the way in which the physical embodiment is formed at the subtle level of the energy channels and energy centres. According to the teachings of tantra the way in which a mind incarnates in a male body is subtly different from the way in which it incarnates in a female body. In the psycho-physical make-up of a male, there is more force, more concentrated and direct energy, whereas in that of a female, there is more spaciousness, signifying Wisdom. These relative differences should always be understood in the context of the ultimate nature of the mind.' His words illustrated the complex and highly scientific nature of Enlightenment, Tibetan style.

Perhaps the most encouraging and most simple confirmation came from an old lama called Kangyur, who lived not far from Tenzin Palmo's cave in Lahoul and who knew the English nun well. Kangyur, a robust figure with a white wispy beard and jolly manner, was known throughout the region for his holiness and for his lifelong habit of sleeping outside on his roof in −35 degree temperatures without any socks. When asked if a woman could achieve Enlightenment he was adamant: 'On the outside there is difference but the heart is the same,' he said, patting the point mid-way between his breasts. 'What is Enlightenment but the heart knowing itself? This is very hard. Just as the eye can see the whole world but cannot see itself, so the heart can know everything but has great difficulty in understanding itself. But Tenzin Palmo was a great practitioner. Everyone here was very surprised how well she did.'

To Tenzin Palmo herself, however, her efforts were nothing special. 'I like to sit and meditate. There is nothing else I like to do,' she said.

TWELVE

Coming Out

Tenzin Palmo may have been content to sit there in her cave meditating indefinitely, but the world literally came knocking. One day in the summer of 1988 she was startled out of her solitude by the appearance of the police. Paying no heed to the boundary fence, erected specifically to keep all visitors out, nor to the accepted etiquette never to disturb solitary practitioners, the policeman barged right into her compound, knocked loudly on the door and demanded to know why she had an illegal visa. He went on to state in no uncertain terms that if she did not appear at the local police station the next day she would be arrested. It was the first voice Tenzin Palmo had heard in three years, the first figure she had seen. By any one's accounts it was a rude awakening. Complying with this onslaught of officialdom, she obediently descended from her mountain to confront the new Superintendent of Police, who told her he was very sorry about the situation but he had no choice but to give her a Quit India notice. She would have to leave the country in ten days.

Patiently Tenzin Palmo explained to the Superintendent that she had been in India for twenty-four years and was not prepared to leave in ten days. Furthermore, she went on, it wasn't her fault that her visa was not in order, as she'd left the matter with the previous incumbent who had been renewing it on her behalf. Faced with her utter reasonableness and obvious sincerity, the Superintendent softened and said that as he was going on holiday for a month he did not have to give her notice immediately, as he had thought, but that eventually she would have to leave. Until the matter was sorted out he graciously gave her permission to return to her cave and resume what she was doing.

Tenzin Palmo climbed her mountain once more but it was no use. She had been seen, she had been forced to speak, and by the spiritual laws laid down, her retreat was thereby irrevocably broken. She could not continue. By rights she should have been furious or at least bitterly disappointed. She had done three years in the last serious bout of retreat but the fruits could not be fully realized, it was said, until the final three months, three weeks and three days had been done. After such sustained dedication and diligence she could well have ranted at the Superintendent or wept silently back in her cave. It would have been reasonable. Instead she laughed and said: 'Certainly, it was not the way you are meant to finish a retreat. You are meant to stay there for a few days and slowly get used to seeing people again.'

Word soon got out that Tenzin Palmo's retreat had ended and friends now sought her out, eager to see for themselves the results of that long period of meditation and solitude. Was she still all right? Had that prolonged period of introspection and isolation sent her mad, or slightly deranged? Maybe she had been transfigured into a glorious being of light, surrounded by rainbows, as the fabulous stories of yore told? If the people who came looking had expected to see a major metamorphosis, however, they were to be disappointed.

'It wasn't so much that Tenzin Palmo had changed, more that her qualities were enhanced. The warmth, the mental sharpness, the humour were all still there, but more so. There was growth. It was as though she already had the talent and the capacity and then put the effort behind it. She is very single-minded,' reported Didi Contractor, the woman who had vetted Tenzin Palmo's cave to make sure it was habitable when she first went to live there and who had known many great spiritual teachers and their followers during her years in India.

'I don't think anyone on the outside can see the results of what she managed in the cave. What she accomplished was between her and the Deity (I'd rather say that than the Nothingness). One can only go by the symptoms. Certainly she has stature and an integrity of character which is very developed. She also has a completeness. Tenzin Palmo is always completely consistent and always completely kind. But I don't know whether that is either a proof or a fruit of her spiritual search. It could be part of who she is that makes it possible for her to take up the search. I would say, however, that Tenzin Palmo has got further than any of the other many western seekers I've met,' she commented.

Another visitor was Lia Frede, a German woman who lived in a beautiful house in the hills of Dharamsala, and who had known Tenzin Palmo for some years. She also had had a long interest in spiritual matters, particularly Vipassana meditation, and had conducted several retreats herself. Coincidentally Lia was leading a small trek in Lahoul, studying the ecology of the region, when she heard the news that Tenzin Palmo was 'out'.

'I was delighted to have the chance to talk to her because I wanted to know what she had accomplished,' she said frankly. 'The day is etched clearly on my mind. I had terrible trouble finding the cave, it was so well blended in with the rest of the mountain – but we eventually got there. I was a little shy about intruding so I left my two companions at the gate and went inside and called. Immediately Tenzin Palmo came out, smiled happily and said, "Come in, come in, bring your friends, I've just baked bread. Would you like tea?" It was as though she had seen me yesterday. She was totally normal. I remember sitting there thinking it was all so incongruous. There we were in the cave having this delicious fresh bread with roasted sesame on it and chatting away. It was as though we were in the middle of England having afternoon tea.

'As she walked us back down the path I asked her what results she had got from her retreat. I didn't like to ask her outright if she'd got Enlightened but I was waiting for her to tell me of some transcendent experience she'd had. It was certainly what I would have expected. Instead she looked at me and replied, "One thing I can tell you – I was never bored." That was it. I was waiting for more, but nothing else was said. It has always puzzled me that that was the only statement she made.' Tenzin Palmo was obviously being as tight-lipped as ever.

If Tenzin Palmo was revealing nothing, Lia, like Didi, could see for herself clearly her friend's exceptional qualities. 'Tenzin Palmo has deep-seated purity and, I would say, innocence. And the other thing is that she has true equanimity. Things that happen to her she neither objects nor supports – she neither pushes nor obstructs. She has this neutrality. She deals with what is happening without attaching any ego involvement to it. It's not that she's trying, the ego is just not there. I was amazed by her reaction when she was trapped in her cave and she thought she was going to die. I know if I had been in that situation I would have panicked. Instead she calmly did her death meditations. And when I heard that her supplies didn't arrive and she almost starved, I was furious! I would have wanted to know why. She never bothered to find out though. Nor did she blame the Superintendent for breaking up her retreat. She knows that people have their karma. Still, to me that amount of equanimity shows a definite degree of spiritual advancement.'

More relevant than people's impressions of Tenzin Palmo was her response to them. Having been isolated from people and the ways of the world for so long, what was it like suddenly coming into contact with them again, having to make conversation, having to deal with the noise and mundanity of everyday life? According to the testimonies of other Western retreatants, who had ventured into shorter periods of silence and seclusion, re-entry into the world was a shocking experience, an assault on the senses and the psyche which left them reeling. They reported that it took weeks for them to recover and reintegrate back into society. Tenzin Palmo had been cut off from human contact for infinitely longer and had, by her own admission, been removing layer upon layer of outer coverings. Her sensitivity must have been honed to finer levels than ever before. 'At first talking to people was exhausting, not at the time, but afterwards I found myself very tired. But after a while it was OK,' she conceded.

Curiously, rather than making her less capable of dealing with people, less willing to enter into relationship with the world as one might expect, the cave seemed to have the opposite effect. Tenzin Palmo was not traumatized by meeting the world again, and was witnessed being exceptionally sociable, very chatty, and super-sensitive to the needs and suffering of humanity. It was as big a sign as any that her meditations in the cave had worked.

'Tenzin Palmo has a large compassion – an unruffled compassion,' commented Lia Frede. 'She's really very unjudgemental and gives her ear and advice to anyone, be it a sinner or a saint. She's neutral – she doesn't mind whether someone has just affronted her or been nice to her. It is something I've noticed in other spiritually advanced beings. Anyone who comes to her with a problem, she's always willing to help. That's why people seek her company, because it has a purifying influence when you are with a person like that.'

'I have the kind of mind that wherever I am that's where I am,' was Tenzin Palmo's attitude. 'I think I have two sides to my nature – one is this basic need to be alone, the love of isolation, the other is a sociability and friendliness. I don't know if I am particularly warm towards others but I do know that whoever I am with I feel they are the most important person in the world at that time. Internally there is always this feeling of wishing them well. So although I love to be alone, when I'm with others that's fine too.'

Now, thrust into the mainstream of the world once more, Tenzin Palmo could see for herself if she had changed. Had there been a transformation? That, ultimately, was the only valid test of her spiritual practices, for no amount of retreat could have been said to have worked unless there was a fundamental shift, a turning around of your old, habitual ways of seeing and being. Up there on her mountain, in splendid isolation, she may have been thoroughly absorbed in the eternal verities but could that experience stand up to the challenge of everyday life?

'There is a kind of inner freedom which I don't think I had when I started – an inner peace and clarity. I think it came from having to be self-sufficient, having nothing or no one to turn to whatever happened,' she said. 'Also while I was in retreat everything became dreamlike, just as the Buddha described. One could see the illusory nature of everything going on around one – because one was not in the middle of it,' she continued, using the impersonal pronoun in order to deflect attention from any realizations she may have had! 'And then when you come out you see that people are so caught up in their life – we identify so totally with what we've created. We believe in it so completely. That's why we suffer – because there's no space for us.'

'Now I notice that there is an inner distance towards

whatever occurs, whether what's occurring is outwards or inwards. Sometimes, it feels like being in an empty house with all the doors and windows wide open and the wind just blowing through without anything obstructing it. Not always. Sometimes one gets caught up again, but now one knows that one is caught up again.'

While being like 'an empty house' may seem desirable to a meditator, to the average person, brought up on the notion that passion and emotional involvement is what gives life its colour and verve, such a state could seem vapid and remote. Was being an 'empty house' the same as being a 'shell' of a person – cold and unfeeling? And what is the difference between detachment and being cut off from your emotions anyway? A study conducted at a London hospital among children who were left for weeks without visitors showed that it was at the point when they stopped crying and became in the eyes of the staff 'good', that the harm was done. Follow-up studies showed that these children had developed the potential for psychotic behaviour. The stage at which they stopped crying was when some vital feeling part of them had 'died'. Was being detached being alienated?

Tenzin Palmo, as might be expected, refuted all such insinuations. 'It's not a cold emptiness,' she stated emphatically, 'it's a warm spaciousness. It means that one is no longer involved in one's ephemeral emotions. One sees how people cause so much of their own suffering just because they think that without having these strong emotions they're not real people.

'Why does one go into retreat?' she went on hotly. 'One goes into a retreat to understand who one really is and what the situation truly is. When one begins to understand oneself then one can truly understand others because we are all interrelated. It is very difficult to understand others while one is still caught up in the turmoil of one's emotional involvement – because we're always interpreting others from the standpoint of our own needs. That's why, when you meet hermits who have really done a lot of retreat, say twenty-five years, they are not cold and distant. On the contrary. They are absolutely lovely people. You know that their love for you is totally without judgement because it doesn't rely on who you are or what you are doing, or how you treat them. It's totally impartial. It's just love. It's like the sun – it shines on everyone. Whatever you did they'd still love you because they understand your predicament and in that understanding naturally arises love and compassion. It's not based on sentiment. It's not based on emotion. Sentimental love is very unstable, because it's based on feed-back and how good it makes you feel. That is not real love at all.'

It may not have been psychological but there was severing going on in Tenzin Palmo's life just the same. As it turned out, the Superintendent's edict had a far more dramatic effect than terminating her retreat. It brought to an end an entire era. Now the utterly unexpected happened. After a lifetime of being enamoured with the East in general and Tibetan Buddhism in particular, she began to feel the pull of her own culture. For the first time in the twenty-four years that she had been living in India, the West beckoned.

She explained: 'I felt my time in India had drawn to a close, that I needed to get back to the West and rediscover my roots. After all, I am not Tibetan. When I worked in the library in Hackney I had a boyfriend who was into classical music, architecture, art, old churches, that kind of thing. He loved to talk about it all and go to concerts and galleries. I was very fascinated. Then I became a Buddhist when I was eighteen and renounced all that! My whole focus turned. After twenty-four years of being in India and reading nothing but dharma books, however, I felt there was this huge void in my life and that I hadn't finished what I was supposed to have done.'

Having no idea of where she wanted to go, Tenzin Palmo did what she always did in such situations – remained still and waited for the 'voice' to speak to her. In the meantime her many friends, scattered all around the world, began to write inviting her to their countries. She contemplated America, Australia, England, but none seemed right. Then an American friend, Ram, whom she had met in India, wrote saying he had found the perfect place – Assisi. Why didn't she join him and his wife there? She had never been to Assisi, but once she read the name the voice spoke out loud and clear.

'That's it,' she said, clicking her fingers.

Without sentimentality or sadness Tenzin Palmo prepared to

leave the Cave of Great Bliss. It had consumed a colossal chunk of her life, her 'prime years' between the ages of thirty-three and forty-five, but to her it seemed nothing. 'The thing that struck me most was where had all the time gone? Time just condensed. The last three years in particular just flew past. It seemed like four months at most,' she commented.

Without haste she packed her few belongings, bade farewell to her Lahouli friends and made her way to the West and the cradle of the greatest flowering of Western culture, Italy, birthplace of the Renaissance. She had come full circle. Coming into the world, leaving it, and then returning. She arrived at the pretty medieval town of Assisi, built on the flanks of Mount Subasio in Umbria, in the dead of night but knew instantly she'd made the right choice. It could have been the small clusters of picturesque houses perched on mountain-tops so reminiscent of Lahoul, or the aura of sanctity left by St Francis which still hung in the air, or even the fact that there were several Indian ashrams in the area, but the moment Tenzin Palmo arrived she felt at home.

'I felt a very strong connection with Assisi. To this day it's the only place I miss, including my cave. There's a special, ineffable quality about it which is palpable in spite of the millions of tourists who flock there each year. It's not an ordinary place. It's the centre for world peace and holds a lot of inter-faith conferences. And many people have reported having spiritual experiences there, strong transformative experiences,' she said.

She moved into the bottom floor of a house belonging to a friend of Ram's and proceeded to rediscover her Western roots with delight. She roamed the charming, narrow streets of the town, often at night and alone, feeling quite safe. She visited the famous double basilica housing St Francis's tomb, marvelling in the exquisite frescoes, especially those by Giotto. And she climbed the mountain, curious to see another cave, the one inhabited by St Francis who had prayed so hard to God to let him know the suffering of Jesus that not only did the stigmata appear on his hands and feet but actual nails manifested too. Over the five years she lived in Assisi Tenzin Palmo developed a strong devotion to St Francis and would spend hours meditating in his cave when there were no tourists around.

'It was a very different cave from mine because it has this church built over it. But it was great! There are still doves in the tree outside, descendants of ones St Francis bought from a seller and left there to multiply. I loved his animal stories. Do you know he had a cicada and they'd sing to each other? He was a very vivid saint,' she said.

Once Tenzin Palmo revealed that she felt she had been a Christian monk in one of her many lifetimes. 'The feeling when I go into cloisters is very strong. It's almost déjà vu. And I've always had an affinity with the enclosed orders. I think I probably decided to go to the East when the Christian tradition stopped going anywhere. It would make sense,' she divulged.

The austerities that she had submitted herself to for so long now gave way to a few indulgences. She learnt to eat pasta and developed a liking for cappuccino and tiramisu (although she claimed her favourite dish was still rice, vegetables and dhal). She watched videos, especially old black and white 1940s movies. More than this, she buried herself in her friends' vast library and music collection, soaking up her European heritage like a dry sponge. 'It was as though the whole Western part of myself had been ruptured and needed to be healed and put back together again.' She now allowed herself to read novels, veering towards French authors and stories with a religious plot like Umberto Eco's The Name of the Rose. And she devoured anything she could find on medieval history, devoting herself to this new learning with the same thoroughness with which she had tackled Buddhism. The period around the twelfth and thirteenth century, the time when St Francis lived, particularly appealed to her. 'There was a lot of intellectual ferment and scholastic debate going on then – a lot of stuff coming from the Arabs and Jews and they were slowly beginning to discover the Greeks. It was also the time of the growth of the mendicant orders when very great saints and artists were around,' she explained.

She also plunged into the biographies and writings of the Christian saints and philosophers: St Teresa of Avila, St John of the Cross, Thomas Aquinas, the Desert Fathers, Thomas Merton, the Philokalia, the scriptures from the Orthodox

Church, and much much more. As she read, her appreciation for the religion she had once dismissed grew and with it came a new understanding and pride in her Western identity.

'The Tibetans generally regard us as barbarians. They think we're very good at inventing the motor car, but have nothing much inside, and so in terms of real culture are barren. At a certain point that is very disempowering. It is just like when the Christian missionaries went abroad and denigrated whatever culture they found themselves in, thinking theirs was the only true one,' she said. 'I began to see it isn't true. We are not all McDonalds and Coca Cola. We have incredible philosophy and art and an incredible spiritual tradition. Western thought is very sophisticated and I discovered that in matters of the religion it was all there. Personally, I still found the Buddhist analysis of the Path the most clear and complete for someone like me, but it was so good to see the same insights being stated albeit in a different way. These things are important to know.' Then she added with a wry smile, 'Interestingly when Buddhism first went to Tibet the Indians thought the Tibetans were "barbarians" too. They didn't want to hand over the precious Buddha dharma to them because they thought they would mess it up!'

Most of all Tenzin Palmo discovered the pleasure of music, which fed some long-neglected part of herself. She steeped herself in the classical composers – Bach, Handel, Haydn and her favourite, Mozart. 'It was a wonderful thing to find Mozart. I completely fell in love with him,' she declared. 'It was something quite profound at a certain level. It was very moisturizing. I think I had become extremely dry, somewhere,' she said candidly.

Knowingly or not, Tenzin Palmo was balancing East with West, asceticism with sensuality, solitude with sociability – giving herself a more rounded personality. In this way she was following the exact advice given by one of her new-found Christian mentors, the great thirteenth-century German mystic, Meister Eckhart, who had written: 'I say that the contemplative person should avoid even the thought of deeds to be done during the period of his contemplation but afterwards he should get busy for no one can or should engage in contemplation all the time, for active life is to be a respite from contemplation.'

At this time another aspect to Tenzin Palmo's life began to open up – one that would develop much further in the future. The Christians soon got wind of her presence in Assisi and became highly interested to see and hear for themselves the woman who had spent so long in retreat alone. Her effort was beyond anything their orders ever attempted. She was asked to talk at seminars and at one point received an embossed invitation from the Vatican Council, no less, asking her to speak at an inter-faith conference in Taiwan. She was also invited to conduct workshops in seminaries and convents to tell the enclosed orders precisely what she had done, and how she had done it. Tenzin Palmo happily accepted, as she was now well receptive to inter-faith dialogue and was keen to give whatever knowledge she had in exchange for Christian methods of contemplation. But it didn't work out like that at all.

'At one Benedictine monastery I was told that mass was at 5 a.m. and so I thought I would join in. When I got to the chapel, however, there were only one or two people inside. I asked where everyone was and was told that they were in a small room that had been set aside for my meditation course. When I got there I found all these shoes neatly lined up outside the door and all the inmates inside sitting there on the floor cross-legged. They had set up an altar with a Buddha statue on it, flowers and water bowls and asked me if it was all right. "It's lovely, thank you," I told them.

'They were only interested in learning about Buddhism. They'd been studying it, had met the Dalai Lama and were keen to know more. I wanted to encourage Christian meditation but they weren't having any of it. They told me that there were so few masters of the inner life in Catholicism which was why the young people were falling away. They said the young were asking for ways of obtaining inner peace and a spiritual path to put meaning back into their lives. The nuns and monks felt that if they could get themselves together they could become guides to bring the young people what they needed.

'They wanted methods, because they had lost their own. They wanted directions: what to do, what not to do, descriptions of the problems that can arise in meditation and how to deal with them. Tibetan methods are excellent because they don't require

any particular faith structure. Anyone can make use of them –
including psychologists. So I told them what to do and they
would sit there nodding their heads. Afterwards one elderly
Carmelite nun said: "If only someone had told me how to
meditate years ago. It's so simple.'"

From her side, Tenzin Palmo enjoyed being with the nuns
enormously. They swapped methods of robe-wearing, she told
them about her life, they explained theirs. In spite of the
differences, their pleasure in the commonality of the habit was
mutual. From the Christian nuns she also picked up methods
of a different kind which were to be extremely useful in a
few years' time. In turn the Christian fraternity so appreciated
Tenzin Palmo that they invited her to their monasteries to do
long retreats whenever she wanted. She thanked them kindly
and declined.

As time went by her name became known and her influence
began to spread. She was invited to talk in Rome, north Italy,
Umbria, Devon, Poland. While she was in Poland she visited
Auschwitz and saw for herself the place which had been the
site of so much human suffering. 'One of the things that moved
me most of all were the photographs of the people who had
gone to the gas chambers. So many of them were bright-eyed
and beautiful. Some were even smiling. I found that incredibly
painful,' she said.

For all of her appreciation of Western culture, she had not
relinquished her Buddhism, nor her meditation. Far from it. She
continued to do her daily practices and conducted several short
retreats. Before she knew it she was also caught up in a project to
start a nunnery for Western Buddhist nuns in Pomaia, near Pisa.
She had met the women at a summer course and, recognizing
in them a reflection of her own dire experience when she was
first ordained, was touched by their plight. 'The nuns had no
place of their own, and no one was looking after them. The
monks were OK – they had their monastery, but the nuns were
moving from centre to centre. It was not good for their spiritual
development at all,' she said.

Later, when the opportunity came for her to join her friend
Ram on a pilgrimage to Mount Kailash, in Tibet, she jumped
at it. She had never been to the land which had fostered the

strongest impulses in her present life, and Mount Kailash was regarded as the most sacred pilgrimage site of all. Situated in a remote region of western Tibet, in one of the most desolate places on earth, Mount Kailash was hailed as the very centre of the tantric universe by Buddhists and Hindus alike. At its peak, which soared more than 21,000 feet into the rarefied atmosphere, lived the gods abided over by Tara herself. Tenzin Palmo had wanted to go to Kailash ever since she first read about the mystical mountain in Lama Govinda's inspirational book *The Way of the White Clouds*, but had never seriously thought she would make it in this lifetime.

'It was incredible to be in Tibet finally – so much of my life had been spent thinking and reading about it. The surroundings absolutely lived up to my expectations – but there was also the anguish of seeing all that had been destroyed under the Chinese. There were huge monasteries which were just ruins. It was terribly sad,' she said.

They hired four yaks to carry their tents and cooking gear while they travelled by the more modern method of Land Cruiser. The journey took ten days, as there were no roads and the going was incredibly hard. When she eventually got there it was worth it. 'Kailash itself was wonderful. We had to go over the 18,000 feet Dolma Pass in a snowstorm to get to it and Ram and I were both exhausted and got disorientated. Then this big black dog appeared. We gave it some soggy biscuits and he showed us the way down. We were incredibly happy. It was very special and a great blessing. It took us two and a half days to circumambulate Mount Kailash once, prostrating at the holy places. Some Tibetans do it in a day. They get up at 3 a.m. and finish at 10 p.m. Some do twenty to thirty rounds in a month! Some go for 108, the numbers of beads on their malas (rosaries). And some prostrate all the way around, which takes them about two weeks. It's very flinty so it's not easy.'

'The nearby Lake Manasarovar is very special too. We were there for my fiftieth birthday. Ram insisted on bathing in it, so I did too. It almost killed me. It was freezing, with this icy wind blowing. You have to drink the water too, otherwise it doesn't count!'

She met the nomads, gentle people still clinging to a way of life that had been going on for millennia. She heard their longing for the Dalai Lama, saw their poverty, but thought they were better off than the Tibetan town-folk, who were humiliated daily by the Chinese overlords. 'For all their suffering I was astonished by the indomitable spirit of the Tibetans and how they managed to stay cheerful in such awful circumstances,' she said. 'It was bliss to be there, one of my peak experiences even though I felt terrible with splitting headaches and altitude sickness! I had a sense of fulfilment – I had dreamt of it for so long.'

There was no longing to stay, however. Tenzin Palmo may have had the strongest connections possible with Tibet and its religion, but now she was a Westerner, who had furthermore discovered Western music. In the midst of the stony wastes of West Tibet, under the shadow of the sublime, mystical Mount Kailash, Tenzin Palmo played Mozart. 'You can take Mozart anywhere,' she enthused. 'To me it's the perfect music. It's incredibly moving and gives me great joy! My Desert Island Discs would be almost all Mozart. If you could think of heaven with music, it would have Mozart there.'

She was also longing for some decent food. 'I got sick to death of greasy noodles. I was longing for rice and dhal,' she said. Her home was no longer Tibet.

Tenzin Palmo sincerely believed that Assisi would be her base for the rest of her life. With this thought in mind she set about building a small two-roomed wooden house in the grounds belonging to her friends with money given to her through donations. She meant to go back into retreat, for she had certainly not forgotten her pursuit of perfection. She had actually begun when, Italian-style, building permission was suddenly withdrawn. Once again it seemed that fate, or 'karma', was stepping in and taking a hand in Tenzin Palmo's life. She may have been ready to settle down but her days of 'going forth into homelessness', as decreed by the Buddha as the ideal state for his monks and nuns, were far from over. She had work to do. Much work.

THIRTEEN

The Vision

The month was March 1993. The place Dharamsala, the former British hill station in Himachal Pradesh, north India, now the home of the Dalai Lama and his government in exile. As senior nun and burgeoning teacher, Tenzin Palmo had been invited to attend the first Western Buddhism conference, aimed at discussing the issues involved in the phenomena of transmitting the Buddha-dharma to the West. With her were twenty-one other leading representatives of the major Buddhist traditions in Europe and America, as well as eminent lamas from the different Tibetan schools. The discussions went back and forth – the role of the teacher, the differences between the Eastern and Western psyche, ethical guidelines – when suddenly 'the role of women in Buddhism' came up.

An attractive German laywoman, Sylvia Wetzel, took the floor. With a small but discernible gulp she invited His Holiness the Dalai Lama and the assembled throng of luminaries to join her in a visualization. 'Please imagine that you are a male coming to a Buddhist centre. You see the painting of this beautiful Tara surrounded by sixteen female arhats and you have the possibility to see too Her Holiness the fourteenth Dalai Lama who, in all of her fourteen incarnations, has always chosen a female rebirth,' she began. 'You are surrounded by very high female rinpoches – beautiful, strong, educated women. Then you see the Bhikshunis coming in, self-confident, outspoken. Then you see the monks coming in behind them – very shy and timid. You hear about the lineage lamas of the tradition, who are all female, down to the female Tara in the painting.

'Remember you are male,' she reminded them, 'and you approach a lama, feeling a little bit insecure and a little bit irritated, and ask, "Why are there all these female symbols, female Buddhas?" And she replies, "Don't worry. Men and women are equal. Well, almost. We do have some scriptures which say that a male rebirth is inferior, but isn't this the case? Men do have a more difficult time when all the leaders, spiritually, philosophically and politically are women."

'And then the male student, who is very sincere, goes to another lama, a Mahayanist from the Higher Vehicle School, and says, "I am a man, how can I identify with all these female icons?" And she replies, "You just meditate on Shunyata (Emptiness). In Shunyata no man, no woman, no body, nothing. No problem!"

'So you go to a tantric teacher and say, "All these women and I am a man. I don't know how to relate." And she says, "How wonderful you are, beautiful Daka, you are so useful to us practitioners helping us to raise our kundalini energy. How blessed you are to be male, to benefit female practitioners on their path to enlightenment."'

It was outrageous but delivered in such a charming way that everyone, including the Dalai Lama, laughed. 'Now you have given me another angle on the matter,' he said. In effect Sylvia Wetzel had voiced what millions of women down the centuries had felt. In spite of the mirth, the dam holding back more than 2,500 years of spiritual sexism and pent-up female resentment was beginning to burst.

Others began to join in. A leading Buddhist teacher and author, American nun Thubten Chodron, told how the subtle prejudice she had met within institutions had undermined her confidence to the point that it was a serious hindrance on the path. 'Even if our pain was acknowledged it would make us feel better,' she declared.

Sympathetic male teachers spoke up. 'This is a wonderful challenge for the male – to see it and accept it,' said a Zen master.

American Tibetan Buddhist monk Thubten Pende gave his views: 'When I translated the texts concerning the ordination ceremony I got such a shock. It said that even the most senior nun had to sit behind the most novice monk because, although her ordination was superior, the basis of that ordination, her body, was inferior. I thought, "There it is." I'd heard about this belief but I'd never found evidence of it. I had to recite this text at the ceremony. I was embarrassed to say it and ashamed of the institution I was representing. I wondered, "Why doesn't she get up and leave?" I would.'

The English Theravadan monk Ven Ajahn Amaso also spoke up: 'Seeing the nuns not receiving the respect given to the monks is very painful. It is like having a spear in your heart,' he said.

Then it was Tenzin Palmo's turn, and with all her natural eloquence she told her tale: 'When I first came to India I lived in a monastery with 100 monks. I was the only nun,' she said, and paused for several seconds for her words to sink in. 'I think that is why I eventually went to live by myself in a cave.' Everyone got the point. 'The monks were kind, and I had no problems of sexual harassment or troubles of that sort, but of course I was unfortunately within a female form. They actually told me they prayed that in my next life I would have the good fortune to be reborn as a male so that I could join in all the monastery's activities. In the meantime, they said, they didn't hold it *too* much against me that I had this inferior rebirth in the female form. It wasn't too much my fault.'

Seizing her chance, she went on to fire her biggest salvo. An exposé on the situation of the Western Sangha, particularly the nuns whom she had befriended in Italy. 'The lamas ordain people and then they are thrown out into the world with no training, preparation, encouragement, support or guidance – and they're expected to keep their vows, do their practice and run dharma centres. This is very hard and I'm surprised that so many of the Western monastics stay as long as they do. I'm not surprised when they disrobe. They start with so much enthusiasm, with so much pure faith and devotion and gradually their inspiration decreases. They get discouraged and disillusioned and there is no one who helps them. This is true, Your Holiness. It's a very hard situation and it has never happened in the history of Buddhism before.

'In the past the sangha was firmly established, nurtured and cared for. In the West this is not happening. I truly don't know why. There are a few monasteries, mostly in the Therevada tradition, which are doing well, but for the nuns what is there?

There is hardly anything, quite frankly. But to end on a higher note, I pray that this life of purity and renunciation which is so rare and precious in the world, that this jewel of the sangha may not be thrown down into the mud of our indifference and contempt.'

It was an impassioned, formidable cry from the heart. When she had finished a great hush fell over the gathering. No one was laughing now. As for the Tenzin Gyatso, the Great Ocean of Wisdom, regarded by his people as an emanation of Chenrezig, the Buddha of Compassion, he was sitting there, head in his hands, silently weeping. After several minutes he looked up, wiped his eyes and said softly, 'You are quite brave.' Later the senior lamas commented that such directness was indeed rare and that in this respect the conference had been like a family gathering where everyone spoke their mind frankly.

That speech marked yet another radical turning point in Tenzin Palmo's already remarkable life. She had stood up and spoken out (to the top man, no less), but it was as if she knew words were not enough. Complaining about the system was one thing, doing something about it was another. And if the women who felt wronged couldn't act, who would? Now the backlog of her own personal unhappiness as a nun in Dalhousie came to the fore and began to be used for positive ends. She had waited almost thirty years but it was not a moment too late. The time for women's spiritual liberation had come. And Tenzin Palmo was to take a leading active role. It was as far away from her cherished life as a recluse as she could get, but still it seemed peculiarly apt. She knew at first hand the difficulties that women on the spiritual path faced. She had suffered, had known spiritual rejection and the heavy weight of discouragement, but now it seemed it had all been for a purpose.

'I think that is why I was born as a woman this time,' she said.

She began by helping to arrange a conference for Western nuns in Bodhgaya, where they could air their problems, exchange views and establish a much-needed feeling of community and support. After this she joined forces with a small but committed group of women agitating to bring full ordination to the nuns. She knew more than most how essential this was for elevating their status in the eyes of society and boosting their self-esteem. It was a delicate, complex issue, however, bound up with centuries of ecclesiastical red tape, circuitous theological argument and layers of entrenched male prejudice. It would take years of persistence and gentle persuasion to overturn the existing order and to persuade the lamas to move over on their high thrones. But at least the movement had started.

And when these projects were under way and Tenzin Palmo started to think yet again of returning to a life of serious retreat, she was presented with another scheme – one much closer to her own heart. One infinitely more difficult to achieve. The building of a nunnery for the women of her own order, the Drukpa Kargyu School. The idea had been put into her head back in the seventies by her lama, Khamtrul Rinpoche. He had pointed in the general direction of the lush Kangra valley, where his own monastery of Tashi Jong had been rebuilt, and said, 'You can build a nunnery here.' At the time she had dismissed it as a brilliant but impossible ideal. Now she was older, had done her twelve years of meditation in a cave, and was back out in the world. The time might be right.

Her plans to help the Western Buddhist nuns build a nunnery had fallen through, and Tenzin Palmo knew how urgently the Tibetan nuns needed help. Like the Western nuns they had nowhere to go, for they had been forgotten in the haste to rebuild the monasteries for the refugee monks. Consequently they were reduced to cooking in monastery kitchens for the monks or returning home to take up a life of domesticity in order to earn their keep. It was a pitiful situation which made Tenzin Palmo very sad.

'The nuns are so young and fresh, with so much devotion and enthusiasm, and yet they're given so little encouragement. They're open and incredibly diligent. We're talking about girls who prostrate all the way from Kham to Kailash, hundreds of miles, and then do prostrations around Mount Kailash itself. They don't even think about it! It's that kind of total dedication to the path,' she said. 'Even the rare nun who does manage to get some philosophical training is handicapped on account of the fact that she is a woman. I know of one case where a nun managed to win a place at a prestigious university in Sarnath, in India, and although she came top she was pulled out after two years on the grounds that she had had enough learning for a woman and any further study would be a waste of time and money.'

Still, she shuddered. Starting a nunnery was a huge undertaking. It would take years of planning, organizing, worldly endeavour, and more to the point, personal investment. Retreat was what she was good at. Retreat, to her, was easy. As she was hesitating she met a Christian monk, a wise man, who pointed out that the difficult choice was always the one that offered the more growth.

She returned to Assisi and over the coming months formulated her plans for the kind of nunnery she wanted to create. First and foremost it was to be a place where women could go to develop their spiritual potential to the full. Female Enlightenment was still the goal. It would be a place of female spiritual excellence. A place which would not just educate women in religious dogma but turn them into yoginis, women who had actualized the truth within. Only women of wisdom, as opposed to women of knowledge, would hold true spiritual power and thus be able to touch and transform the lives of others.

And the only women she knew of who had such attainments were the Togdenmas, the female counterparts of those great yogis of Tashi Jong, the Togdens. The Togdenmas had been following spiritual techniques specially devised for female practitioners by one of Milarepa's leading disciples, Rechungpa in the twelfth century. Methods which were reputed to turn women into Buddhas, quickly! Even in Tibet, where systems for attaining Enlightenment abounded, Rechungpa's method had been regarded as unique. But the Togdenmas had not been seen or heard of since the Chinese occupation. All was not completely lost, however. Tenzin Palmo knew that the old Togdens, living in the present Tashi Jong in India, had the key to this ancient treasure chest of instructions. If she could find the right nuns to train, the precious Togdenma lineage might be resurrected.

'These teachings are incredibly precious. They are a living flame which must be passed on by living transmission. If it is not done before the Togdens die then they are in danger of dying out for ever. Once this lineage is no longer practised it is finished – it cannot be revived. If I could bring the practice and the nuns together it could be of enormous benefit to many, many sentient beings in the future,' she reasoned.

She started to streamline her plans. The nunnery, which would be called Dongyu Gatsal Ling (Delightful Grove of the True Lineage), would take women aged between seventeen and thirty who had already finished their general education. She did not intend running an orphanage, nor a basic school. The initial intake would be restricted to ten to fifteen to ensure that there was a core of well-trained nuns who in turn would be able to teach others. After that was accomplished the numbers could be increased to maybe 100 or 200 nuns. It was absolutely vital, therefore, that at the outset two or three mature nuns were found to act as role models and teachers for the younger women.

The initial five-year training programme would consist in studying classic texts and logic as well as becoming familiar with specific ritual practices and religious services. The nuns would also learn English as part of their foundation course. When this was completed those nuns with the required aptitude, and who wanted to continue, would be chosen to undergo the Togdenma training – the *raison d'être* of the nunnery.

Westerners would not be forgotten. Beside the nunnery she would build an international retreat centre, where women from all over the world could go to practise in a conducive atmosphere alongside other like-minded women. They would receive general Buddhist and meditation instruction from the Dongyu Gatsal Ling nuns. If they wanted to train as Togdenmas, however, they would have to undergo all the prerequisite schooling, be psychologically suitable, and be able to speak Tibetan, the lingua franca of the nunnery. At this stage, while the profound realizations still rested in the traditional practices of old Tibet, there was no other way.

Apart from the monastic college and the international centre there would also be a temple, individual retreat huts and a guesthouse for short-stay female and male visitors.

As the blueprint for Tenzin Palmo's nunnery grew in mind's eye, certain revolutionary ideas began to be introduced – ones she'd gleaned from the Christian communities she'd taught in Europe. She would do away with the traditional system of individual sponsorship, which had been in place for centuries in Tibet, whereby monks and nuns got the money needed for their keep from family members or wealthy patrons. This, she pointed out, was an invidious practice as it not only created competition and cunning (as the monastics vied to see who got more), but produced a mundane, worldly mind-frame which took the focus away from the spiritual life. Instead she proposed that the nuns of Dongyu Gatsal Ling would strive for economic independence. There would be work periods where they would learn to earn their living through businesses such as craft. (Their brother monastery Tashi Jong could provide ample tuition.) This would give them economic stability, financial independence and relieve them of the anxiety of continually having to find funds. Working together co-operatively would also create harmony. All the money that came in would go into a pool and each nun would be given her robes, her food and a small weekly stipend for personal items. This would do away with the rivalry.

There was more to come: 'Although there will be a certain hierarchy it will not be obvious. The senior nuns will be the teachers but all the jobs will be rotated. Everyone has to be a scullery maid with the appreciation that it is just as important as being the teacher. I am going to instruct them that sweeping the courtyard with awareness is a spiritual practice. And the cook is probably more indispensable than the teacher! This way everyone understands each other's problems. I want to make this nunnery a harmonious place, an environment in which everyone can flower,' she said.

One of the many criticisms directed at women seeking Enlightenment down the ages was that they were handicapped by not being able to get on well together. It was said, by the men, that they squabbled, were bitchy, were not able to live cohesively together and thus their spiritual focus was seriously undermined. This, they cited, was one of the reasons why nunneries hadn't flourished in Tibet, unlike the great monasteries.

'It's absolute nonsense. Women have been cohering for millenia,' was Tenzin Palmo's attitude. 'I have noticed that when women are working together on a project there is a tremendous energy, a very special energy. Women like the idea of all-women retreats. When we are feeling fulfilled, doing some inner work, we get along just fine. And women like each other's company. My aunt goes off to Paris with her women friends, leaving her husband behind, and they all have a great time. In my view bitchiness is not an intrinsic part of female nature. Sometimes men don't pull together either.'

She continued with her radical plans. She would introduce Hatha yoga (which had helped her so much on her long retreat) to counteract the long periods of sitting and help align the body for meditation. Physical exercise of any sort was a novel idea for Tibetan nuns. 'Yoga is very suitable. You don't need equipment or much space, and it's quite dignified,' she said. 'There might be a little resistance but if it is introduced right from the beginning it should be all right. I think it is really important.'

The more she thought about it the more the nunnery took shape. When she had decided precisely what she wanted to do she took her scheme to the collective spiritual heads of Tashi Jong monastery, including the young Khamtrul Rinpoche, and put before them precisely what she had in mind. When she had finished she said: 'To date monks have received so much help but there is a great need for women to be assisted too. It's important that women help themselves. Women need confidence to become teachers so that they can become self-sufficient and don't have to rely on men. And women need women teachers, other women they can talk to, who can understand their problems from a female perspective. I truly believe that women can become Enlightened – it's just the opportunity that has been lacking. So this is what I want to do. By creating this nunnery I serve not only my lama, who suggested the idea to me in the first place, but the lineage and women also. These are the three most important things I can do in this life.'

There was one important proviso. She had no intention whatsoever of being the abbess. She would get the nunnery up and running, she stated, and then she would return to what was her chosen path in this life – the way of the contemplative.

The assembled panel from Tashi Jong heard her through and much to her amazement agreed to all she had proposed. They gave her their full blessing to proceed. The only problem was, they said, that being refugees and trying to build up their own community they had little funds to spare and consequently she would have to take charge of the project herself. It was a tall order but, they said, she should not despair. They had done their observations and predicted that Dongyu Gatsal Ling nunnery would come into being and be a great success.

Nevertheless, it was an ambitious plan to say the least. To get such a scheme up and running needed a multitude of factors which seemed completely impossible: land, building permission, architectural plans, bricks, mortar, expertise in a range of areas and money. A lot of money. Only finding inmates of the nunnery would be easy. Tenzin Palmo was homeless, penniless and had been out of the workplace and the ways of the world for thirty years. But that was no reason not to try. With her customary boldness and faith in the Buddha, dharma and sangha to whom she had given her life, she now launched herself on a most unexpected career path, the role of international fundraiser. Her plan was to give dharma talks wherever she was invited and hope that someone would be out there to listen, and drop a few pennies in her begging bowl.

FOURTEEN

The Teacher

By the most unlikely turn of events Tenzin Palmo found herself
thrust into the role of teacher. She had neither planned this
strange development, nor particularly enjoyed it, solitude and
introspection being her calling, but the financial demands for
building a special nunnery where women could go to achieve
spiritual excellence necessitated it. Hundreds of thousands of
dollars were needed to buy the land near Tashi Jong, purchase
the bricks and mortar, and there was nothing for it but to
travel the world, going from one Buddhist centre to the next,
from one interested group to the next, dispensing wisdom that
had been garnered and crystallized over thirty years of intense
inner journeying in order to raise funds. It was a painfully slow
process, the charge at each event being by donation only. In
spite of the weeks, the months, the years of talking, Tenzin
Palmo remained peculiarly unruffled and unhurried, treating
each offering, be it 5 dollars or 5,000 dollars, with the same
genuine gratitude. Neither the slowness nor the enormity of
the task seemed to faze her.

'Well, the high lamas have given the project their blessing
and say it will be accomplished. So, I have faith. I continue,'
she reasoned. Still, the radical change in her lifestyle bemused
her. 'How I got myself into this I just don't know! If anyone
had told me a few years back I would be travelling the globe
teaching and raising money, I would have thought them crazy,'
she said, leaning over and putting her arms over her head. 'But
if I'm not going to do it, who is? And it's one way to repay the
kindness of my lama.'

Even though it had changed course somewhat, the river was
still flowing through Tenzin Palmo's life and had her firmly in

its current. As always she surrendered to it, bouncing along where it obviously wanted to take her, being guided every step of the way. She had started in Singapore in 1994 a year after her impassioned speech to the Dalai Lama. Initially things had not gone well. She had chosen Singapore at random, but had set nothing up in advance. Nobody knew she was in town, nor who she was, and she had absolutely no experience of self-promotion. Just when she was beginning to think it was hopeless, she had bumped into an old friend, a Chinese woman named Wong Pee Lee. It must have been a remarkable reunion, for only the night before Pee Lee had had a most vivid dream. In it she had seen Tenzin Palmo surrounded by Dakinis wearing beautiful silks. During the dream a voice had said: 'Now is the time for you to help women.' Tenzin Palmo told Pee Lee of her mission to build the nunnery. The dream came into focus, Pee Lee went into action, and the first of hundreds of lectures was organized. From Singapore Tenzin Palmo would travel throughout south-east Asia, touring Malaysia, Taiwan, Brunei, Hong Kong, Sarawak, Indonesia, Cambodia, the Philippines, then to England and France and on to the United States, where she crisscrossed her way between Washington, Seattle, New York, Maryland, Vermont, Hawaii, and up and down the coast of California before returning to Asia and doing it all over again. Each time someone would take up the baton of organizing a meeting. There was no shortage of venues, no shortage of attendees. Everywhere she went the crowds gathered, as word had spread about the English woman who had spent twelve years meditating in a cave in the Himalayas and people were curious to see the phenomenon for themselves. Many, and there were quite a few, were also eager to learn how that experience would translate into words.

They were not disappointed. For all her reluctance to take the stage, Tenzin Palmo proved to be an inspired teacher. She spoke from the heart, without notes, without preparation, and the words came tumbling out crystal clear. More than anything else they revealed the true extent of her spiritual maturity and what she had achieved in the cave. Displaying that quintessential feminine quality of cutting through abstract theories and ossified intellectual constructs, she ignored all traditional approaches and went straight to the heart of the matter. She was practical, down-to-earth, brilliantly lucid. Those in front of her lapped it up. Here was someone who could deliver the Buddha dharma in fluent, articulate English, someone who knew the nuances and hidden agendas of the Western psyche and who, most significantly, could speak from experience rather than from the textbook. It was a potent mix. Most significantly, she was a female in robes speaking from a platform – a novelty indeed.

It was what many had been waiting for. The Tibetan lamas, who first brought the Buddha's words to the eager Western ears, had inspired more often than not by the force of their spiritual presence rather than by their broken English. The beauty on the outside was so obviously a reflection of exquisite states generated within and people were drawn like moths to the light. Extracting the meaning behind the awkward delivery and ornate cultural context, however, had demanded exceptional hard work. Confusion and problems arose, for the lamas, used to addressing the very specialized congregation of monks, had no precedent of how to deliver the Buddha dharma in terms applicable to householders, professionals, and women of the West. Only the truly dedicated who sat around long enough, or bothered to learn Tibetan, unwrapped the packaging to elicit the essence of what lay within.

With Tenzin Palmo all was made easy. She moved from Tibetan meditation centres to Zen groups, to dedicated Vipassana practitioners, to Christian communities, even to non-religious organizations dispensing wisdom, common-sense, and her own hard-won insights. And as she travelled her influence spread and her fame increased, in spite of herself.

'Our minds are like junk yards. What we put into them is mostly rubbish! The conversations, the newspapers, the entertainment, we just pile it all in. There's a jam session going on in there. And the problem is it makes us very tired,' she tells a group of occupational therapists in Seattle, who have heard she is in town and have invited her to address them, believing that her experience may help them with the stress-loads they carry. 'I congratulate you all on the job you are doing,' she continues. 'You chose it not just because you need to earn a living. There are easier ways to earn a buck.

Somehow you chose this job because you wanted to help. You people are giving out, giving out and you need to replenish – otherwise you will just become like empty vessels.' We need to take in as well as give out,' she tells them.

'When we normally think of resting we switch on the TV, or go out, or have a drink. But that does not give us real rest. It's just putting more stuff in. Even sleep is not true rest for the mind. To get genuine relaxation we need to give ourselves some inner space. We need to clear out the junk yard, quieten the inner noise. And the way to do that is to keep the mind in the moment. That's the most perfect rest for the mind. That's meditation. Awareness. The mind relaxed and alert. Five minutes of that and you'll feel refreshed, and wide awake,' she assures them.

'People say they have no time for "meditation". It's not true!' she goes on. 'You can meditate walking down the corridor, waiting for the computer to change, at the traffic lights, standing in a queue, going to the bathroom, combing your hair. Just be there in the present, without the mental commentary. Start by choosing one action during the day and decide to be entirely present for that one action. Drinking the tea in the morning. Shaving. Determine, for this action I will really be there. It's all habit. At the moment we've got the habit of being unaware. We have to develop the habit of being present. Once we start to be present in the moment everything opens up. When we are mindful there is no commentary – it's a very naked experience, wakeful, vivid.'

At every given opportunity she stresses that to lead a spiritual life one doesn't have to emulate her. 'Meditation is not just about sitting in a cave for twelve years,' she pronounces. 'It's everyday life. Where else do you practise generosity, patience, ethics? How much patience did I have to have sitting up in my cave listening to the wolves howl?' The point goes home. 'Ultimately the Buddha dharma is about transforming the mind, which in Buddhist parlance includes the heart. The transformation of the heart/mind cannot be achieved if we only sit in meditation and ignore the dharma of our everyday life,' she stresses.

She peppers her talks with quotations from the Sutras, stories she has heard, her own experiences, modern-day life: 'The film

Ground Hog Day was a very Buddhist movie,' she says. 'It was about a man who had to live the same day over and over again. He couldn't prevent the events occurring, but he did learn that how he responded to them transformed the whole experience of the day. He discovered that as his mind began to get over its animosity and greed and as he started to think of others his life improved greatly. Of course, it took him a long time to grasp this idea because at the beginning of the movie he was learning to play the piano and by the end he was playing a sonata.'

To specifically Buddhist audiences she expands her theme, going into greater depth and at the same time revealing the extent of her own wisdom and scholarship. 'Mindfulness can be interpreted in two ways,' she says. ' "Concentration", which is narrow and laser-like, or "awareness" which is more panoramic. One could take as an example listening to music. If one is really listening to music it is as if one is absorbed into the music. As the poet T.S. Eliot put it, "Music heard so deeply that it is not heard at all, but you are the music while the music lasts." That is concentration. But to know one is absorbed in the music is awareness. Do you see the difference? When we are aware, we are mindful not only of what we are doing but the feelings, the emotions that are arising, and what's happening around us as well.

'It's so simple we miss it. We think it has to be something bigger, more spectacular. What do people think spiritual development is? It's not lights and trumpets. It's very simple. It's right here and now. People have this idea that Enlightenment and realization is something in the distance – a very fantastic and magnificent happening which will transform everything once and for always. But it's not like that at all. It's something which is sometimes so simple you hardly see it. It's right here in front of us, so close we don't notice it. And it's something which can happen at any moment. And the moment we see it, there it is. It's been there all the time, but we've had our inner eye closed. When the moments of awareness all link up – then we become a Buddha.

'The Sanskrit word for mindfulness is "Smriti", in Pali it's "Sati", and in Tibetan "Drenpa",' she continues. 'Significantly, they all mean "to remember". It's what the Catholics call "being in a state of recollection". And it's extremely difficult. If we can be aware for a few minutes that's already a lot. If mindfulness is synonymous with "remembering" it follows that the enemy of awareness is forgetfulness. We can be aware for a few short moments and then we forget. How do we remember to remember? That's the issue. The problem is we have this tremendous inertia. We simply don't have the habit of remembering.'

She searches for an analogy to illustrate her meaning. 'At the moment it's as though we're looking through a pair of binoculars and the perspective is blurred. When we experience anything we do so through the filter of ideas, preconceptions, judgements. For example, when we meet somebody we don't see them as they actually are. We see them in relationship to what we're thinking about them – how much we like or dislike them, how they remind us of somebody else, what sort of qualities they have. We're not experiencing them in themselves. Everything we perceive is like that – everything we see, eat, hear, touch. It's immediately interpreted back to ourselves in conformity with our thoughts and experiences.

'We might think, "So what?" It's not important. But what happens is that we're living several paces back from the experience itself and therefore we become more and more conditioned, more and more robotic. We become increasingly computer-like. Someone "pushes our buttons" as they so aptly put it and out comes the conditioned response.

'What we have to do is bring everything into sharp focus, to see things as they truly are as if for the very first time – like a small baby looking at the murals in a shrine room, as the Tibetans say. The baby sees the colours and shapes without judgement, its mind is fresh. That's the state of mind we have to bring into our everyday life. If we can learn to do that, without doing anything else, it will transform the situation automatically,' she promises.

She goes on to give a comprehensive description of the various ways 'ordinary' people can begin to achieve Mindfulness. Once again the instructions are specific, and eminently practical. She tells people how to watch their breath, their bodies, their thoughts. The instructions are detailed, clear. At times her voice becomes animated, lyrical, taking on that 'bubbly' quality that she was known for in her youth when an idea excited her.

'People have this idea that to become a spiritual person you have to become this cosmic blob, which is what we're frightened of. But it's not like that at all,' she continues. 'It doesn't mean you no longer feel, that you're emotionally flat. One still has one's identity, one's personality – it's just that one no longer believes in it. When we meet the high lamas they're the most vivid people possible. That's because so many of the knots that we have in our minds and which keep us so inhibited have fallen away and the actual spontaneous nature of the mind can shine through. The Buddha's mind is not a blank nothing – it's filled with compassion, joy and humour. It's wonderfully light. It's also extremely sensitive and very deeply intelligent,' she says and pauses to think of an example to amplify her meaning.

'Awareness is like a surfboard. If you are a surfer you don't want a quiet lake, you want the big wave. The bigger the wave, the more fun, right? Milarepa said, "The greater the disturbance, the greater the joy," because he was riding on top of it, skilful and balanced. From a spiritual point of view it's not advantageous to be a rabbit. It's better to be a tiger,' she continues, switching metaphors. 'Rabbits are very nice and cuddly but they don't have much potential for breaking through. Tigers, on the other hand, are very wild but that pure energy, if used skilfully, is exactly what's needed on the path. All the great saints were very passionate people. It's just that they didn't dissipate their passions into negative channels. They used them as fuel to send them to Enlightenment.'

And at these points she seems to come close to that greatest cave meditator of all, Milarepa, the founder of her lineage, whose experience lead him beyond dogma.

Accustomed long to meditating on the whispered chosen truths.
I have forgot all that is said in written and in printed books.
Accustomed long to application of each new experience to my own spiritual growth,

I have forgot all creeds and dogmas.
Accustomed long to know the meaning of the Word-
less,
I have forgot the way to trace the roots of verbs, and
source of words and phrases.

To more advanced congregations the talks get meatier and
livelier, often spilling over into animated dialogues.

'There is the thought, and then there is the knowing of the
thought. And the difference between being aware of the thought
and just thinking is immense. It's enormous . . . Normally we
are so identified with our thoughts and emotions, that we are
them. We are the happiness, we are the anger, we are the fear.
We have to learn to step back and know our thoughts and
emotions are just thoughts and emotions. They're just mental
states. They're not solid, they're transparent,' she said, before
delivering the bottom line. 'One has to know that and then not
identify with the knower. One has to know that the knower is
not somebody.'

There is a silence while the listeners digest the information.
Tenzin Palmo has ventured out on to profoundly philosophical
ground. A voice from the floor speaks out: ' "The knower is
also not somebody," ' the voice repeats slowly, thinking it over.
'That's difficult!'

'Yes! But that was the Buddha's great insight,' Tenzin Palmo
comes back in a voice quiet with respect.

'You think you've got it when you understand that you are
not the thought or feeling – but to go further and know you
are not the knower . . . that brings you to the question: "Who
am I?",' continues the questioner.

'And that was the Buddha's great understanding – to realize
that the further back we go the more open and empty the
quality of our consciousness becomes. Instead of finding some
solid little eternal entity, which is "I", we get back to this vast
spacious mind which is interconnected with all living beings.
In this space you have to ask, where is the "I", and where is
the "other". As long as we are in the realm of duality, there is
"I" and "other". This is our basic delusion – it's what causes
all our problems,' Tenzin Palmo says with finality. 'Because of

this we have a sense of being very separate. That is our basic ignorance.'

It is quintessential Buddhism – Emptiness, the perennial philosophy – the remedy for all humankind's woes.

The dialogue from the floor continues: 'This duality, this sense of being separate, is the cause of our fundamental pain, the deep loneliness that human beings feel at the core of their being then?'

'Of course,' replies Tenzin Palmo crisply. 'It creates everything. Ignorance, according to Buddhism, is not ignorance about this or that on an intellectual level – it's ignorance in the sense of unknowing. We create this sense of an "I" and everything else which is "Non I". And from that comes this attraction to other "Non I's" which "I" want, and this aversion to everything I don't want. This is the source of our greed, our aversion and all the other negative qualities which we have. It all comes from this basic dual misapprehension.

'Once we realize that the nature of our existence is beyond thought and emotions, that it is incredibly vast and inter-connected with all other beings, then the sense of isolation, separation, fear and hopes fall away. It's a tremendous relief!' she says. And the audience has to believe her. This is the mystic truth that saints from all religions have discovered – the joy of unity that comes when the ego has been shed.

She pauses again while everyone savours the full extent of what it means to be in this state. 'The reason we are not Enlightened is because we are lazy,' she continues, drawing on the discovery she made in the cave of her own greatest 'failing'. 'There's no other reason. We do not bother to bring ourselves back to the present because we're too fascinated by the games the mind is playing. If one genuinely thinks about Renunciation it is not a giving up of external things like money, leaving home or one's family. That's easy. Genuine renunciation is giving up our fond thoughts, all our delight in memories, hopes and daydreams, our mental chatter. To renounce that and stay naked in the present, that is renunciation,' she says, her words becoming more impassioned.

'The thing is we say we want to be Enlightened, but we don't really. Only bits of us want to be Enlightened. The ego which

thinks how nice, comfortable and pleasant it would be. But to
really drop everything and go for it! We could do it in a moment
but we don't do it. And the reason is we are too lazy. We are
stopped by fear and lethargy – the great inertia of the mind.
The practice is there. Anyone on the Buddhist path certainly
knows these things. So how is it we're not Enlightened? We
have no one to blame but ourselves. This is why we stay in
Samsara because we always find excuses. Instead we should
wake ourselves up. The whole Buddhist path is about waking
up. Yet the desire to keep sleeping is so strong. However much
we say we will awake in order to help all sentient beings we
don't really want to. We like dreaming.'

It is heartfelt stuff, made all the more potent because everyone
present senses she is speaking from experience.

At one of America's oldest Buddhist establishments, the
evocatively named Goat in the Road at Muir Beach, California,
she leads a weekend seminar on 'How to Open the Heart'. It's
a topic she feels particularly strongly about, having experienced
a serious lack of warmth in several of the newly opened Western
Buddhist centres she's visited. 'I walk in and the atmosphere
is very heavy, quite cold. I mean, they talk enormously about
compassion and Bodhicitta but they have no real kindness in
their hearts, even towards each other. Something's going wrong.
The dharma isn't working as it should. I see people who have
been sincerely studying and practising Buddhism for years and
they still have the same hang-ups.'

Sitting in front of her sell-out audience, she tries to remedy
the situation: 'So often there's a fundamental division between
the practice and ourselves. The practice remains outside of
ourselves. It's very hard for us Westerners to get out of our
heads. We approach meditation from the brain only and so we
have duality – the subject and the object. The practice has to
come down into the heart, it has to go somewhere deep within
us. Then there is no subject (me) and object (the meditation).
We become the meditation. Then there is a transformation at
a very profound level.

'At the moment we Westerners are looking down into the
heart – into the visualizations we are establishing there. What
we need to do is to learn to come down into the heart, the

seat of our true self. When we indicate "me" we point to our heart, not to our head. It's instinctual. The problem is that we don't make that leap into becoming the meditation. That is why we don't transform. Loving kindness should be so spontaneous that we don't have to think about it. It's not a theory, an idea. It's something you feel. The heart opening up is real,' she says, almost as a plea.

And then she leads the group in a short meditation. She sits there legs crossed, eyes closed, hands cupped together in her lap, and within seconds a blissful, calm look comes over her face and a small smile plays around her mouth. It's obvious it's working, at least for her.

Everywhere she goes people, wanting more of her wisdom, more of her presence, line up to see her. At one event in Madison, New Jersey, she gives interviews for six hours non-stop, with people arriving at fifteen-minute intervals. They come to her with their personal problems, their career dilemmas, their spiritual conundrums, their worries, their woes. She is there for each one of them, listening, dispensing advice, holding their hand, crying when moved. She doesn't seem to get tired, or impatient. One woman asks how she can reconcile her job in the armed forces with her newly found Buddhist belief in non-violence. A young nun spills out her unhappiness at feeling unsupported in her community. A round-faced monk simply wants to tell her of his own spiritual journey. A middle-aged Californian asks how can she be expected to take responsibility for the welfare of all living beings when she has just spent ten years in therapy learning not to be responsible for her alcoholic mother. A man, worried about the gruesome Tibetan Buddhist teachings of the hell realms, wants to know what Tenzin Palmo thinks happens after death. Her reply reveals that even after decades steeped in Buddhism she has retained her independence of mind.

'I once tackled a lama about it as by his definition I was definitely going there. "Don't worry about it," he laughed while slapping me on the back. "We only say that to get people to behave themselves." Frankly I don't think this approach works. We have a hard enough time of it as it is. Frightening people with tales about hell is counter-productive – it just makes them want to give up!'

'The lamas tend to present the after-death state as a reward or punishment for what we have done in this life, which lasts for a certain amount of time until we come back again to Earth and start working for our spiritual development anew,' she goes on. 'It's like we save up our money in this life and then spend it in the next and then have to return to start saving up again. But to me the spiritualist idea is more meaningful. They also believe there are many different dimensions where you can go after death, where you meet up with like-minded people. The difference is that the spiritualists maintain that after death you are able to work helping others who are less fortunate, which creates further spiritual evolution. It's one of the ways we evolve by cultivating love and compassion even while one is in the spirit realm.'

The man goes away relieved.

It is not only the people in the audience who are eager to meet her. Established teachers, also facing the challenge of presenting Buddhism to the West, are also curious to assess her worth. Yvonne Rand, founder of the Goat in the Road, is one. As one of America's leading Zen instructors and an ardent spokeswoman for the feminization of Buddhism, she has an especially keen interest in Tenzin Palmo.

'I appreciate the fact that she's a woman and very confident about delivering the essential core of the teachings in a way people can understand. She is a very gifted teacher. She's also not in any way sentimental, which I like,' she says. 'There's a rapidly increasing number of women teachers and as we collaborate more and more in a non-sectarian way it will lead to more confidence. This collaboration is a highly creative process.'

'She's not ordinary – I think she came in with a pretty pure mind,' said Lama Palden Drolma, a Californian woman who earned her title 'Lama' after completing a three-year group retreat within the USA under the guidance of the eminent teacher Kalu Rinpoche. She had invited Tenzin Palmo to speak at her newly opened Sukhasiddhi Foundation in Mill Valley, San Francisco. 'To me her whole life is inspirational,' she continued. 'The fact that she has stayed a nun for thirty years is an achievement in itself. Her dedication is awe-inspiring. In her you can see that the dharma has truly worked She's warm, natural and personally

I don't sense much ego there. She's also an extraordinarily clear teacher, expressing the dharma in a very direct and meaningful way. So many people have wanted to hear her that we've had to turn a lot away.'

It's ironic, therefore, that for all the undoubted success of her teaching programme, the number of followers she has gathered, and the increasing strength of her reputation, Tenzin Palmo remains singularly unimpressed by her newly-found career. She could so easily become a guru, the position is there so obviously in the offing. But it's a job she simply doesn't want.

'I just don't enjoy it. It gives me no joy,' she admits candidly. 'When I'm teaching there's this little voice inside me which says, "What are you doing?" And so I think it cannot be right. Of course, I meet a lot of lovely people I normally wouldn't meet. Everyone's very kind. Strangers become friends. And I learn a lot from being in different situations, answering questions, teaching. Actually, I often think I learn more than the people I'm teaching. I see things in new ways. It's helpful. But it's just something that I don't want to do with the rest of my life.'

In the meantime she continued. There was a job to do, a need to be met. Other women were seeking Enlightenment and she had to respond. Her Bodhisattva vow, 'to free all suffering creatures and place them in bliss', demanded it. In doing so she had expanded her scope considerably, from seeking her own liberation as a woman, to helping other women achieve the same goal. Just as she had been among the first Westerners to discover Buddhism, to become a nun and to live in a cave in the snow-bound Himalayas, Tenzin Palmo, aged fifty, was still pioneering – still forging the way ahead, this time on a more ambitious scale. And so without any fuss, and just the occasional sigh, she carried on.

FIFTEEN

Challenges

From being a cave-dweller Tenzin Palmo had become a jet-setter. From being entirely stationary she had begun to move across the world at a frantic pace. From being silent she now spoke for hours on end. From living the most simple existence she was now exposed to the full gamut of late twentieth-century life. The world that she had re-entered was a radically different place from the one she had left in 1963 when she had set sail for India. She saw for herself the stress and the insecurity, the job losses and the new phenomenon of homelessness. She read about increased crime, escalating violence and the drug problems. She witnessed her friends pedalling faster and faster in an effort to keep up. She noted governments everywhere swapping the principle of public service for economic rationalism; and now the new luxuries were cited as silence, space, time and an intact ecology. And she experienced first hand the great need for spiritual values in an increasingly materialistic society.

'People are parched with thirst,' she said. 'In Lahoul there was a richness to life in spite of all the hardships. Here people are hungry for some real meaning and depth to their lives. When one has stopped satiating the senses one wants more. That's why people are aggressive and depressed. They feel everything is so futile. You have everything you want, and then what? Society's answer is to get more and more, but where does that get you? I see isolation everywhere and it has nothing to do with being alone. It's about having an alienated psyche.'

More specifically to her own story, by the mid-1990s the Western world had got over the first flush of its love affair with Buddhism and was beginning to take a cooler and more mature look at the complex, exotic religion which had come among them. That it had taken the Occident by storm was no longer in dispute. Thinking people of all ages and from all walks of life throughout Europe, the USA, Canada, Australia and New Zealand had been awed by the profundity of its message and drawn by the quality of the lamas who had delivered it. As a result Buddhist centres, specifically Tibetan Buddhist, had mushroomed all over the globe. But now the honeymoon was over. The early disciples, after thirty years of investigation and practice, began to see a more realistic – and human – face of the religion which had been transplanted into their soil. Flaws emerged, discrepancies arose and while Eastern mores may have forbidden outright criticism of its established religion and spiritual figureheads, the West, with its right of free speech, had no such scruples. By the time Tenzin Palmo hit the world circuit, certain aspects of Buddhism were being loudly and publicly challenged – and with them, by implication, Tenzin Palmo's chosen way of life.

The first object held up for scrutiny was the guru – regarded as the Guardian of the Truth, Infallible Guide and, in Tibetan Buddhism, as one with the Buddha himself. 'Guru is Buddha, Guru is dharma, Guru is sangha also,' went the prayer. The reasoning was logical. The Buddha mind was absolute and all-pervasive but the guru was here on earth in the flesh. The Tibetans had an analogy. The Buddha was like the sun, all-powerful and shining on everything, but still unable to make a piece of paper burst into flames. For that you needed a magnifying glass, a conduit to channel the energy, hence the guru. Even so, it was a precarious position for any human to maintain, let alone a man set down in a distant land among foreign people and strange ways. Inevitably several gurus quickly fell off their pedestals amidst a clamour of publicity.

Tenzin Palmo's old friend and mentor, Chogyam Trungpa, whom she had met when he first arrived in England from Tibet, led the way, with a series of scandals which came to light mostly after his death in 1987. Trungpa, it was revealed, had not only frequently sat on his throne reeking of alcohol, he had engaged in several sexual relationships with his female students as well. It did not matter that he was not of a celibate order, the confusion which ensued was widespread. Many students tried to emulate him by also taking to the bottle and several of his female partners claimed their lives had been destroyed by his philandering. This notoriety was followed horribly quickly by the news that his chosen successor, American-born Thomas Rich, who became Osel Tendzin, not only had AIDS which he had kept secret but had infected one of his many unknowing student lovers.

With the lid off, other 'wronged' parties came to light to blow the whistle on their gurus. One woman brought a $10 million lawsuit against a very popular Tibetan teacher for alleged sexual misconduct. It was settled out of court, but not before rumours of the man's philandering had swept the entire Buddhist world. (In Dharamsala, however, the Tibetans frankly did not believe a woman would dare denounce a lama and put the whole episode down to a political plot.) Zen teachers acknowledged that 'sexual misconduct' was rife among their members. British writer June Campbell, in her book *Traveller in Space*, told eloquently of her secret affair with the highly esteemed lama, the late Kalu Rinpoche, describing how confusing and undermining her clandestine affair had been. Jack Kornfield, one of America's most established Buddhist teachers and authors, added to the controversy by stating, almost casually, that he had interviewed fifty-three Zen masters, lamas, swamis and/or their senior students about their sex lives and had discovered 'that the birds do it, the bees do it, and most gurus do it'. He went on to say: 'Like any group of people in our culture, their sexual practices varied. There were heterosexuals, bisexuals, homosexuals, fetishists, exhibitionists, monogamists and polygamists.' The point he was making was that Eastern spiritual heads are no more special than anyone else, but it didn't help. The issue at stake was the supposed infallibility of the guru and the abuse of spiritual authority and power.

Confronted by the revelations, the Dalai Lama openly declared himself shocked. 'This is very, very harmful for the Buddha dharma. Buddhism is meant to benefit people – that is its purpose, its only purpose. When you really examine it such shameful behaviour is due to a lack of inner strength and shows that in actuality there is a discrepancy between Buddhism and their life, that the Dharma has not been properly internalized,' he stated, before announcing that the only remedy for such a dire situation was for all culprits to be 'outed'. 'You must mention them by name, publicize them, and no longer consider them as a teacher,' he avowed.

The Western Buddhist world, with its idealistic new converts, was rattled as disclosure followed hard on the heels of yet another disclosure. It was true that hundreds of followers were perfectly happy with their Tibetan teachers, finding in them supreme examples of morality, wisdom and compassion. Some disciples of Trungpa even spoke in his defence.

'My teacher did not keep ethical norms and my devotion to him is unshakable. He showed me the nature of my mind and for that I'm eternally grateful,' stated eminent American nun and teacher Pema Chodron, director of Gampo Abbey, Nova Scotia, in the Buddhist magazine *Tricycle*. 'Trungpa Rinpoche taught me in every way he could that you can never make things right or wrong. His whole teaching was to lead people away from holding on to some kind of security, to throw out the party line. However, we're always up against human nature. The teacher says something and everyone does it. There was a time when he smoked cigarettes and everyone started smoking. Then he stopped and they stopped. It was just ridiculous.'

But these defenders of the faith were the silent majority. The disaffected were making all the noise and the scandals were tarnishing Buddhism's previously squeaky-clean image. Those whose lives had been touched by the fallen gurus rushed off to the psychiatrists (and the press) to tell of their anguish and doubt. In particular the new breed of articulate emancipated females were especially vociferous, claiming that this was one more instance of male power exploiting and betraying women.

They had a point. While religious teachers of any faith engaging in sexual activity with their disciples was morally and ethically questionable, within the context of Tibetan Buddhism it was arguably more so. Tibetan Buddhism had tantra, the legitimate sexual coupling between spiritual partners which was said to inspire both parties to higher levels of attainment. To be chosen by a guru as a consort for such a mystic union, therefore, was to establish you as a very special woman indeed. In many cases it was irresistible. With the guru seen as Buddha, how could a woman resist?

Tenzin Palmo arrived in the midst of the storm. In the dock was the guru, dubbed by one American commentator 'this poor dysfunctional model'. This was the pillar that Tenzin Palmo had trusted her entire spiritual life on. To her mind the guru was the heart of the matter. Khamtrul Rinpoche had been, quite simply, the most important person in her life, the only 'thing' she had missed in all those years in the cave, the man whose memory could still induce uncontrollable sobs years after his death. She surveyed the scene with her cool, detached eye.

'Of course where a lama is acting dishonourably it is extremely damaging. It creates an atmosphere of rivalry, jealousy, secrecy and chaos. I have heard of some lamas creating a harem situation, or having one or two secret liaisons. In such circumstances the women have a right to feel humiliated and exploited. It's also hypocritical. The lama is posing as a monk, yet he's not. I don't see how that benefits the dharma or sentient beings. It's a very different situation from a lama who has not taken celibacy vows having a consort openly, and a decent steady relationship,' she stated.

The woman who had laughed off Trungpa's sexual advances when she was just nineteen, and who still managed to remain friends with him, was hardly going to take the high moral ground, however. 'Some women are very flattered at being "the consort", in which case they should take the consequences. And some women only know how to relate to men in this way. I sometimes feel we women have to get away from this victim mentality,' she said crisply. 'It is also necessary to understand the strange situation these lamas have found themselves in. They were brought up in a monastic setting among hundreds of like-minded men and now find themselves in a strange land being the only lama in a community of Westerners. There's no one for them to turn to for companionship and advice, and they're surrounded by devoted disciples who are only too willing to please. With the very heavy sexual prominence in the West, I believe many lamas misread the signs and are surprised to find the women are taking their advances towards them seriously. It's a lot of misread messages which is leading to confusion all round.'

Much of the current problem, she deduced, was due to the fact that Westerners had little experience and no education about how to look for and find their real guru. Nor did they understand what the function of a true guru was. Eastern masters were fashionable, Westerners' thirst for spiritual leadership, any leadership, was immense. Their naïvety and susceptibility therefore made them easy prey to misunderstandings and in some cases spiritual and sexual exploitation. In Tenzin Palmo's experience the business of finding a guru was, in fact a highly specialized task indeed.

'In Tibet it was understood that when you meet your root guru there is this instant, immediate mutual recognition – and instant trust. You inwardly know. The problem with the West is that people might meet a charismatic lama, have a surge of devotion and think this is it! Even if they had a connection with Tibet in past lives the chances of meeting up with their lama again are actually very slim. Their root guru could be anywhere, or even dead, as most of the high lamas perished in the aftermath of the Chinese invasion. Previously, it was much easier. The lamas were reborn in their own districts and so it was much more likely that you would refind your guru again,' she explained.

'Many Westerners have false ideas about what a guru is,' she went on. 'They think that if they find the perfect master with the perfect teachings they'll immediately get it. They believe that the guru is going to lead them through every step of the way. It's a search for Mamma. But it's not like that. A genuine guru is there to help people to grow up as well as wake up. The real function of a guru is to introduce you to the unborn nature of your mind and the relationship is one of mutual commitment. From the side of the disciple she or he should see whatever the guru does as perfect Buddha activity, obey whatever the lama says, and put into practice whatever the lama instructs. The lama, on his part, is committed to take the disciple all the way to Enlightenment, however many lifetimes that may take. In that lies its glory and its downfall. If it is a genuine lama you have the certainty of never being abandoned. If it is not a genuine lama you open yourself to all sorts of exploitation.'

The Dalai Lama had his own recipe for distinguishing between an authentic guru and a fake: 'You should "spy" on him or her for at least ten years. You should listen, examine, watch, until you are convinced that the person is sincere. In the meantime you should treat him or her as an ordinary human being and receiving their teaching as "just information". In the end the authority of a guru is bestowed by the disciple. The guru doesn't go out looking for students. It is the student who has to ask the guru to teach and guide,' he said.

Tenzin Palmo had other ideas, especially when it came to lamas suggesting sexual liaisons. 'One way to judge if he's bona fide is to see if he's pursuing old, unattractive women as well as the young, pretty ones!' she suggested. 'If he were a genuine lama he would see all women as Dakinis, young and old, fat and thin, pretty and ugly, because he would have pure view! And if the guru were genuine you can always say no without feeling you've blown it. A true guru, even if he felt that having a tantric relationship might be beneficial for that disciple, would make the request with the understanding that it would not damage their relationship if she refused. No woman should ever have to agree on the grounds of his authority or a sense of her obedience. The understanding should be "if she wished to good, if not, also good", offering her a choice and a sense of respect. Then that is not exploitation.

'Actually real tantric liaisons are extremely rare,' she continued. 'I once asked Khamtrul Rinpoche, "Seeing as sexual yoga is such a fast way to Enlightenment, how come you are all monks?" And he replied, "It's true it's a quick path but you have to be almost Buddha to practise it." To have a genuine tantric relationship first there must be no feeling of lust. Then there must be no emission of sexual fluids. Instead you must learn to send the fluids up through the central channel to the crown while doing very complicated visualization and breathing practices. All this requires tremendous control of body, speech and mind. Even yogis who have practised tumo for many years say they'd need one or two lifetimes of practice to accomplish sexual yoga. So these tantric weekends on offer in the West

these days may give you a jolly good time, but little else!'
she said.

For all the accusations, the distrust, and the general uneasiness,
Tenzin Palmo's own feelings towards Khamtrul Rinpoche never
wavered, not for a second. 'I can say that Khamtrul Rinpoche
was the one person I felt I could trust completely. One of the
greatest blessings of my life is that never for a single moment
did I doubt him as a guru, and as my guru. He guided me
infallibly. I never saw anything I needed to question. He was
always completely selfless and wise,' she said emphatically.

To many Western Buddhists, however, the guru had been
mortally wounded. It was not just the scandals that had eroded
his position, it was the times themselves. In the last seconds of
the twentieth century it was being stated by some that the
guru–disciple relationship had run its course. The figure of
the guru was, they said, a product of the patriarchy with
its emphasis on structure and hierarchy, and with the rise
of female spiritual power the patriarchy's days were rapidly
coming to an end.

Andrew Harvey, former Oxford scholar and poetic writer,
spent many years seeking spiritual truths at the feet of a variety of
prominent masters of different faiths, including several eminent
lamas, the Christian monk Father Bede Griffiths, who established
an ashram in India, and the Indian woman guru Mother Meera.
He summed up the new feeling eloquently: 'I am very grateful for
all my relationships with my teachers but I've come to understand
that you can be frozen by that relationship into a position of
infantilism. It can enforce you in all sorts of inabilities to deal
with the world. It can also corrupt the master. We're being
shown that many of the people we've revered are in fact very,
very flawed,' he said in a recent radio interview. 'We're trying
to come to a new understanding, a new paradigm of what the
relationship between teacher and pupil should be. I think it will
change very dramatically in the next ten to fifteen years. We will
not keep holding on to the old Eastern fantasy of avatars and
masters. It's too convenient a fantasy now. We need something
that empowers us all directly.'

What the new thinkers were suggesting in the place of the
guru was the spiritual friend. A figure who did not claim

to be Enlightened, who did not wish to be regarded as
infallible and given total obedience, but who would walk
the path with the seeker, side by side. It was a democratic
solution befitting Western culture. Tenzin Palmo agreed. She
may have gained invaluable experience from her relationship
with her own guru, but she was extremely fortunate – and
most unusual.

'Frankly, at this point I think it's more important for the
West to practise Buddhism and rely on having good teachers,
rather than gurus. They're not necessarily the same thing,' she
said. 'A guru is a very special relationship but you can have
many, many teachers. Take Atisha (a tenth-century founder of
Tibetan Buddhism). He had fifty teachers. Most teachers are
perfectly capable of guiding us. And we're perfectly capable of
guiding ourselves. We've got our innate wisdom. People can put
off practice for ever, waiting for the magic touch that is going
to transform them – or throwing themselves on someone who
is charismatic without discriminating whether or not they are
suitable. We should just get on with it. If you meet someone
with whom you have a deep inner connection, great, if not
the dharma is always there. It's not helpful to get off on
the guru trip. It's better to understand Buddha, dharma and
sangha.'

As it had done with priests in the Christian religion, the
whole spate of sex scandals around the lamas had brought
into focus another area of radical questioning – celibacy itself.
This was an issue very close to Tenzin Palmo's heart, and the
difficult choice she had made. Was it relevant in the 1990s?
Was it possible? Was it even desirable? Tenzin Palmo had no
doubts.

'Celibacy is still extremely relevant,' she insisted. 'There's
a point to it. It not only frees the body but clears the mind
as well. By not being engaged in a sexual relationship your
energies can be directed into other, higher directions. It also
frees up your emotions too, allowing you to develop great love
for everyone, not just for your family and a small circle of close
friends. Of course it's not for everybody, and that's where the
problems arise. Far too many men become Buddhist monks,
because it's a good life and they have devotion. The Dalai

Lama has publicly stated that only ten out of 100 monks are true candidates.

'And from what I see many Roman Catholic priests are in a very difficult position. I think they should have a choice whether to marry or not. For some it would help a lot to have a close relationship in order for them to learn the laws of marital existence before handing out advice to others. In Tibet there were many married lamas who were incredible. Lama just means guru, it doesn't necessarily mean monk. Even nowadays many have married, like Sakya Trizin and Dilgo Kheyntse Rinpoche. They started training at a very young age, and did several years of retreat before taking a consort. Often they only do so on the instructions of their guru and live in the monastery with their wife, and children, by their side. That can be very nice because with a wife and daughters they understand women, and have an appreciation for the female point of view. You don't have to be celibate, it's just that for many people it's beneficial.'

She had noted the sexual revolution that had taken place while she was in the cave. How could she have missed it? The world that she had emerged into was ablaze with naked, entwined bodies, on billboards, on television, in movies, in newspapers, and in magazines in every high street newsagent. The taboo had been well and truly broken and to prove it sex was discussed, displayed and disseminated like never before. Logos of condoms were paraded on T-shirts, the sex industry had replaced prostitution, people no longer 'made love', they 'had sex'. It was a far cry from the days when an Elvis Presley record sent shivers down a teenager's spine.

'There's no doubt that the West is obsessed with sex, thinks that you can't live without it and that if you do it's going to make you warped and thwarted. It's absurd! Some of the most glowing and fulfilled people I've met have been chaste,' she continued. 'When I look at the monks of Tashi Jong and the laymen of the community the difference in the physical and spiritual quality is stunning. The monks look healthy, clear, happy and the laymen often look quite sickly and dark. This is a generalization, of course, but it's quite appropriate. You can see a different look in their eyes.

'I remember that once a high Indian official came to Dalhousie shortly after I had just arrived there and said to me, "You're a woman of the world, so where are the monks getting it?" "Getting what?" I asked, naïvely. "Well," he replied, "I have eight children and I still can't do without it so how come these monks look so happy?" He found it quite unbelievable that a celibate monk could look so well. And you should have seen him, he was a complete wreck! I have also met plenty of Christian monks who keep their vows purely and who certainly aren't warped or troubled either. The Trappists live very long lives – and they only eat vegetables and cheese,' she added.

By 1997 Tenzin Palmo herself had been celibate for thirty-three years. At the age of twenty-one she had made the radical decision to live without any form of sexual contact or sexual fulfilment, without any comfort of physical intimacy – all in the name of her vocation. She was now fifty-four and still very much alone. At best it seemed heroic, at worst unnatural. What had happened to the girl in the stiletto heels who had a retinue of boyfriends? 'I think she got integrated. I like music, I enjoy seeing beautiful art, being in beautiful scenery. I like being with friends and laughing – which are expressions of the sensuous side of my nature. I am not nearly as serious as I used to be and no longer see "the other girl" as a threat,' she said.

As for her own celibacy, she had no regrets: 'I feel absolutely fine! Now I just don't think that way towards men. They know it and say I'm the only woman they've met who has no sexual vibration. For better or worse that's how I am. I have lots of men friends and enjoy male company. Actually I love men – I think men are very interesting. (I also love women and find them very interesting too.) One of the joys of being a nun is that it makes one's relationship with men in some ways much deeper because they don't feel threatened. They can talk to me and tell me things which they probably wouldn't be able to tell many other people. Actually, I tend not to think in terms of male and female any more. As for physical affection, that's what I missed out all those years when I was in the monastery. Now the need has gone. If people want to hug me (which they do a lot in America), it's OK. But it's perfectly fine also if they don't. As Masters and Johnson said in their conclusion, sex is one of the joys of life but it's certainly not the only one, nor is it the most important. In my opinion there's so much more to life than relationships.'

There were other challenges to face, apart from sex, celibacy and gurus. By the time Tenzin Palmo was travelling across the world on her dharma circuit, the new disciples were beginning tentatively to form 'Western Buddhism', prising the golden nuggets of the Buddha's wisdom out of their eastern casing to adapt them to their own culture. It was a quieter, infinitely more substantial revolution than the more sensational events that were grabbing media attention. It was also one that was absolutely in keeping with Buddhist history. Throughout the ages Buddhism had travelled from one Asian country to the next and such was the flexibility of its thought that it had changed its colour, chameleon-style, to suit whatever environment it found itself in. As a result Japanese Buddhism looked very different from Sri Lankan Buddhism, which in turn looked radically different from Thai, Burmese, Vietnamese or Tibetan Buddhism. Underneath the surface the fundamental truths were the same – the suffering of cyclic existence and the necessity to find the path of escape. Now, for the first time in 2,500 years, the Buddhist tide had turned irrevocably westward and hit the many shores of Europe, the Americans, and Australasia, all of which carried their own distinctive culture and psyche. Each in time would endow Buddhism with its own unique characteristics.

Now senior students began to rewrite the liturgy, attempting to imbue the powerful symbolism of Tibetan imagery and language with words that had more meaning for Western audiences. They began teaching, finding ways of putting the ancient truths into a contemporary context. It was a delicate business, requiring much gentle sifting if the baby was not to be thrown out with the bathwater. At the same time the greatest influences of Western thought started to be grafted on to the Eastern religion in an organic way. It was not just East meeting West, but West meeting East. The ethos of social service, of compassion in action (rather than just on the meditation cushion), was introduced. Buddhist hospices and home-care services for the dying sprang up everywhere, as did leper clinics and refuges for the homeless. Buddhist centres inaugurated meditation sessions for stress relief, counselling services, and programmes for alcohol and drug abuse. And the insights of the West's Masters of the Mind, Jung, Freud and other psychotherapists, were galvanized to add a fresher meaning to the Buddha dharma. The process had begun, a new form of religion was in the making. It was an exciting time.

Tenzin Palmo, who had had no choice but to weld herself to Tibetan Buddhism in its purest form, looked on in fascination at the changes that were unfolding. 'I believe the West is going to make some really important contributions to Buddhism. Tibet was a very unique and special situation and they created a kind of Buddhism which was ideal for them. But the circumstances which Buddhism is facing now in the West are obviously very different and the dharma has to change. Not the essence of course but the way it is presented and its emphasis,' she said.

'I think the skilful incorporation of certain psychological principles is going to be very significant. I also like the idea of social involvement, of genuinely going out there to help others rather than just sitting on the meditation cushion thinking about it. It's opening the heart through practical application and it suits the West. Actually, it's not inimical to the dharma, it's always been in there, but lying a little bit dormant. Different aspects of the dharma emerge when they resonate with certain qualities in the psyches of the people it is meeting. It's an absolutely necessary process if Buddhism is going to be applicable to one's own country.'

'But these are very early days. The dharma took hundreds of years to get rooted in Tibet. There's no Western Buddhism yet. Buddhism will not be rooted in the West until some Western people have gone and taken the dharma and eaten it and digested it and then given it back in a form which is right for Westerners. At the moment it is like that period in Tibet when they went to India to bring scriptures back and Indian masters visited Tibet. Only gradually did the Tibetans evolve it into a form which was right for them, just as the Thais or the Burmese did. Westerners are going to do that too eventually, but it has to come very naturally.'

In the context of Tenzin Palmo's story, however, it was the rise of feminism in the West which brought with it the most interesting rewards, and the sharpest challenges.

SIXTEEN

Is a Cave Necessary?

While Tenzin Palmo had been secreted away in her cave doggedly pursuing the path to perfection, the women of the West had been busy out in the world organizing their own revolution. By the time she came out they had made significant inroads into the male strongholds of both the public and private sector and were turning their determined and increasingly confident eye on the last bastion of male domination, religion. Buddhism was not spared. It might not have had a 'God the Father' to contest, believing as it did in a genderless Absolute, but like all the world's great faiths it had been formulated by men according to men's rules in a time when men were the undisputed leaders. But times were rapidly changing and the old order was giving place to the new. The emerging breed of powerful feminist Buddhists began to query some of the very fundamentals that lay at the heart of the ancient tradition that Tenzin Palmo was following so faithfully, and started to demand a more feminine face for the Buddha.

Their questions were sharp and far-ranging. Instead of the masculine hierarchical structure, which had been in place for millennia, which placed the head at the top and the rest of the community fanning out underneath in a triangle, why shouldn't the head be in the centre of the circle with everyone else at equidistance all around? Why were places of worship always built in straight lines? Why weren't they round instead, following the more feminine principles of the circle and the spiral? Why wasn't the quality of nurture included in the practice? Why wasn't there more emphasis on the sacredness of the body and embodiment, rather than the ideal perpetually being depicted as something transcendent? Why wasn't earthiness as holy as the de-material? Why weren't relationships more honoured? And why were the female consorts of divine art always depicted with their back to the viewer, their role thereby being subtly projected as secondary to the man's, although in effect they were as essential to the process of spiritual unfolding as their male partner?

More significantly to Tenzin Palmo's quest, they asked, is a cave necessary? A cave, they said, was a male prerogative which seriously disadvantaged women with children, spouse and house to care for. While men can (and do) walk away from their families, as the Buddha himself had done, to engage in long bouts of solitary meditation to improve their spiritual chances, women cannot, or do not want to. Why should the maternal instinct, which after all was responsible for bringing forth all beings into the world, including the Buddha, the Christ and all the other holy beings, thus be regarded as a handicap? The cave (or the forest hut), with its call for total renunciation of the world, was, they said, a patriarchal ideal which had held dominance for too long.

As had happened in other fields of feminism, spiritual women now stated they wanted it all. Spirituality and family. The cave and the hearth. To this end they began to initiate practices which included children and families. They introduced emotional healing as a way of meditation rather than the enemy of it. They made moves to change the liturgy and the sexist language of the prayers and ritual. And they brought home the point that the kitchen sink was as good a place to reach Enlightenment as the meditation hall or the remote Himalayan cave. It was revolutionary stuff, which promised to change the face of Buddhism for ever.

Tsultrim Allione, an American woman, was at the forefront of the movement. She had been ordained in 1970 but had disrobed four years later to get married and have children. She went on to write *Women of Wisdom*, one of the first books to laud the place of the feminine in Buddhism, and later established the Tara Mandala Retreat Centre in Pagosa Springs, Colorado, which she set up along the new, experimental feminist lines. She was in a prime position to know both sides of the story.

'I disrobed because I was the only Tibetan Buddhist nun in

the USA at that time and felt very isolated and unsupported,'
she said from a loft in Seattle, where she was presenting a
talk and slide show of her recent visit to female holy sites
in India and Nepal. 'I was twenty-five, my sexual desire was
there, and celibacy began to feel like suppression. What came
out of that was that I went from being a nun to a mother and
a writer in a year. It was an intense experience – and definitely
the best decision for me. From having all the time to myself I
had no time to myself. From thinking I'd overcome jealousy
and anger, and all those negative emotions, they were now all
thrown back in my face. It made me realize that as a nun I
was protected from feeling them. I had to grind deeper into
the layers of the five poisons to see what they were and learn
to work directly with them and not cover them up. If I had
stayed a nun I could have become very arrogant, thinking I
was above them all,' she said.

Tsultrim Allione went on to have four children in five years
(one of whom died in infancy), an experience which made her
dispute the rigid 'official' line that motherhood was an obstacle
to spiritual progress. 'We have to ask ourselves what spiritual
realizations are. The whole maternal impulse is the same as the
urge of love and self-sacrifice. Realizations have been defined by
men and as such they are events which are "up there and out
there". They are not the experience of embodiment. The giving
instinct of a mother is detachment. And there's a quality of really
understanding the human condition from being a mother and a
lay person which you do not get as an ordained person. As a
mother I was constantly disillusioned with myself. I chose how
I failed, not if I failed.'

For herself she had no doubts that a cave was unnecessary. 'I
believe women can become Enlightened in the home,' she said.
'That's the whole point of tantra. There's a story about a woman
who always used to do her practice while carrying water. One day
she drops the water and as she does so her consciousness breaks
open and she experiences Enlightenment. The tantric teachings
actually came out of a protest movement of the lay community
against the monastics which resulted in two systems with two
different sets of ideals. There is both the tantric paradigm and
the monastic paradigm which one can follow.'

At Tara Mandala she has inaugurated the concept of a round place of worship by placing the shrine holding twenty-one figures of the female deity Tara in the centre. 'You walk into a space of wholeness. It's very difficult to describe but everyone feels how different it is. No one yet knows how women will change Buddhism because it is such early days and we have never lived in a society where the feminine was honoured, so we don't know what it would be like. Women are only just beginning to take little steps out of the shadow of the patriarchy. It's a very interesting time.'

Yvonne Rand, one of America's leading Zen teachers, who invited Tenzin Palmo to conduct a weekend seminar at her centre in Muir Beach, California, is also feeling her way. She knew first-hand the difficulties facing women with spiritual aspirations. Before setting up her own independent centre she was chairman of the Board of the San Francisco Zen Centre, a position she found conflicted with her role as a parent.

'As a woman I was expected to take on a lot of responsibility, but I felt like a second-class citizen. There wasn't a lot of understanding about the issues for a single mother and I was always being dismissed for not being very serious about practice. For example, there was a lot of pressure to get up early in the morning and sit in the meditation hall, but for me to do that would have meant leaving young children alone in an apartment,' she said. Eventually she deduced that the rules she was trying to follow came out of the Japanese psyche rather than Buddhism itself, and that the home was as good a place to practise as the formalized group gatherings. 'I finally realized that what I am is a lay, ordained priest, a householder who practices periodically as a monastic. For the first time I saw how I fit in and it was a tremendous relief.'

She pondered on the question of how far a woman can get practising in the home. 'I don't know about Enlightenment but I'm sure women can get very far. Liberation becomes possible when I begin to experience the possibility of being in the moment, when I'm not still carrying the baggage of yesterday or when I was two,' she said. 'The most important thing is constancy. If you pick up a practice, say a mindfulness practice, you have to do it often. Twelve times a day can be very effective. For instance, there's a great little practice called the half-smile where you slightly lift the corners of your mouth and hold it for three breaths. If I do it six or more times a day within three days it makes a surprising difference to the body and mind. You can do it during any time of waiting, when you're kept on hold on the telephone, at the grocery store, in the airport at the stop lights,' she added, sounding remarkably like Tenzin Palmo.

'There are so many things that you can do at home,' she continued. 'You can follow the practice of developing patience or using obstacles as your teacher. I used to sit with people who were dying, and then being with the body afterwards. That was an incredible teaching. I learnt not only about impermanence and the links between the breath and the mind, but that the way we die is the way we have lived. The issues of our living will arise during our dying. When you have chosen your practices and done them for some years you can go back and refine the ground. You don't have to keep adding new ones until you've perfected the ones you've got. One of the hazards of being American is that we're not very modest. We're always in a rush, wanting it all at once.'

The Kitchen Sink Path still has its pitfalls, as Yvonne Rand, practitioner and householder for over thirty years, testified. While not as dramatic as confronting starvation or wild animals, they were equally real, she declared, and had to be worked out with the same diligence and constancy. 'There are two main ones – confusion with priorities, and an unwillingness to give things up so that you become overwhelmed trying to do it all. In order to practise, study and teach, as well as being available to my husband and family, I have given up going out much. In fact, I have become a chicken. I get up at 5.30 a.m. and often go to bed by 7.30 p.m. It's relatively easy for me because my children are now grown up and my husband is a dharma practitioner also. Those hours to myself in the early morning make a huge difference. I do sitting and walking meditation, and I take precepts such as not lying, not taking anything that is not freely given, and not killing or harming a living being. I have done these practices for such a long time that they've become part of my life.'

It wasn't only feminists who were asking the difficult questions. Male practitioners were also challenging the value of the cave. Vipassana teacher Jack Kornfield, one of America's most renowned meditation masters, introduced the concept of a 'few months in' and a 'few months out' as an alternative to years of uninterrupted retreat in isolated places. He was also advocating half-way houses when the retreat was finished. His argument was that prolonged periods of meditation away from mainstream life made it extremely difficult for the person to reintegrate back into society. The Western psyche was unsuitable for such austere practices, he said, as the many who were beginning to try it on their own home soil had found out. Prolonged solitary retreat was causing psychosis and alienation.

In England another well-known Buddhist teacher, Stephen Bachelor, director of studies at Sharpham College for Buddhist Studies and Contemporary Enquiry, tended to agree. He had been a monk for ten years both in the Zen and Buddhist traditions, before becoming one of Buddhist's most famous sceptics, openly questioning such fundamental doctrinal principles as reincarnation. As a friend of Tenzin Palmo he was in a good position to comment on whether a cave was necessary for advanced spiritual practice.

'It doesn't make a lot of sense to make generalizations. So much has to do with the temperament of the person who is going to the cave,' he said. 'Knowing Tenzin Palmo it has obviously been an experience of enormous value, something which has had its knock-on effect afterwards. She is so clearly warm, outgoing, engaging in life. But Tenzin Palmo doesn't conform to the standard norm of the solitary hermit, who is usually introverted and world-denying. I can think of other instances where people are not so psychologically solid and where prolonged periods of meditation in complete solitude can lead to psychotic states. People go in looking for answers for their insecurity and alienation and can get locked into their neurotic perceptions rather than going on beyond them. You have to be wired in such a way to be able to cope with this sort of isolation.'

As a monk, Stephen Bachelor had conducted his own retreats, on one occasion doing three months in, three months out for a period of three years. He knows the kind of traumas such an exercise can induce. 'You do confront your own demons (if you have any), which is of enormous value. You come up against yourself and you have to respond to your reality using the tools you have been given. My long retreat eroded my belief system,' he acknowledged. 'I was in a Zen monastery where all we did was ask the question, "What is this?" My retreat was about unlearning. It was a very different approach from Tenzin Palmo's. In Zen there is no devotion to a particular teacher. One of Tenzin Palmo's great strengths is that she has great faith in her guru and the tradition she is part of. Frankly it is a faith which I find inconceivable.'

All this put Tenzin Palmo's twelve years of determination and extraordinary effort in the cave on the line. Had she wasted her time? Could she have performed her great retreat in London or Assisi? Was she an anachronism? If she had not disappeared to the East when she was twenty would she have done it any differently? As always she stood her ground and put up a compelling credo for the cave.

'It's a poverty of our time that so many people can't see beyond the material,' she said. 'In this age of darkness with its greed, violence and ignorance it's important there are some areas of light in the gloom, something to balance all the heaviness and darkness. To my mind the contemplatives and the solitary meditators are like lighthouses beaming out love and compassion on to the world. Because their beams are focused they are very powerful. They become like generators – and they are extremely necessary.

'Even as I travel around the world I meet people who say how inspired they've been by my being in the cave,' Tenzin Palmo continued. 'I got a letter from a woman who said that her son was dying of AIDS and that in the moments of her deepest depression she'd think of me up in my cave and that would give her solace. It's true of many people leading this life. I know Catholics who feel inspired that Christian contemplatives are praying for the world's sinners. What people have to remember is that meditators in caves are not doing it for themselves – they're meditating on behalf of all sentient beings.' And her words were reminiscent of that old Eastern saying that if it weren't for the meditators directing their prayers to the welfare of all humanity the sun wouldn't rise every morning in the East. And didn't Pascal say that the whole of the world's troubles was because man could not sit still in his room?

But for Tenzin Palmo, the woman, the option had been easy. She had never for a second yearned for a child. She had never known the ache of maternal instinct unfulfilled. Nor had she ever had to balance the demands of motherhood and domestic responsibility with the call for spiritual development, like so many women were trying to do. Western mothers like Tsultrim Allione tried to get round the problem by allowing her children into her meditation sessions (where they climbed all over her). Other women were reduced to getting up before dawn to get in the prescribed hours of practice before getting their children off to school. They would then juggle other sessions between the cooking and the laundry and would finish off late at night doing their final session after the children were in bed. Tibetan mothers like Machig Lobdron (the famous yogini of Tibet) solved the problem by simply leaving her children with her husband for months on end in order to practise. In reality therefore was motherhood a disadvantage to spiritual progress?

'We do different things in different lifetimes,' Tenzin Palmo answered. 'We should look and see what in this lifetime we are called to do. It's ridiculous to become a nun or a hermit because of some ideal when all the time we would be learning more within a close relationship or a family situation. You can develop all sorts of qualities through motherhood which you could not by leading a monastic life. It's not that by being a mother one is cutting off the path. Far from it! There are many approaches, many ways. What is unrealistic, however, is to become a mother or a businesswoman and at the same time expect to be able to do the same kind of practices designed for hermits. If women have made the choice to have children then they should develop a practice which makes the family the dharma path. Otherwise they'll end up being very frustrated.

'Actually, everything depends on one's skilful means and how much determination and effort one puts into it,' she went on. 'Whether one is a monk, a nun, a hermit, a housewife or a businessman or woman, at one level it's irrelevant. The practice of being in the moment, of opening the heart, can be done wherever we are. If one is able to bring one's awareness into everyday life and into one's relationships, workplace, home, then it makes no difference where one is. Even in Tibet the people who attained the rainbow body were often very "ordinary" people who nobody ever knew were practising. The fact is that a genuine practice should be able to be carried out in all circumstances.' She paused for a moment, then added: 'It's just that it's easier to do these advanced practices in a conducive environment away from external and internal distractions. That's why the Buddha created the sangha. Very close relationships can be very distracting, let's admit it.'

It was an essential codicil. What Tenzin Palmo was in fact saying was that while much spiritual development can be achieved within the home or the office, the cave remained the hothouse for Enlightenment. It was what they had always said.

'The advantage of going to a cave is that it gives you time and space to be able to concentrate totally. The practices are complicated with detailed visualizations. The inner yogic practices and the mantras also require much time and isolation. These cannot be done in the midst of the town. Going into retreat gives the opportunity for the food to cook,' she said, ironically launching into the language of the kitchen to get her meaning across. 'You have to put all the ingredients into a pot and stew it up. And you have to have a constant heat. If you keep turning the heat on and off it is never going to be done. The retreat is like living in a pressure-cooker. Everything gets cooked much quicker. That is why it is recommended.

'Even for short periods, it can be helpful. You don't have to do it all your life. I think it would be very helpful for many people to have some period of silence and isolation to look within and find out who they really are, when they're not so busy playing roles – being the mother, wife, husband, career person, everybody's best friend, or whatever façade we put up to the world as our identity. It's very good to have an opportunity to be alone with oneself and see who one really is behind all the masks.'

In this light, she declared, the hermitage or cave would never be an archaic ideal, as some were suggesting. And for as long as certain individuals, like herself, had the yearning to pursue the lonely inner path, away from the hustle and bustle of ordinary life, then the cave would always exist, in one form or another. 'Is the search for reality old-fashioned?' she stated more than asked. 'As long as the search for spiritual understanding is valid, so is the cave.'

Tenzin Palmo, out in the world, had come into contact with many of the new women agitating to put a more feminine face on the Buddha, and applauded their efforts. 'The push by the women to introduce these changes is going to be one of the greatest contributions the West is going to make to the dharma,' she said. Over the years she had developed an interesting relationship with the strongest proponents. Like them, her goal was equality of opportunity for all women in the spiritual arena. Like them, she abhorred the latent misogyny of the Patriarchal system. Like them, she was fiercely independent, intent on forging her own way ahead regardless of the obstacles. Like them, she was outspoken against discrimination and injustice wherever she found them. But, unlike them, she did not think the full-frontal attacks often employed by the feminists worked. And, in her inimical fashion, she told them so.

'These angry feminists! I come up against them all the time. They have this whole idea of righteous indignation which they use as fuel to oppose whatever they think is unjust. They direct an enormous amount of anger towards men, as though they were the perpetrators of all evil. Frankly I don't think all this anger helps. And I tell them so. Anger is simply anger, we use it to justify our own negative states. We all have a huge reservoir of anger in us and whatever we direct it to only adds oil to the fire. If we approach something with an angry mind what happens is that it leads to antagonism and defensiveness in the other side. The Buddha said hatred is not overcome by hatred, but only by love.

'Admittedly men have done some pretty awful things but they have often been aided and abetted by women. If one looks at the situation fairly, the people keeping women down are often other women! It's not men against women, but women against women. After all, the greatest opponent of the suffragettes was

Queen Victoria! If the women stood together what could men do? The whole issue is not a matter of polarizing the human race. It's more subtle than that.'

Her words had wisdom. If the last several thousand years of patriarchy had been a backlash against the previous millennia of matriarchy when the Earth Goddess had reigned supreme (as many pundits were saying), what was the point of having another radical pendulum swing back again? If a new order was emerging then balance between male and female (as well as East and West) was obviously the best solution. And because she spoke sense the women listened and told her they hadn't thought of it that way before.

Tenzin Palmo had thought out her own way of bringing about the revolution. A much quieter way. 'It should be based on open discussion, patience, compromise, lots of equanimity and a soft, warm heart.' They were the classic Buddhist values. 'The Buddha said we must love all sentient beings. How can we then set sentient beings up as the enemy?' Most especially, she advocated a calm, non-strident voice. 'Of course you can raise your voice but first you have to check your motivation. Is it out of love for other women and their needs or out of anger? If we're speaking out of negative emotions the result will only be worse,' she repeated. 'On the other hand we don't have to be simpering.'

In her mind she knew what spiritually powerful women looked like. There was her favourite painting, by Piero della Francesca, of the Madonna, standing with her cloak wide open giving shelter to a multitude of people underneath. 'She looks straight out at the viewer. She's strong, confident, in no way simpering but in no way angry either. There is love there, compassion, and gravitas. She's a very powerful lady,' she said.

There was also a young Tibetan woman who had begun to teach on the world stage called Khandro Rinpoche, whom Tenzin Palmo had high regard for. 'She is as sharp as can be, absolutely clear and at the same time completely feminine. I have never seen her angry yet everyone respects her enormously. She has inner authority and when she sits on the throne she sits there with complete confidence, an egoless confidence. There's no pride there. Along with her precise wisdom she also has a warm, nurturing side. She's absolutely in control, not at all weak or sentimental.'

She paused for thought, then added: 'What is our image of woman? To me, it comes down to poise and inner strength. When you have those you have natural authority, and people will automatically want to follow you. These are the qualities that I shall try to encourage the women at Dongyu Gatsal Ling nunnery to develop.'

And with that Tenzin Palmo continued on her way, moving quietly across the world, collecting alms for a nunnery where it could all be possible.

SEVENTEEN

Now

It has been nine years since I first met Tenzin Palmo in the grounds of that Tuscan mansion and was catapulted into the slow but inexorable business of writing her life story. In that time much has changed. She has lost some of that luminous glow she had when she first came out of the cave, though her eyes are as sparkling and her manner as animated as ever. The years on the road, forever on the move, teaching incessantly, have taken their toll. It has been a long, tough haul. At the time of writing she has collected enough money to buy the land and lay the foundations. By anyone's standards it's a tremendous achievement, but for one woman to have to have done it single-handed, without the aid of professional fundraisers, it is extraordinary. Still, there is a long way to go, and so she travels on, gathering yet more funds to boost the coffers for her nunnery. For all the slowness of the process she remains strangely unconcerned, showing no signs of impatience to hurry things along and get the job done. She has no personal ambition in this scheme. At one level she really doesn't mind.

'My life is in the hands of the Buddha, dharma and sangha, literally. I've handed it over. Whatever is necessary for me to do to benefit all beings, let me do it. I don't care,' she admits. 'Besides, I've discovered that if I try to push things the way I think they should be done everything goes wrong.'

Having surrendered to the Buddha, the practicalities of her life curiously seem to take care of themselves. People are only too pleased to have her company for as long as she can be with them – offering her plane tickets, their houses, food, transport, money, so that all her physical needs are met. This is how she says it should be. 'A true monastic lives without security, dependent on the unsolicited generosity of others. Contrary to what some Westerners might think, this is not being a parasite, this is going forth in faith. Jesus also said, "Give ye no thought unto the morrow what ye shall eat and what ye shall wear." We should have faith that if we practise sincerely we won't starve, we will be supported not just materially but in every way.'

And so, living out her faith absolutely, Tenzin Palmo stands in a strange counter-flow to the rest of twentieth-century society with its emphasis on acquisition and satisfaction of desire. She has no home, no family, no security, no partner, no sexual relationship, no pension plan. She has no need to accumulate. She still owns nothing except the barest of essentials – her robes, some texts, a jumper, a sleeping-bag, a few personal items. Once she splashed out and bought a luxury, a neck pillow for travelling, but lost it soon afterwards. 'It serves me right. I was getting far too attached to it,' she comments with a laugh. Her bank balance remains as meagre as ever, Tenzin Palmo refusing to touch any of the donations intended for the nunnery – even for travelling to raise funds. She is as meticulous as ever regarding money given for religious purposes. For all her penury she remains as sanguine as ever, money having no interest to her. She'll happily open her own purse and given whatever she can to whoever asks her. She's following the life of renunciation that she has always wanted and in doing so demonstrates eloquently that restraint and simplicity can bring happiness and peace of mind.

Travelling in various parts of the world with her I witness an alluring but enigmatic figure, a mixture of curious contradictions so that you can't quite grasp her. She is eminently practical, down-to-earth, plain-speaking, and at the same time other-worldly and fey, her eye focused on a horizon too distant for most of us to see. She is content to wait for hours, days even, without complaint, for people, planes, events, so that you think she is passive and easily swayed. But no one can be more determined nor put their foot down more strongly when an issue is at stake that she cares about. She will bluntly tell anyone why they should not eat meat, sigh heavily when the conversation turns to Thanksgiving turkeys, scowl openly at a row of fishing books displayed proudly on a bookshelf. And woe betide anyone who crosses her on theological issues; then the full force of her formidable logic and rhetoric is galvanized, leaving her opponent winded and running for cover. She is infinitely kindly yet you tread warily, for in spite of her humility there is something awesome about her. And sometimes, when she looks at you, maybe after you have said something you thought significant, she can make you feel like a very small child indeed.

There are other anomalies. For all her efficiency and the demands of her teaching schedule, her pace is slow and there is an uncommon air of leisure about her. Somehow she seems to have bypassed that 1990s lore that decrees that busy is better, and that unless we are working a sixty-hour week, and going to the gym in our spare time (in order to perform better at work), we are wasting our time. She pays no heed to today's lore that to sit and simply stare out of the window is a sin. And so, in stark contrast to the emotionally stressed and physically exhausted people who flock to her, she remains an oasis of tranquillity. As such, she teaches that 'being' is often better than 'doing' and that taking time out to be still and think is often a better investment for future productivity than cramming every waking moment with feverish activity.

Her most outstanding characteristic, however, remains her overt and spontaneous sociability. For all her mounting status and the thousands of people she has met, she has not tired of human company. Her circle of friends is immense, and once anyone has entered into her domain they are never forgotten. She keeps up with childhood friends and with nearly all her family, including her brother Mervyn and his wife Sandy, who was at school with her. She is warm and welcoming to all, especially to those who come in genuine search. Her warmth is genuine, her concern for the litany of problems she hears real, her ability to listen and give advice unflagging. Yet you know in your heart that if she never saw you again she really would not miss you. And her lack of emotional need is disconcerting, for the ego likes to be flattered, wants to be wanted. From her, however, you'll never get it. This is her hard-earned 'detached engagement', which allows her to wander freely in the world without the entanglement of close personal relationships.

'I don't think it's a bad thing,' she says. 'It doesn't mean that one doesn't feel love and compassion, that one doesn't care. It just means that one doesn't hold on. One can be filled with joy to be with someone but if one is not it doesn't matter. People, especially family, get upset if you are not attached to them but that's only because we confuse love and attachment all the time.'

She still sees the young Khamtrul Rinpoche whenever she is at Tashi Jong, in the lush hills of north India. He is now a solemn and rather shy teenager. She teaches him words of English and tries to infiltrate Western books into his strict and, in her opinion, too isolated world. Now that her great mentor, the previous Khamtrul Rinpoche, has gone, she feels her guidance coming from another source. 'I think I am being led by the Dakinis,' she says, referring to those powerful female spiritual forces with whom she has always had a particularly close association.

There have been changes in the wider feminist Buddhist field too. Since 1993, when she and the other women at the Dharamsala Conference confronted the Dalai Lama with the sexual discrimination they had faced, the nun's lot has started to improve a little. One team of accomplished nuns has begun to tour the globe making sand mandalas of the Kalachakra deity in the cause of world peace – a task traditionally undertaken by monks. A new nunnery, Dolma Ling, has opened in Dharamsala, where the nuns are learning the art of debating. It is a huge leap forward, the intellectual business of dialectics being customarily regarded as the exclusive domain of the monks. At one point last year the nuns plucked up enough courage to debate in the courtyard of the Dalai Lama's temple itself, in front of the monks. They stood there, small, young, enthusiastic figures stamping their feet and clapping their hands in the ritualized gestures of point scoring – and Western onlookers testified that the sight brought tears to their eyes. And the matter of introducing full ordination gets closer and closer. The Dalai Lama has sent emissaries to Taiwan to investigate the Chinese Bhikshuni tradition, with the hope of making it available to Tibetan nuns. After 1,000 years it is about time.

Still, there is a long way to go. There are as yet no

women sitting among the massed ranks of robed figures in the Great Temple. Depressingly, the new influx of recognized reincarnations of the former masters and lineage holders are all boys – thereby promising little hope of a breakdown in the patriarchal hierarchy. And the average Eastern man in the street will still gawp in frank disbelief at the very suggestion that a woman can attain Enlightenment.

Over the years Tenzin Palmo, the nun, has risen to legendary status, with younger Western nuns staring in awe whenever she comes among them. She is an icon. A woman who proved them wrong. A woman (and a Western woman) who survived in a cave, all alone, for twelve years, engaging in serious meditation without cracking or diminishing her purpose. A woman whose subsequent words of wisdom are an inspiration to people, lay and ordained alike. As such, Tenzin Palmo continues to be a role model and a torch-bearer for spiritual women everywhere.

Her plans for the future, as much as she will allow herself to have any, revolve around a single theme, the one she has had all her life, to gain Enlightenment. With this goal still set firmly in her mind, she intends, once her task of building the nunnery is done, to go back to the cave. As such she will have come full circle. Leaving the world, returning to it, and then departing once more to live in solitude to follow the inner life. For all the brave new assertions that Enlightenment can be achieved out in the world, she feels that the cave is still relevant in our modern world, and that is ultimately where she belongs.

'I would like to gain very deep realizations,' she says softly. 'And all my teachers, including the Dalai Lama, have said that retreat is the most important thing for me to do during this lifetime. When I am in retreat I know at a very deep level that I am in the right place doing the right thing,' she says.

And so she continues to be rare. As Richard Gere, the actor and committed Buddhist, put it recently: 'Most of us Westerners would get brain cancer if we went into caves. We are such active people that our karma has to work itself out. Not many of us are far along enough to have spiritualized our mind streams sufficiently to handle a cave.'

Although she has undoubtedly travelled far along the spiritual path, she declares she still she has a long way to go. 'I've hardly even started. There are a lot more barriers I have to break through in my mind. You see, a flash is not enough. You have to repeat and repeat until the realizations are stabilized in your mind. That is why it takes so long – twelve years, twenty-five years, a lifetime, several lifetimes.'

She will not return to the same cave in Lahoul, however. Her body is too old to withstand the extreme physical hardship of living 13,200 feet high in the Himalayas, she says. Nor can she trudge up mountains carrying fifteen kilograms of supplies, as she did before. In any case, her old home in the mountain no longer exists. After she left in 1988, none of the nuns or monks of the area had the will or the courage to move in and carry on where Tenzin Palmo had left off. Consequently the cave was pulled apart – the door and windows being carried down to the town to be used again and the stones scattered back over the hillside where they had come from. The overhang re-emerged and for many years it looked as though no one had ever sat, and gardened, and prayed up there. Years later, however, the cave briefly came back to life through another determined Western woman. In 1995 a German nun called Edith Besch refound the spot made famous by Tenzin Palmo and built the cave up again – on a much grander scale. A room was added and the front wall built out. There was even a separate kitchen and an outside toilet. Edith only managed one year in the cave, however, before being taken ill with cancer and dying in a monastery in the valley below, aged just forty-three. The local people attested that she had been notoriously hot-tempered when she arrived, but after twelve months of retreat had emerged serene and patient in spite of her sickness and had died a peaceful death. The cave, it seemed, had worked its magic once again.

For Tenzin Palmo her next cave will be more metaphorical than actual. 'More likely it will be a little retreat hut in a place which is quiet and peaceful but not so remote. Maybe a small hermitage on someone's land where it is not so difficult to get supplies. This place could be anywhere, although certainly not England! I still do not feel at home there. It might well be the East – I have always had the feeling that I will die in the East,' she mused.

The location is irrelevant. Wherever it is, she has only one purpose in mind: to continue pursuing the path to perfection in the body of a woman.

Bibliography

Allione, Tsultrim, *Women of Wisdom* (Arkana, 1986)

Armstrong, Karen, *The Gospel According to Woman* (Fount Paperbacks, 1986)

Batchelor, Stephen, *The Tibet Guide* (Wisdom Publications, 1987)

Blofeld, John, *The Wheel of Life* (Shambala, 1972)

Chagdud Tulku, *Lord of the Dance* (Padma Publishing, 1992)

Crook, John and Low, James, *The Yogins of Ladakh* (India, Motilal Banarsidass, 1997)

Dalai Lama, His Holiness, Tenzin Gyatso, *Beyond Dogma* (Souvenir Press 1994)

Dalia Lama, His Holiness, Tenzin Gyatso and Carriere Jean-Claude, *The Power of Buddhism* (Newleaf, 1996)

David-Neel, Alexandra, *Magic and Mystery in Tibet* (India, Rupa, 1989)

Dowman, Keith, *Sky Dancer* (Snow Lion, 1996)

Evans-Wentz, W.Y., *Milarepa* (Oxford University Press, 1969)

Hardy, Justine, *The Ochre Border* (Constable, 1995)

Harvey, Andrew, *Hidden Journey* (Bloomsbury, 1991)

Hixon, Lex, *Mother of the Buddhas* (Quest, 1993)

Humphreys, Christmas, *Both Sides of the Circle* (Allen and Unwin, 1978)

Kornfield, Jack, *A Path with Heart* (Rider, 1994)

Lama Yeshe, *Introduction to Tantra* (Wisdom, 1987)

Nydahl, Ole, *Entering the Diamond Way* (Blue Dolphin, 1985)

Satprem, *Mother or The Divine Materialism* (Institute for Evolutionary Research, 1980)

Pema Chodron, *Start Where You Are* (Shambala, 1994)

Rahula, Walpola, *What The Buddha Taught* (Gordon Fraser, 1967)

Shaw, Miranda, *Passionate Enlightenment* (Princeton University Press, 1994)

Sogyal Rinpoche, *The Tibetan Book of Living and Dying* (Harper Collins, 1992)

Therese of Lisieux, translated by Ronald Knox, *Autobiography of a Saint* (Fountain, 1977)

Trungpa, Chogyam, *Born in Tibet* (Unwin 1987)

Tweedie, Irina, *Daughter of Fire* (The Golden Sufi Center, 1986)

Whitmont, Edward C., *Return of the Goddess* (Crossroad, 1984)

Acknowledgements

I would like to offer my heartfelt thanks to: Robert Drew for his invaluable encouragement; Monica Joyce, intrepid fellow traveller; Ngawang for hauling me up to the cave; David Reynolds for believing in me; Ruth Logan and all the Bloomsbury team for their tremendous effort; Andrew Doust for brushing me down when the going got tough; and, of course, Tenzin Palmo, who so generously allowed me into her life.

Author's Note

If you would like to make a donation towards the funding of Tenzin Palmo's Dongyu Gatsal Ling nunnery, please send a cheque or Postal Order payable to Tenzin Palmo c/o Vicki Mackenzie at Bloomsbury Publishing Plc, 38 Soho Square, London W1V 5DF

A Note On The Author

Vicki Mackenzie was born in England, and as the daughter of a naval officer spent her childhood gaining an eclectic education in various parts of the world. After graduating from Queensland University she joined the news desk of the *Sun* in Sydney as a cadet reporter. She soon moved on to Fleet Street, where she became a features writer – first on the *Daily Sketch* and then on the *Daily Mail*. She went on to write for the *Sunday Times*, the *Observer*, the *Daily Telegraph*, the *Sunday Telegraph*, the *Daily Express*, the *Mail on Sunday* and many national magazines. For several years she was also a contributor at the Australian Consolidated Press bureau in Fleet Street.

In 1976, on a whim, she attended a month-long meditation course run by two Tibetan Lamas in Nepal. This ignited a deep interest in Buddhism which resulted in her writing the best-selling *Reincarnation: The Boy Lama* and its sequel, *Reborn in the West: The Reincarnation Masters*.

She now divides her time between Australia and England.